Mary Ann Dwight

Grecian and Roman Mythology

Mary Ann Dwight

Grecian and Roman Mythology

ISBN/EAN: 9783337008666

Printed in Europe, USA, Canada, Australia, Japan

Cover: Foto ©Thomas Meinert / pixelio.de

More available books at **www.hansebooks.com**

ENDYMION.

GRECIAN AND ROMAN MYTHOLOGY.

BY M. A. DWIGHT.

WITH A SERIES OF ILLUSTRATIONS.

SECOND ABRIDGED EDITION

NEW YORK:
PUBLISHED BY A. S. BARNES & BURR.
51 & 53 JOHN STREET.
1860.

CONTENTS.

INTRODUCTION,	7
ANCIENT DEITIES,	19
MODERN, SUPERIOR DEITIES,	67
GENII AND INFERIOR DEITIES,	183
DEMI-GODS AND HEROES,	211
MYTHIC FICTIONS,	294

Entered according to Act of Congress, in the year 1849, by
M. A. DWIGHT,
In the Clerk's Office of the District Court for the Southern District of New York.

PREFATORY NOTE.

A KNOWLEDGE of Mythology is of so much importance in connection with ancient history, that the subject should be made a study in every school. To render it accessible to all, this work is offered to the public in an abridged form. The information necessary to an understanding of the character and attributes of each deity is retained, and the more general treatment omitted. This method was adopted on the supposition that at the recitations of his class, the teacher would have the larger work to which he could refer.

LIST OF ILLUSTRATIONS,

ENGRAVED ON WOOD, BY J. D. FELTER.

	Page		Page
FRONTISPIECE,	See p. 139	MINERVA'S SHIELD,	155
PAN,	23	VULCAN,	162
PARCÆ,	26	MERCURY,	179
FURIES,	30	COUNCIL OF JUPITER,	181
HARPY,	33	ONE OF THE LARES,	183
RIVER-GOD,	44	SILENOS,	193
JUPITER AMMON,	73	CLIO,	201
JUPITER PLUVIUS,	74	GANYMEDES,	203
JUNO,	81	ÆSCULAPIUS,	205
VESTA,	84	TELESPHOROS,	206
CYBELE,	92	PERSEUS,	213
NEPTUNE,	96	MEDUSA,	220
PLUTO,	98	BELLEROPHONTES,	221
DEMETER,	112	HERCULES AND SERPENT,	226
APOLLO MUSAGETES,	130	HERCULES AND CERBERUS,	234
DIANA TRIFORMIS,	139	CASTOR AND POLLUX,	262
MINERVA,	152	CENTAUR,	263

INTRODUCTION.

The word Mythology is compounded of two Greek words, Muthos, a fable, and Logos, a discourse; and signifies a system of fables, or the fabulous history of the false gods of the heathen world.

Fable is divided into various kinds; and the following is an example of the instructive, as used for the purpose by a famous orator: When Philip's son, the hereditary enemy of the liberty of Greece, demanded eight of their leading men to be delivered up to him, as the great impediment of mutual amity, "On a time," said Demosthenes to his fellow-citizens, "an embassy came from the wolves to the sheep, assuring them that the dogs by which they were attended were the sole occasion of the war; wherefore, if they would give them up, all would be well, and end in lasting peace. The sheep were persuaded, gave up the dogs, and henceforth the wolves devoured them at pleasure."

A second sort is political, as the following: When Jupiter heard of the death of his son Sarpedon, in the rage of grief he called Mercury, the messenger of the gods, and gave him orders to go instantly to the Fates, and bring from them the strong box in which the eternal decrees were laid up. Mercury obeyed, went to the sisters, and omitted nothing that a wise and well-instructed minister could say to make them pacify the will of Jove. The sisters smiled, and told him that the other end of the golden chain which secured the box with the unalterable decrees, was so fixed to the throne of Jove, that were it to be unfastened, his master's seat itself might tremble."

A third sort of mythology consists in a material representation of virtue and vice, or instruction conveyed by wood and stone, instead of a tale. Such in some respects are all the badges and ensigns of the gods, when carved or cast in metal;—and such the secret symbols delivered to the initiated in the several mysteries, which they carefully kept from vulgar eyes, showing them only upon certain signs. The example which best illustrates this material species of mythology, contains at the same time a beautiful moral: It was the temple of Honor, that had no entrance of its own, and the only passage to it was through the temple of Virtue. Happy the man who truly worships in the first, even if the ignorance of his contemporaries prevent him from entering the second; he will yet, sooner or later, possess the station due to his merit

But Mythology is a vast and various compound; a labyrinth through which no one thread can conduct us; since all the powers of heaven and earth, whatever is, whatever acts, whatever changes, and whatever remains the same, is, by some image congruent to its peculiar nature, variously painted in the mimic mirror of the universe. The primary great gods represent its principal parts and powers; and the numerous inferior train exhibit either the lesser powers of nature or their influences; or, they belong to human passions, and human transactions as connected with them. The rest are men adopted among the gods, and frequently blended with the original deities.

The course of time since the commencement of the world has been divided into three periods; the unknown, the fabulous, and the historical, which may be considered as the origin of mythological fables. The unknown comprehends all that space which the ancients supposed to have passed since the beginning of things, and of which we have no knowledge. In their opinion, all that was then transacted escaped the keenest sight. The fabulous began with the earliest notices of things; that is, in ancient style, with the births and marriages of the gods, and continued through the heroic ages until records and history introduced certainty and unfabled truth. Then commenced the historical period, which preserves its evidence to the present time.

Instead of this accurate division, the early poets sang, that Saturn (by whom they represent time) lurked long out of sight of heaven, and likewise devoured his own progeny as soon as they were born. This is plainly the unknown period. Jupiter, Saturn's son, together with Juno, Ceres, Pluto, Neptune, and Vesta, were produced without his knowledge, and preserved against his will. They conspired against their relentless parent, seized and bound him with a cord of wool never to be loosed, while almighty Jove holds the reins of government. Here is the fabulous period comprehending the birth and adventures of the gods, and the historical in the conclusion.

Religion, law, and philosophy united, were first taught to mankind in the form of fables; but these ancient fables convey no such ideas to the modern reader "The most ancient theology," says Plutarch, " both of the Greeks and barbarians, was natural philosophy involved in fables, that physically and mystically conveyed the truth to the learned;—as appears from the poems of Orpheus, the Egyptian rites, and the Phrygian traditions." A remark which it is necessary to keep in mind, in order to distinguish the pure, primitive doctrine from later inventions; for the regions of fable are wide and fertile, resembling Rabelais' iron work island, where swords grew from the trees, and mushrooms sprang from the earth so exactly under them, that every ripe sword fell precisely into its own scabbard, without missing it a hair's breadth.

Nature is the parent of real mythology. She was associated with philosophy in the great work of civilizing the rude tribes of the early ages. Her robe of triple tissue, is a monstrous tale of feigned, allegorical personages engaged in action, who speak and act so much in character, as at once to represent causes and narrate transactions, which by striking the fancy and winning the heart, convey instruction agreeably to the mind. The history of the creation, or rise of the universe, that the moderns call natural philosophy, and the ancients theogony, or the generation of the gods, was the groundwork of the fabric; the powers that govern the world furnished the figures, and constitute the design; while the human character (moral philosophy), the passions of men as they glow or languish, become tarnished or bloom with life, gave a gloss and coloring to the whole. But this system of pure, primitive mythology was corrupted as soon as it spread beyond the nations with whom it originated, and soon became blended with history, and historical personages

Structures for the worship of heathen deities may be considered as among the most ancient monuments of antiquity. As soon as a nation had become in the least degree civilized, they took care to appropriate and consecrate particular spots to the worship of their deities.

In the earliest instances, they were contented with erecting altars in the open air, either of earth or ashes, and sometimes resorted, for purposes of worship, to the depths of solitary woods. At length, they acquired the practice of building cells, or chapels, within the enclosure of which they placed the images of their divinities, and there assembled to offer their supplications, thanksgivings, and sacrifices. These places of worship bore some resemblance to their own dwellings. The Troglodites adored their gods in grottoes; and the people who lived in cabins, erected edifices, the form of which was more or less assimilated to that kind of habitation. Herodotus and Strabo contend that the Egyptians first erected temples to the gods; and the first one erected in Greece, is attributed by Apollonius to Deucalion. Clemens Alexandrinus and Eusebius refer the origin of temples to the sepulchres built for the dead.

According to Pausanias, the oracle of Delphi in remote ages was consulted in a kind of arbor formed of laurels. That of Jupiter at Dodona, at a similar era, rendered its oracles by an old oak, as we learn both from Pausanias and Herodotus. In the vicinity of Magnesia, upon the Meander, was a grotto consecrated to Apollo, wherein was to be seen a very ancient statue of that god.

The first statues erected for the ancient gods hardly deserve the name, being only great stones set on end; generally square, sometimes conical, sometimes pyramidal, or semicircular, and frequently quite rough, without even the touch of a tool. The oldest statues of Mercury were originally large square stones. The statue of the mother of the gods, brought from Phrygia, was a large black square stone.

The ancient Phœnicians had an image of the sun, which they believed not to have been formed by human art, but to have fallen immediately from heaven. It was a large black stone, round and broad at the base, but diminishing by degrees towards the top, and terminating in a slender point. The Megareans worshipped a large stone in the form of a pyramid, under the name of Apollo. Their more elegant neighbors, the Athenians, worshipped him in human shape, but with a head long and sharp, like a pyramid. A small globe split in two, and one of the halves set on a pole, was a symbol adored by the ancient Peönians.

When the Greeks, at a subsequent period, surpassed all other people in cultivating the arts, they devoted much time, care, and expense, to the building of temples, rendering them in every way worthy of their destination. In every city of Greece, as well as its environs, and in the open country, was a large number of sacred temples; and the most costly temple of each place was especially dedicated to its tutelary deity. Instances of this are found in the temple of Minerva at Athens, that of Diana at Ephesus, of Apollo at Delphi, of Jupiter at Olympia, of Venus at Paphos and Cytherea; and of Jupiter Capitolinus at Rome. At Panionium, was a temple of Jupiter Heliconius erected by the Ionian colonies, and imported into Attica from Asia Minor. The Dorian colonies of Asia Minor had likewise a common sanctuary, the temple of Apollo Triopius. Near to Mylassa was a temple sacred to Jupiter Carius and common to the Carians, the Lydians, and the Mysians. In the territory of Stratonice was the temple of Jupiter Chrysaoreus belonging to the Carians. In the immediate vicinity of these edifices, the people, at fixed seasons, held assemblies for the purpose of sacrificing to the gods; they also celebrated their fêtes on the same spot, and deliberated respecting the affairs of the entire nation.

The most ancient Greek temples were very small. The *cella* was barely large enough to contain the statue of the presiding deity of the temple, and occasionally an altar in addition. Even in succeeding ages, when the riches and power, as well as the taste and skill of the Grecian states were augmented, they were not built on a great scale; for their object did not render extent necessary, since the priests alone entered the cella, and the people gathered in masses outside the walls. Exceptions were made in those dedicated to the tutelary divinities of towns, of those of the supreme gods, and of those appropriated to the common use of various communities. But this increased extent was chiefly displayed in the porticoes surrounding the cella, and was again enlarged by the peribolos, or enclosure within a wall, which separated it from the adjoining ground, as a sacred place appertaining to the temple. This enclosure was generally adorned with a profusion of statues, altars, and monuments. Sometimes it contained other smaller temples, or even a grove. The elevation and retirement of these Sacred Enclosures, gave additional beauty, dignity, and sanctity to the temples contained within them.

The Grecian temples had, for the most part, possessions of their own, which served to defray the expenses incurred in the service of the god. These possessions consisted partly in votive presents, which had been consecrated (especially where the divinities of health and prophecy were adored) by the hopes or the gratitude of the suppliants for advice or counsel. We know from several examples, especially from that of the temple of Delphi, that treasures were there accumulated, of more value, probably, than those of Loretto, or any other shrine in Europe. But as they were sacred to the gods, and did not come into circulation, they were for the most part unproductive treasures, possessing no other value than that which they received from the artist.

The Greeks used three kinds of altars in their mythological worship; one, upon which they burned incense and made libations; another served for their sanguinary sacrifices; and the third received their burnt offerings and sacred vases. Originally, they were made of heaps of earth, and sometimes of ashes, as that of the Olympian Jupiter, mentioned by Pausanias. There was also an altar of ashes at Thebes, consecrated to Apollo. In process of time, they were formed of brick and stones; such was the material of the famous altar at Delos. They were at first erected in groves, in the highways, and streets, as well as upon the tops of mountains; but after the introduction of temples, they were of course transferred to those edifices.

The form of altars, as well as their height, was various among the ancients; sometimes a perfect cube, which was the most common among the Greeks; at others, a parallelopipedon; sometimes round, at others octangular, triangular, &c., according to the material of which they were formed; and from some ancient medals we find there were altars of a circular form. Those which were constructed of metal, were generally triangular and formed like a tripod; those constructed of brick or stone were mostly cubical, and some have sculptured bases and pedestals like candelabra. According to Pausanias, some were constructed of wood; but by far the greater number that have been preserved to our times, are of marble.

On solemn festivals, the ancients decorated the altars of their deities with leaves or the branches of trees that were sacred to them; as those of Minerva with the olive; Venus with the myrtle; Apollo with the laurel; Pan with the pine, &c. And it was from these temporary decorations, that the ancient sculptors drew those elegant elements of foliage, which embellish the altars of antiquity. On others, that were intended for their sanguinary oblations, and were hollowed at the top to receive the blood of their victims, and the offered libations, are found heads and sculls of animals, vases, pateræ,* and other instruments; also, vessels of sacrifice mingled with garlands of flowers, such as were used to bind the victims; also, bands and other sacrificial accessories. When inscriptions were added, they alluded to the epoch of their consecration, the names of those who erected them, the motive of their erection, and the name of the deity to whose honor they were dedicated.

Altars as well as temples were considered so sacred by

---

* *Patera*—A round plate or saucer used at the sacrifice.

the ancient Greeks, that most of them had the privilege of protecting malefactors and debtors, and even rebellious slaves who fled to them for refuge. Plutarch informs us, that those who killed Cylon and his followers, when holding by the altars, were afterwards stigmatized with the epithets impious and profane; and Justin, in his history, observes, that the murder of Laodamia, by Milo, who had fled to the altar of Diana for protection, was the cause of his death, and of the public calamities of Æolia. In the comedy of Mostellaria, by Plautus, the inviolability of altars and temples appears to have existed among the Romans. Every temple, however, was not a sanctuary; but only those which had been made so by consecration. The first asylum is generally supposed to have been founded at Athens by the Heraclidæ, but some writers assert that there was one previously erected at Thebes, by Cadmus.

Independent of the public altars, the Greeks and Romans had private or domestic altars, which were dedicated to the lares and penates, the household gods of the ancients.

All the nations of antiquity were at some period of their history addicted to the custom of offering sacrifices to the deities whom they worshipped. The origin of the practice is attributed by some to the Phœnicians, and by others to the Egyptians; while Ovid imagines, from the import of the words *victim* and *hostia*, that no bloody sacrifices were offered before the prevalence of wars, when nations became victorious over their enemies. These, however, are mere hypotheses not borne out by historical research or tradition, and are entitled to little regard.

The principal sacrifices among the Hebrews consisted of bullocks, sheep, and goats; but doves and turtles were accepted from those who were not able to bring these animals, which were to be perfect and without blemish. The rites of sacrificing were various, and all are minutely described in the books of Moses

The manner of sacrificing among the Greeks and Romans was as follows. In the choice of a victim they took care that it was without blemish or imperfection, and the bull was to be one that had never been yoked. Having pitched upon a victim, they gilded the forehead and horns, especially if a bull, heifer, or cow; the head was adorned with a garland of flowers, a woollen infula,* or holy fillet, from which hung two rows of chaplets with twisted ribbons; on the middle of the body was a kind of stole, which hung down on either side; the lesser victims were also adorned with garlands, and bunches of flowers, together with white tufts, or wreaths.

The victims thus prepared were brought before the altar; the lesser being driven to the place, and the greater led by a halter; if they made any struggle, or refused to go, the resistance was considered an ill-omen, and the sacrifice frequently set aside. The victim thus brought, was carefully examined to see that it was without defect; then the priest, clad in his sacerdotal habit, and accompanied by the sacrificers and other attendants, and being washed and purified according to the ceremonies prescribed, turned to the right and passed round the altar, sprinkling it with meal and holy water, and also sprinkling those who were present. The crier then proclaimed, with a loud voice, "Who is here?" To which the people replied, "Many and good." The priest then having exhorted the people to join with him, by saying, "Let us pray," confessed his own unworthiness, acknowledging that he had been guilty of divers sins, for which he begged pardon of the gods, and

---

* *Infula.*—A flock of white and red wool, which was tightly twisted, drawn into the form of a wreath or fillet, and used by the Romans as an ornament on festive and solemn occasions. In sacrificing, it was tied with a white band to the head of the victim, and also of the priest, more especially in the worship of Apollo and Diana. The "torta infula" was worn also by the vestal virgins.

his hope that they would be pleased to grant his requests, accept the oblations offered them, and send them all health and happiness; and to this general form, the priest added petitions for such particular favors as were then desired. Prayers being ended, he took a cup of wine, and having tasted it himself, caused his assistants to do the like; and then poured forth the remainder between the horns of the victim. The priest or the crier, and sometimes the most honorable person in the company, then killed the beast by knocking it down, or cutting its throat. If the sacrifice was in honor of the celestial gods, the throat was turned up towards Heaven; but if they sacrificed to the heroes or infernal deities, the victim was killed with his throat towards the ground. If by accident the beast escaped the stroke, leaped up after it, or expired with pain and difficulty, it was thought to be unacceptable to the gods. The victim being killed, the priest inspected its entrails and made predictions from them. They then poured wine, together with frankincense, into the fire to increase the flame, and then laid the sacrifice on the altar, which in the primitive times was burnt whole to the gods, and thence called a holocaust; but in after times, only part of the victim was consumed in the fire, and the remainder reserved for the sacrificers; the thighs, and sometimes the entrails were burnt to their honor, and the company feasted upon the rest. During the ceremony, the priest and the person who gave the sacrifice jointly prayed, laying their hands upon the altar. Sometimes musical instruments were played during the time of sacrifice, and on some occasions, the people danced around the altar singing sacred hymns in honor of the gods.

The barbarous practice of human sacrifices followed that of offering brutes. When men had gone so far as to indulge the fancy of bribing their gods by sacrifice, it was natural for them to think of enhancing the value of so cheap an atonement by the cost and variety of the offering; and when oppressed with suffering, they never rested until they had offered what they conceived to be the most precious of all, a human sacrifice.

The Gauls and Germans were so devoted to this shocking custom, that no business of any moment was transacted among them without being prefaced by the blood of men. They were offered up to various gods; but particularly to Hesus, Taranis, and Thautates. These deities are mentioned by Lucan, where he enumerates the various nations who followed the fortunes of Cæsar.

PART FIRST.

ANCIENT DEITIES.

CHAOS.

CHAOS (*void space*), a heterogeneous mass, containing all the seeds of nature, was first, according to Hesiod; then came into being the broad-breasted Earth, the gloomy Tartarus, and Love.

From Chaos were produced Earth, Love, Erebus, Night, and the Universe.

TERRA OR EARTH.

Earth was one of the most ancient oracles and deities in mythology. She produced the mountains, the sea, and the heavens.

Eros, or Love, was probably understood by the ancients to be that attractive principle in nature, by which homogeneous bodies are united; and to this principle, they poetically ascribe the attributes of reason and wisdom, to intimate, that in the formation of the world, all things were constituted by harmonious laws.

According to some mythologists, Love is of all gods the most ancient, and is said to have existed before all generations, and first incited Chaos to bring forth darkness, out of which sprang Ether and Day—and also, that his union with Chaos gave birth to men, the animals which inhabit the earth, and that even the gods themselves were the offspring of Love, before the foundation of the world.

Among the ancients, Love was worshipped with great solemnity, and as his influence was supposed to extend over the dead as well as the living, his divinity was universally acknowledged, and vows, prayers, and sacrifices, were offered to him.

Erebus, properly speaking, is the abode of Night; in conjunction with which he produced Day. This is the commencement of mythological fictions;—the opposite extremes of things are brought together;—from shapelessness and deformity arise form and beauty, and light is made to spring out of darkness.

Ancient mythologists and poets say, that the various parts of which the wondrous world consists, would have lain for ever in the abyss of being, if the breath of the tremendous Erebus, the spirit that dwells in eternal darkness, had not gone forth and put the mass in vital agitation. Then, the congenial parts began to sever from their heterogeneous associates, and mingle together. Matter appeared, and inseparable from it, attraction; different degrees of powers, and all active principles of nature continued and increased.

Order, Figurability, Succession, and Retention, were passive in the genial contest; but Intention and Aptitude mildly interfered, and begot Providence (*or foresight*), who, being joined with his bride, Measure (*or perfection*), the daughter of Contemplation, presided over the forming world, called to light the vegetable and animal race, and then crowned his wondrous work with the formation of man.

NOX OR NIGHT.

Night covers and conceals, and for this reason she is made the mother of the horrible, as well as the charming.

From uncreated Night, Daylight arose, by which all formations are developed, and all creatures enjoy life. She is likewise, according to some, the mother of the inexorable Parcæ, of the avenging Nemesis, who punishes hidden crime; of the Furies, who torment the wicked; of Charon, the Ferry-man of Hell; and of the twin brothers, Sleep and Death.

Night is also the mother of Dreams; of the Hesperides, who guard the golden apples;—of Deceit, enveloping himself in darkness;—of malicious censure;—of fretting grief; —of trouble and hunger;—of destructive war;—of duplicity of speech;—and finally, of perjury. Among the children of night are comprised all those things which she conceals; or which Fancy, herself, would fain cover with nocturnal darkness. In night, there is something of which even the gods stood in awe: for Homer says, " When Jupiter was angry at the god of sleep, Night covered him with her veil, and the thunderer restrained his wrath, fearing to offend swift Night."—(Il. xiv. 256.)

The nightly, mysterious darkness, in which something hidden exercises superior power and influence over gods and men, was not clear to the conception of the ancient poets. They understood not the supreme, over-ruling power, before which all other powers vanish; but believed in the hidden rule and authority that were apparent in the many miseries which mingled with the happiness of mortals. And as danger, fear, and mystery, have their attractions, as well as light, peace, and security, they delighted in the representations of dreadful events and wasting destruction, allowing their imaginations to stray far away into the dominion of night and the world of shadows.

Night was considered among the ancients as one of their oldest divinities, and was worshipped by them with great solemnity In the temple of Diana, at Ephesus, was a famous statue of her, to whom, as the mother of the Furies, black sheep were offered in sacrifice; and also a cock, as that bird proclaims the approach of Day, during the darkness of Night.

On antique gems we find Night represented in a female figure of youthful beauty; either holding in her arms two handsome boys, Death holding an extinguished torch in his hand, and Sleep with the stem of a poppy; or sitting beneath a shady tree, distributing poppies to Morpheus and his brothers. Morpheus, the son of sleep and the god of dreams, stands before her in youthful beauty, receiving the poppy from her hands, while his brothers are behind her, bent to the ground gathering the falling leaves.

It appears from these representations, poetical, as well as plastic, how carefully the ancients endeavored to transform gloom and terror into soothing images. And, on the other hand, what a high conception of tragical subjects, considering the night born, inevitable Fate, as the power that rules over gods and men, and whose old dominion and concealed future, lie far beyond the penetration of human knowledge and foresight.

PAN.

Various origins have been given to Pan (or the Universe), one of which is, that he sprang from Chaos; that is to say, Chaos contained the seeds of all things.

Among the most learned of the ancients, Pan was considered as one of the oldest divinities; and, according to the Egyptians, and the most learned of the Grecian sages, he had neither father nor mother, but sprang from Demogorgon (the genius of the earth) at the same instant with the fatal Parcæ. A beautiful way of saying that the universe derived its origin from a power unknown to them, and was formed according to the unalterable relations, and eternal aptitude of things, as were the Fates, daughters of Necessity.

The figure of Pan represents the universe, and is a delineation of nature and the rough face which it first wore, while his spotted robe of a leopard's skin represents the starry heavens. His person is a compound of various and opposite parts, rational and irrational, a man and a goat; so is the world;—an all-governing mind and heterogeneous, prolific elements pervade and constitute it.

Pan's symbol of the pipes is most eloquently expressive of nature's divine, harmonious constitution, and of the order and measure that govern all her works, producing that solemn movement called the music of the spheres; imperceptible indeed to our material organ, but so delightful and pleasing to the ear of the mind. This wondrous reed on which he incessantly plays, is composed of seven pipes, unequal among themselves, but fitted together in such just proportion as to produce the most unerring and melodious notes, calling forth the echo, which poets have made the object of his love.

The worship and the different functions of Pan, were derived from the mythology of the Egyptians. This deity was one of the eight great gods that they worshipped, ranking before the other gods, which the Romans called Consentes. They regarded him as the emblem of fecundity, and the principle of all things; therefore the Greeks gave him the appellation of Pan. He was worshipped with great solemnity at Mendes.

By the Arcadians he was venerated as the chief of the rural deities. Herdsmen and shepherds are said to have dreaded the sight of Pan, yet they regarded him as the tutelary deity of themselves, and of their flocks and herds, and brought him frequent offerings of milk and honey. Sacrifices were offered to him in a deep cave in the midst of a wood. The Athenians had a statue of him like that of Mars, and in some antique gems and sculptures his figure is nearly as formidable as that of the Medusa.

At Rome, there was a yearly festival celebrated in honor of Lupercus, or the Grecian Pan, with whom he was identified. This celebration took place on the 15th of February, and was called Lupercalia. The priests who officiated, and who were dedicated to the service of Pan, were called Luperci. This order of priests was the most ancient and respectable of all the sacerdotal offices. It was divided into two separate colleges, called Fabiani and Quintiliani, from Fabius and Quintilius, two of the high priests. The former were instituted in honor of Romulus, and the latter of Remus.

A goat was sacrificed to Pan, to which a dog was added because as god of shepherds he protected the sheepfold from the devouring wolf. The priests touched with a bloody knife the foreheads of two illustrious youths, who were obliged to smile during the ceremony; the blood was then wiped off with a bit of wool dipped in milk. After this, the skins of the victims were cut into thongs, with which whips were made for the youths, who ran about the streets, using them freely on all whom they met.

According to Baronius, Pope Gelasius abolished the Lupercalia in the year 469 of the Christian era.

PARCÆ OR FATES.

The Parcæ were daughters of Night, or an invisible, overruling power. According to some, the daughters of Necessity, or the necessary connection of things—by which is meant the Creator's eternal and immovable essence, to which the fable of her daughters, and their fatal spindle plainly points.

This necessary connection of things, or necessity itself, called by the Greeks Moira and Heimarmene, and by the Romans Fatum, was that mysterious power, which, with invisible sceptre, ruled over gods and men. The inexorable Parcæ were the attendants of this unknown being, and presided chiefly over the life and fate of mortal men.

They were three in number, according to the triple division of time into past, present, and future. Their everrunning thread is partly spun and wound up, partly just drawn out and twisting, and partly as yet on the distaff. Clotho holds the distaff, and is ever furnishing the present; Lachesis (allotment) spinning the thread of life, lays out the future; and Atropos (irreversion) with the fatal scissors cuts it off, severing the past; so that the grand transaction of time is not badly represented in the fable. But as Plato has nobly said, "All this is nothing but God himself, who, according to the ancient tradition, having the beginning, middle, and end of all things in his power,

keeps one straight, steady course according to nature, with his inseparable adherent, Justice, who is ever ready to avenge the least deviation from his divine law."

Although the Parcæ signify that terrific power which governs as it were from the dark, whose decrees are passed as soon as conceived, and against which there is no resistance, yet, they are represented as beautiful females, spinning, and joining at the same time in the song of the Sirens. In high and unlimited power, all things are easily accomplished; and the resistance even of the mighty finds in this height its termination. To prescribe bounds to all revolutions, only the slightest touch of the fingers is requisite, and to manage the mysterious course of events is made the easiest work of a female hand. This beautiful representation of the thread of life, delicately spun and easily severed, cannot be equalled by any other. The thread does not break, but is cut off; and the cause of this lies in a superior power, which has already firmly and irrevocably disposed of what gods and men still strive to accomplish in their own way.

Ancient representations of the Parcæ by the hand of art are seldom found. Upon the gems which antiquity has left us, Lachesis, who spins the thread of life, and is sometimes called the handsome daughter of Necessity, is represented in youthful beauty, seated, and spinning, having one distaff before and another behind her, and at her feet lie a comic and tragic mask. These masks are among the happiest allusions to human life, if we behold it with all its serious and comic scenes. Unaffected by either, she cannot be diverted from her purpose; but, during their course, the tender and delicate finger of the goddess never ceases to turn the fatal thread.

Another gem shows Lachesis leaning against a pillar in a quiet posture, carelessly holding a distaff in her left hand, and playing as it were with the thread of destiny. This quiet attitude in which the sublime goddess of destiny looks down upon the far extended designs of men, is an extremely beautiful idea of the ancient artist. For while gods exert all their power, and mortals all their strength to bring their plans and views to bear, this goddess, smiling, playfully holds the thread on which depend the limits of all things, even the proudest projects of gods and men.

In vain, for instance, does Jupiter endeavor to preserve the life of his son, Sarpedon, in the battle of Troy, against the will of Fate. "Wo's me," he exclaims, "that my son, Sarpedon, must fall under the hand of Patroclos, according to the doom of Fate." And although he would gladly rescue his son, yet his power must yield before that of the inexorable goddess. Nothing is left to his own will, but to deliver the body to his messengers, Death and sweet

Sleep, who carry it to his native land, where the friends and relatives may weep over it. (Il. xvi. 431.)

In the same manner Ulysses was doomed by destiny to wander ten years over foreign seas and countries, and at last to reach home without his companions. And in the history of his wanderings it may be seen, that where circumstances appear to afford the greatest pleasure, happiness, and security, there the greatest dangers lie concealed. As, for instance, in the quiet harbor of the Lestrigons, on occasion of the song of the Sirens, and in that of Circe's magic cup.

It is the history of human life in general. However near at hand Ulysses beholds the accomplishment of his wishes, all recedes; his tears and fervent prayers are in vain, until it is the will of Destiny that he shall again find his home, and he reaches his native island—sleeping.

The worship of the Parcæ was well established in some cities in Greece, and though mankind were convinced that they were inexorable, and that it was impossible to mitigate their will, yet they wished to show a proper homage to their divine power by raising to them temples and statues. They received the same worship as the Furies, and their votaries yearly sacrificed to them black sheep; during which ceremony the priests were obliged to wear garlands and flowers.

NEMESIS.

Nemesis, like the Parcæ, was the daughter of Night. Her office was to baffle pride and haughtiness, and to punish secret vice. She presided over the distribution of retributive justice, and her vengeance, if once provoked, was sure to fall on the offender at last, however long delayed In this fable is plainly seen the idea of retributive justice, which, though slow in its course, never fails, sooner or later, to overtake the wicked, who must inevitably suffer the consequences of their own wrong-doing. As a personification of the moral reverence for law, of the natural fear of committing a guilty action, and hence of conscience, she is mentioned in Hesiod's Theogony in connection with Shame.

Having belonged with the original deities, those mysterious beings who were regarded with awe and veneration by gods as well as men, she is allowed the same rank among the modern heathen deities, and was particularly worshipped at Rhamnus in Attica, where she had a celebrated statue.

The Greeks celebrated a festival in memory of their deceased friends, called Nemesia—as the goddess Nemesis was supposed to preserve the memory and relics of the dead from insult.

The Romans, also, were particularly attentive to the worship of Nemesis, whom they solemnly invoked, and to whom they offered sacrifices before declaring war against their enemies, to prove to the world that they did not act without the most just occasion. Her statue at Rome was in the Capitol.

THE ERINNYES OR FURIES.

The Erinnyes were originally a personification of the curses pronounced upon a guilty criminal. In this sense the word Erinnys is often used in the Homeric poems; and the poet, conceiving them as distinct beings, considered them as among the inhabitants of Erebus, whence they were called to life and activity, when some curse is pronounced upon the guilty.

The crimes which they are represented as punishing, are, disobedience to parents, violation of the respect due to old age, violation of the laws of hospitality, and improper conduct towards suppliants. As ministers of the vengeance of the gods, they were stern and inexorable. Upon earth they were employed to inflict vengeance by wars, pestilences, and dissensions, and by the secret stings of conscience ; and in hell they punished the guilty by continual flagellations and torments. Gradually they assumed the character of goddesses who punished crime after death, and seldom appeared on earth.

Neither Homer nor the Greek tragedians designate the Erinnyes by any particular names but the later poets make them three in number, viz. : Tisiphone, the avenger of murder ; Megæra, the wrathful ; and Alecto, the restless ; and so great was the awe in which men stood of these inexorable sisters, that they scarcely ventured to mention their names, or fix their eyes upon the temples dedicated to the Furies. They had a temple in Achaia, which no one guilty of crime could enter without being suddenly deprived of reason and made furious ; and whoever was conscious of having secretly perpetrated an unlawful action, endeavored to propitiate the Furies by prayers and offerings.

Their temple at Athens was near the Areiopagos, and few even of the superior deities received so much homage as the three avenging sisters ; and their priests formed a tribunal before which no one dared to appear, until he had sworn upon the altar of the Eumenides to tell nothing but the truth.

Their worship was almost universal ; and in their sacrifices the votaries used branches of cedar and of alder, hawthorn, saffron, and juniper. The victims were generally turtle doves and black sheep, with libations of wine and honey.

They were represented with snakes around their heads instead of hair, and wearing funereal robes fastened with girdles formed of snakes and scorpions. With one hand they grasp a dagger with whips of serpents and scorpions; in the other is held a flaming torch; and thus they are represented as pursuing the perpetrators of crime and wickedness. The Grecian artists, however, frequently represented the Furies as young and beautiful; sometimes with, and sometimes without serpents around their heads.

The Furies were also called Eumenides; but the term Eumenides, that is, the kindly disposed goddesses, is applied to them by a euphemism, or antiphrasis.

Helicon was consecrated to the Muses; but Cithæron was the mountain of the Erinnyes, and rang with the frantic yells of the wildest nocturnal orgies of Bacchanalian revelry. The aspect of Cithæron is the reverse of that of Helicon; it is savage, cold, gloomy, and inhospitable. All the mythological traditions connected with it, partake of the physical sternness which characterizes the mountain itself.

THE HESPERIDES.

The Hesperides are called daughters of Night, that is to say their origin and existence are veiled in darkness. Their names were Ægle, Erytheia, and Arethusa;—and they were appointed to guard the golden apples, which were the gift of Earth to Juno on her wedding day.

The celebrated gardens of the Hesperides abounded with fruits of the most delicious kinds, and were carefully guarded by a dreadful dragon, which never slept. By Hesiod, these gardens were placed beyond the Atlantic Ocean in the dusky horizon of the west, where they rested upon the shoulders of Atlas. By geographical writers they are placed near the ancient Berenice, now Bengazi in Cyrenaica on the Mediterranean coast of Africa.

MORS OR DEATH.

Mors, born of Night and without a father, was one of the infernal deities. By the ancients she was worshipped with great solemnity, and was represented by them, not as an actually existing power, but as an imaginary being.

The face of Mors, when they gave her any face, seems to have been of a pale, wan, dead color. The poets describe her as ravenous, treacherous, and furious, and as roving about open-mouthed and ready to swallow up all who came in her way. They give her black robes and dark wings; and often make her of a colossal stature. From the epithets *pallida* and *lucida*, pale and wan, she must have been represented with a pale face and meagre body, instead of the bare skull and skeleton of some modern painters.

The description of Death by the ancients was more frightful and dismal than that of modern artists and poets. They describe her as thundering at the doors of mortals to demand the debt they owe her. Sometimes as approaching their bedsides; and sometimes pursuing her prey; or as hovering in the air, and ready to seize it.

Death is sometimes represented as a skeleton, wearing a black robe, covered with stars, and having wings of an enormous length, and her fleshless arms supporting a scythe. No temples were dedicated to her, and no sacrifices offered, because Death is inexorable, inaccessible to entreaties, and unmoved by prayers and offerings.

SOMNUS.

Somnus, the son of Night, presided over sleep. According to some mythologists, his palace was a dark cave, where the sun never penetrates; at the entrance are a number of poppies and somniferous herbs. Virgil places him in the entrance to the infernal shades, on account of his relation to Lethe; but Ovid and Statius give him a place on our Earth.

The God of Sleep is represented as a child stretched on a couch in a profound slumber, holding in his hand a bunch of poppies, which serve also for a pillow. The Dreams stand by him; and Morpheus, as his attendant, watches to prevent the disturbance of his repose. Sometimes his head rests upon a lion's skin and sometimes on a lion, with one arm either a little over or under his head, and the other hanging carelessly by the side of the couch, having placed in it poppies, or a horn full of poppy juice.

He is often winged; and so like Cupid as to be frequently mistaken for him, notwithstanding the lizard at his feet, the proper attribute of Somnus, as it sleeps during half the year. The lizard is not mentioned by the poets, and may have been used by artists merely for the sake of distinction, though the poppy seems sufficient for the purpose, except in some few pieces, where the distinguishing attributes of both are blended together. In that case, it may be intended to represent Cupids under the character of Somnus.

Poets speak often of the wings of Somnus and of their being black, as most proper for the god who chiefly rules at night. For the same reason, the figures of him are of ebony, basalt, or dark-colored marble.

MORPHEUS.

Morpheus, the God of Dreams and son of Night, can assume any shape at pleasure, presenting dreams to those who sleep. To the palace of Somnus there are said to be two gates, one of ivory and the other of horn, out of which dreams pass and repass—the false through the ivory, the true through the transparent horn.

Morpheus is sometimes represented as a man advanced in years, with two large wings on his shoulders, and two small ones attached to his head.

MOMUS.

Momus (*Mockery*), a son of Night, was the god of raillery and repartee; at the feasts of the gods he played the buffoon. His office was to reprove the faults of the gods, which he did in so sarcastic a manner as to put himself out of favor. He blamed Vulcan, because in the human form which he made of clay, he had not placed a window in the breast, by which whatever was done or thought there might easily be brought to light. He censured the house made by Minerva, because it was not movable, by which means a bad neighborhood might be avoided. Of the bull which Neptune made, he observed, that the blows might have been surer, if the eyes were nearer the horns. Venus herself was exposed to his satire; and when the sneering god could find no fault in the figure of the goddess, he observed as she retired, that the noise of her feet was too loud, and very improper in the goddess of beauty. For these illiberal reflections upon the gods, he was driven from Heaven.

Momus is generally represented raising a mask from his face, and holding a small figure in his hand.

CHARON.

Charon, a god of Hell, and son of Erebus and Night, conducted the souls of the dead in a boat over the rivers Styx and Acheron, to the infernal regions. But he conveyed no one without their tribute, and it was a custom among the ancients in preparing the dead for burial, to place a piece of money under the tongue for Charon.

When a departed soul presented herself for a passage in his boat he first inquired whether the traveller could furnish the requisite fee; and if it should happen that the obolus had been forgotten, the poor soul was left to wander on the gloomy shores a hundred years before being conducted over the river; and such as had not been honored with a funeral, were subjected to the same penalty.

Among the ancients, it was considered an inexpressible cruelty to deny to the dead a burial; and for this reason, all great commanders were careful, after a battle, to inter the bodies of those whose lives had been lost in their service.

No living person was received into Charon's boat, unless he could show a golden bough which he had received from the Sybil as a passport. Yet it is said that Æneas by his piety, Hercules and Theseus by their valor, and Orpheus by his music, obtained the privilege of passing to and fro in old Charon's ferry boat.

Charon is represented as an old man with a ragged garment, a long grey neglected beard, and his forehead lined with wrinkles.

NEREUS.

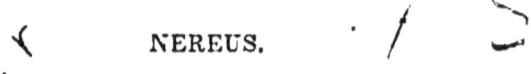

Nereus, the son of Pontos and Terra, was the personification of the smooth sea.

He married Doris, the daughter of Oceanos, and their children were the Nereïdes, or the nymphs of the sea. They are said to have been fifty in number, and their names are all mentioned; yet but few of them are introduced into the history of the gods. The greater part of them are represented as forming a splendid retinue when Thetis and Amphitrite, the principal ones, appeared on the sea.

The imagination of the ancients allowed no place to remain uninhabited, and therefore formed a multitude of creatures, and a variety of abodes, in regions which none but immortals could inhabit; and the rising of the marine deities from their crystal palaces to the surface of the waters afforded a subject for some attractive fables among the ancient poets. When on the sea shore, the Nereïdes resided in grottoes and caves, which were adorned with shells and shaded with vine branches.

They are represented as young and handsome virgins, sitting on dolphins, and holding Neptune's trident, or sometimes garlands of flowers. Their duty was to attend upon the more powerful deities of the sea, and to be subservient to the will of Neptune.

The Nereïdes were implored as well as the rest of the deities. Their altars were chiefly on the coasts of the sea, where the piety of mankind made them offerings of milk, oil, and honey, and often of the flesh of goats; as they had the power of ruffling or calming the waters, they were always addressed by sailors, who implored their protection, and that they would grant them a favorable voyage and a prosperous return.

Nereus was represented as an old man, with a long flowing beard, and hair of an azure color, and sometimes crowned with sea weed. The chief place of his residence was in the Ægean Sea, where he was surrounded by his daughters, who often danced around him in chorus.

He had the gift of prophecy, and informed those who consulted him of the different fates that awaited them.

AMPHITRITE. THETIS. GALATÆA.

Amphitrite became the wife of Poseidon, and Thetis was married to the Thessalian king, Peleus. Galatæa loved Acis, the handsome shepherd, and the monstrous Cyclop Polyphemos, sued in vain for her favor. On a certain occasion, the monster beheld the nymph at the foot of Mount Ætna, embracing his handsome rival. He became distracted with furious jealousy, and tearing up a rock from its roots, raised it in the air, and hurled it upon the lovers in order to bury them under its weight.

The nymph swiftly escaped into the sea, but Acis, overwhelmed by the massy stone, sprang forth from beneath

it as a purling brook, the waters of which produced a
meandering stream that bore his name.

THAUMAS.

Astonishment at the grand spectacles of nature rises out
of the sea, and with a few leading features, is personified
in Thaumas, a son of Pontos.

Thaumas is the father, and the Oceanide, Electra
(*Brightness*), the mother of Iris or the rainbow; that wonderful being, who, on account of the rapidity with which
her feet touch the earth, ere her head has left the clouds,
is represented as the female messenger of the immortals.
She shared with Mercury the honor of conveying to the
inhabitants of the earth the mandates of the superior
divinities; especially of Juno, to whose service she was
particularly attached, and whose person she constantly
attended.

Her most serious charge was to cut the thread of life
which seemed to detain the soul in the expiring body; she
is thus represented by Virgil, as being sent by Juno from
Olympus to release the struggling soul of Dido.

HARPIES.

Children of the same parents are the swift-winged Harpies, Aëllo, Ocypete, and Celæno; who, like raging torna-
does, rush forth from the sea and seize their prey—a horror to mortals who are unable to resist their rapacious
claws. They are represented as having the faces of virgins,
the bodies of vultures, and the claws of lions.

They were sent by Juno to plunder the tables of Phineus.
whence they were driven to the islands called Strophades.
They plundered Æneias during his voyage towards Italy.
and predicted many of the calamities which attended him.

According to Damm, the term Harpya signifies properly
a violent wind, carrying off any thing that is exposed to

its fury; in other words, a furious whirlwind. Hence the fable of the Harpies. To the vivid imagination of the Greeks, the terrors of the storm were intimately associated with the idea of powerful and active dæmons directing its fury. The names given to the Harpies indicate this; viz. Ocypete, *rapid ;* Celæno, *obscurity ;* and Aëllo, *a storm.* With Homer, the Harpies are goddesses who suddenly carry off persons unseen and unheard.

GRÆÆ.

Phorcys, and his wife Ceto, are the children of Pontos and parents of the monsters. Grææ (*Gray-maids,*) Perphredo (*horrifier*), Enyo (*shaker*), and Deino (*terrifier*), three decrepit virgins, who were grey with age from their very birth. Their abode was at the end of the earth, where reigns eternal night.

THE GORGONS.

The Gorgons, Euryale, Stheïno, and Medusa, were daughters of the same parents. Instead of hair their heads were covered with serpents. They had the faces and breasts of women, and their bodies, which terminated in the tails of serpents, were covered with scales. Their very looks had the power of turning the beholder to stone. Medusa, who was killed by Perseus, was the only one of them subject to mortality.

We find the Graeae always united with the Gorgons, whose guards they were, according to Æschylus. This poet describes them as " three long-lived maids, swan formed, having one eye and one tooth in common, and on whom the sun with his beams nor the mighty moon ever looks." Perseus, he says, intercepted the eye as they were handing it from one to the other, and having thus blinded the guard, was enabled to approach the Gorgons unperceived.

CHRYSAOR.

From the blood of Medusa, sprang Chrysaor with the golden sword, and the winged Pegasos.

Chrysaor married Callirrhöe, a daughter of Oceanos; and they became the parents of the triple-bodied Geryon, and Echidna, who was upwards a beautiful nymph, but terminated below in a hideous coiling dragon.

With Echidna, the giant Typhoeus produced the triple-headed dog Cerberos, that watched the gates of Pluto's dismal realm, the two-headed dog Orthrus, the Lernaean Hydra, and the fire-vomiting Chimaera. Echidna is also said to be the mother of the Nemaean Lion and the mysterious Sphinx.

CERBEROS.

Cerberos was variously described by the ancient mythologists and poets. According to Hesiod he had fifty heads, and according to others only three. He was stationed at the entrance of Hell as a watchful keeper, to prevent the living from entering the infernal regions, and the dead from escaping their confinement. It was usual for the heroes, who in their lifetime visited the dominions of Aides, to appease the barking mouth of Cerberos with a cake.

HYDRA.

The celebrated Hydra, which infested the lake of Lerna in Peloponnesus, had, according to Diodorus, a hundred heads; according to Simonides, fifty; and according to the more received opinion of Apollodorus, the number was nine. As soon as one of these heads was cut off, two immediately grew in its place, unless the wound was instantly touched with fire. To destroy the Hydra was one of the twelve labors of Hercules.

CHIMÆRA.

Chimæra was represented as a dreadful monster, having the head and breast of a lion, the body of a goat, and continually vomited forth fire.

This fiction was probably occasioned by a lambent flame of some ignited gas issuing from a small cavity in the side of a lofty mountain of Lycia, and which is still apparent. On the summit of the mountain were lions; in the middle goats pastured; and the lower parts of it were infested with serpents. Bellerophon, a famous hero, made this mountain habitable, and was therefore said to have killed the Chimæra.

THE SPHINX.

The Sphinx was a monster with the face of a woman, the breast, feet, and tail of a lion, and the wings of a bird. Juno, always hostile to the city of Dionysos, sent this monster to ravage the territory of Thebes. She had been taught riddles by the Muses, and from the Phicean Hill propounded one to the Thebans: It was this: "What is that which has one voice, is four-footed, two-footed, and at last three-footed?" The oracle told the Thebans that they would not be delivered from the Sphinx until they had solved her riddle. They often met to try their skill, and when they failed, the Sphinx carried off and devoured one of their number. At length Hæmon, son of Creön, having become her victim, his father, by public proclamation, offered his throne and the hand of his sister Iocasta to whoever should solve the riddle.

Œdipus, who was then at Thebes, hearing this, came forward and answered the Sphinx, that it was man, who when an infant creeps on all fours; when a man, goes on two feet; and when old, uses a staff, a third foot. The Sphinx then flung herself down to the earth and perished.

GIANTS. CYCLOPES. TITANS.

Earth united with Heaven produced Oceanos and the giants with fifty heads and a hundred hands—by which is meant, the personification of the great powers of nature— as their names signify: Cottos (*eruption*), Briareos (*hurricane*), and Gyes (*earthquake*). The Cyclopes which represented the energies of the sky; Steropes (*lightning*), Brontes (*thunder*), and Arges (*the candent bolt*). Also the Titans and Titanides, whose names signify the milder powers of nature, or some of the planets. Titans (so called from Titaia, one of the epithets of Earth), Cœos (*he that begets*), Hyperion (*superior or wandering on high*), Crios (*the ruler*), Japetos (*intention*), Kronos (*time*). Titanides—Phœbe (*the shining*), Rhea (*succession*), Themis (*justice*), Theia (*order*), Tethys (*the nourisher*), Mnemosyne (*retention or memory*).

These productions became formidable to their father, who closely confined them in the grottoes of the earth, and never permitted them to see the light. Earth, displeased at their fate, forged the first sickle or scythe, and giving it to Kronos, the youngest of the Titans, instigated him to limit the power of his father by maiming him. From the drops of blood that Earth received in her lap, arose the giants Porphyrion, Alcyoneus, Cromedon, Encelados, and Rhœtus. What fell into the sea rendered it prolific, and from the foam arose Venus, the goddess of Love and Beauty. She was the first beautiful object that arose from the contest of power against power among the productions of Earth; and deriving her origin from the creative power of Heaven, she is the representation of all that is beautiful and attractive, commanding the homage of gods as well as men.

THE NYMPHÆ.

According to Hesiod, the Nymphs were also the productions of Heaven. The Greeks divided them into various orders according to the place of their abode.

Thus, the Mountain-Nymphs (*Oreiads*) haunted the mountains. The *Napææ*, or Dale-Nymphs, the valleys; the *Leimoniades*, or Mead-Nymphs, the meadows; the *Naiades*, or Water-Nymphs, the rivers, brooks, and springs; the *Limniades*, or Lake-Nymphs, the lakes and pools. There were also the *Hamadryades*, or Tree-Nymphs, who were born and died with the trees; the *Dryades*, or Wood-Nymphs, and the *Meliades*, the Fruit-tree-Nymphs, or Flock-Nymphs, who watched over gardens, or flocks of sheep.

The charge of rearing various gods and heroes was committed to the Nymphs; for instance, they were the nurses of Dionysos, Pan, and even Jupiter himself; and they also brought up Aristæos and Æneias. They were also the attendants of the goddesses; they waited on Juno and Venus, and in huntress-attire, pursued the deer over the mountains in the company of Diana.

One of the most interesting species of Nymphs are the Hamadryades, those personifications of the vegetable life of plants. They possessed the power to reward and punish those who prolonged or abridged the existence of their associate-tree.

A man named Rhœcos, happening to see an oak just

ready to fall to the ground, ordered his slaves to prop it up. The Nymph, who had been on the point of perishing with the tree, came to him expressing her gratitude for having saved her life, and at the same time desired him to ask what reward he would. Rhœcos then requested permission to be her lover, to which the Nymph acceded; charging him at the same time to avoid the society of other women, and told him that a bee should be her messenger. On a time, the bee happened to come to Rhœcos as he was playing at draughts, when he made a rude reply; which so incensed the Nymph that she deprived him of sight.

OCEANOS.

Oceanos, son of Heaven and Earth (*Uranos* and *Ge*, or *Calus* and *Terra*), married Tethys, in connection with whom he produced the Rivers and Fountains, and the Oceanides.

The name of Oceanos is made to signify an immense stream, which according to the rude ideas of the ancients circulated round the terraqueous plain, and from which the different seas ran out in the manner of bays. This opinion, which was also that of Eratosthenes, was prevalent even in the time of Herodotus. This same river Oceanos was supposed to ebb and flow thrice in a single day; and the heavenly bodies were believed to descend into it at their setting, and emerge from it at their rising.

The ancients were superstitious in their worship of Oceanos, reverencing, with great solemnity, a deity to whose care they intrusted themselves when going on a voyage. He presided over every part of the sea, and even rivers were subject to his power. According to Homer, he was father of all the gods, and on that account received frequent visits from the other deities.

Oceanos is generally represented as an old man, with a long, flowing beard, and sitting upon the waves of the sea

He often holds a pike in his hand, and ships under sail appear in the distance.

RIVERS AND FOUNTAINS.

As productions of Oceanos, the Rivers and Fountains belong to the ancient Deities; but in the later history of the gods, imagination has given them personality, and they appear as active beings. As for example, Scamander, Achelous, Peneus, Alpheios, and Inachos. This personification of the running waters has given rise to some beautiful fictions, and the head of a people whose origin is not known, is called a son of the river near the shores of which are found the dwellings of his descendants. Æschylus introduces the Fountains as pitying Prometheus, when he was chained to the rock by Jupiter, and complaining with him of the tyranny to which he was subjected.

There are few streams so celebrated in antiquity as the Alpheios. Its proximity to the scene of the Olympic contests, continually connects its name with the mention of those memorable games.

There is also a pleasing legend connected with this stream. According to the poets, Alpheios loved and pursued the Nymph Arethusa; who was only saved from him by the intervention of Diana, who for that purpose changed her into a fountain. This fountain she placed in the island of Ortygia, near the coast of Sicily. The ardent river-god, however, did not then desist, but worked a passage for himself amid the intervening ocean, and rising again in the Ortygian island, his waters were mingled with those of the fountain Arethusa.

According to another version of the same legend, it was Diana herself, and not the nymph Arethusa, whom the river-god of the Alpheios pursued; and when this pursuit ended in the island of Ortygia, then arose the fountain Arethusa.

This account affords a clew to the true meaning of the entire fable. The goddess. it appears, had an altar at Olympia in common with the god of the Alpheios. To the same Diana water was held sacred; and this part of her worship, having passed from the Peloponnesus into Sicily, the worship of the Alpheios accompanied it; or, in other words, a common altar for the two divinities was erected by the Syracusans in Ortygia, similar in its attendant rites and ceremonies to the altar at Olympia. In the island of Ortygia all water was considered sacred, and Diana was worshipped at the fountain of Arethusa. And from this commingling of rites arose the poetic legend, that the Alpheios had passed through the ocean to Ortygia and blended its waters with those of Arethusa; or, in other words, its rites with those of Diana.

INACHOS.

A considerable portion of ancient history is traced back to Inachos, son of Oceanos. Inachos was a stream that watered the fields of Argolis in Peloponnesus; fiction gave it personality, and made it the author of the people who lived around its shores.

His son Phoroneus taught them the use of fire; and having previously been dispersed in the woods, he persuaded them to unite and build themselves contiguous dwellings. Thus, Phoroneus causing his people to make the first step towards civilization, became one of the earliest and principal benefactors to mankind.

Io, a daughter of Inachos, loved by Jupiter, and persecuted by Juno, was transformed into a cow, and furiously driven over the whole earth, until she found a resting-place in Egypt. There she had a temple erected, and was worshipped as a goddess (Isis). She gave a son to Jupiter, called Epaphos, from whom sprang a royal race, that afterwards reigned in Greece; founding their right of royal authority on descent from old Inachos.

Libya, a daughter of the Egyptian king Epaphos, gave two sons to Poseidon, Belus and Agenor; the latter was king of Tyre. Cadmos, who is said to have brought the first letters into Greece, and to have founded the city of Thebes, was his son; and Europa, the mother of Minos, his daughter.

Belus, the other grandson of Epaphos, was the father of Danäos and Egyptus, the former of whom came over from Egypt to Greece, and reigned in Argos. From him Acrisius descended, the father of Danäe, and the grandfather of the heroic Perseus. Alcæus was a son of Perseus; and a grand-daughter of Alcæus, Alcmena, was the mother of Hercules.

These are the principal personages descended from the heroic family of Inachos. From the impossibility of tracing back any family of kings further than Inachos, arose the common saying of the ancient poets: "Though thou canst derive thy origin from old Inachos, thou still remainest a victim of inexorable Orcus."

10.

Io, daughter of Inachos, was priestess of Juno at Argos, and, unhappily for her, was beloved by Jupiter. When this god found that his conduct had excited the suspicions of Juno, he changed Io into a white cow, and declared with an oath that he had been guilty of no infidelity.

The Goddess, affecting to believe him, asked the cow as a present; and, on obtaining her, set the "all-seeing Argus" to watch her. He accordingly bound her to an olive-tree in the grove of Mycenæ, and there kept guard over her. Jupiter, pitying her situation, directed Mercury to steal her away. The god of ingenious devices made the attempt; but, as a vulture always gave Argus warning of his projects, he found it impossible to succeed. Nothing then remained but open force. Mercury killed Argus with a stone, having first lulled him to sleep with his lyre, and hence obtained the appellation of Argus-slayer.

The vengeance of Juno, however, was not yet satiated; and she sent a gadfly to torment Io, who fled over the whole world from its pursuit. She swam through the Ionian Sea, which was fabled to have hence derived its name from her. She then roamed over the plains of Illyria, ascended Mount Hæmus, and crossed the Thracian Strait, thence named the Bosphorus; she rambled on through Scythia and the country of the Cimmerians, and, after wandering over various regions of Europe and Asia, arrived at last on the banks of the Nile, where she assumed her original form, and bore to Jupiter a son named Epaphos.

The whole story of Io is an agricultural legend, and admits of an easy explanation. Io, whether considered as the offspring of Iasos (the favorite of Ceres), or Peiron (the "experimenter" or "tryer"), is a type of early agriculture, progressing gradually by the aid of slow and painful experience. Jupiter represents the firmament, the genial source of light and life; Juno, on the other hand, is the type of the atmosphere, with its stormy and capricious changes. Early agriculture suffers from these changes, which impede more or less the fostering influence of the pure firmament that lies beyond; and hence, man is obliged to watch with incessant and sleepless care over the labors of primitive husbandry. This ever-watchful superintendence is typified by Argus with his countless eyes, save that in the legend he becomes an instrument of punishment in the hands of Juno.

Juno being the type of the atmosphere, the peacock was considered as sacred to that goddess.

Ovid gives to Argus a hundred eyes, of which only two ever slept at the same time: he also makes Mercury to have slain him with a *harpé*, or short curved sword.

STYX.

Styx, a daughter of Oceanos and Tethys. Also a celebrated river of hell round which it flowed nine times. The waters of this subterranean fountain trickle in nightly gloom from a high vaulted rock, forming the stream over which there is no return; and by this stream the gods swear that inviolable oath, the obligation of which no power of heaven or earth can dissolve. Thus the gods on high swear by the deep where night reigns, and where, according to the ancients, are the foundations of the universe on which depend the preservation of all things.

If any of the gods were guilty of perjury, Jupiter obliged them to drink of the water of the Styx, which for a whole year lulled them to senseless stupidity; for the nine following years they were deprived of the nectar and ambrosia of the gods; after the expiration of this period of punishment they were restored to the assembly of the gods and to the enjoyment of their original privileges.

HYPERION.

Hyperion and Theia unite and produce Eos (*Dawn or Aurora*), Helios, and Luna. Eos married Astræos (*Starry*), the son of the Titan Crios, and became the mother of the strong winds, Zephyros, Boreas, and Notos,* and Eosphoros (*Dawn-bearer*), or the morning star.

Appearing in the grey twilight of morning, Aurora lifts with rosy fingers the veil of Night, sheds a radiant lustre over the earth, and disappears at the entrance of Helios.

She is represented as standing in a magnificent chariot, and sometimes drawn by winged steeds. A brilliant star sparkles upon her forehead, and while with one hand she grasps the reins, she holds in the other a lighted torch.

HELIOS OR SOL.

Helios, or Sol, belonged likewise to the ancient deities; in which, with a few strong features, the grand objects of nature are personified; for it is the shining sun that appears in the image of Helios. His head is surrounded by rays, and he gives light both to gods and men. He sees and hears every thing, and discovers all that is kept secret.

To him were sacred those fat oxen that grazed without herdsmen in the island of Sicily, and at the sight of which he was delighted as he passed through the skies. When, therefore, the companions of Ulysses had killed several of them, the god of the sun threatened Jupiter that he would descend into Orcus and carry light to the dead unless he avenged the injury done him. Jupiter terrified by his threats, immediately dashed the ship in pieces, so that Ulysses' companions became a prey to the sea. (Il. xii. 260.)

Sometimes the god of the sun is called Titan, on account of his belonging to that family; or from his father,

---

* See large edition.

with whom he is sometimes confounded in ancient tales; or Hyperion, a name which signifies height and sublimity; and it is remarkable that a term of precisely the same import (*Ikare*) is applied to the same luminary by the Iroquois of North America.

Sol was an object of veneration among the ancients, and was particularly worshipped by the Persians under the name of Mithras.

HECATE.

Coïos and Phœbe unite and produce Latona and Asteria. The latter married Perses, and became the mother of Hecate; who, although of the Titan family, is highly honored by Jupiter as well as the other gods; for she belonged to that class of beings whose power was supposed to extend throughout the universe. She was considered as one of the fatal deities who distributed either victory or renown according to her pleasure, and in whose hands lies the fate of men. She reigns on earth, in the sea, and in the air; and was called Luna in heaven, Diana on the earth, and Persephone in hell. She was supposed to preside over magic and enchantment; and to her, kings and nations considered themselves indebted for their prosperity.

Hecate is undoubtedly a stranger divinity in the mythology of the Greeks. It would appear that she was one of the hurtful class of deities, transported by Hesiod into the Grecian mythology, and placed behind the more popular deities, as a being of earlier existence.

Jablonski regards Hecate as the same with the Egyptian Tithrambo. Her actions upon nature, her diversified attributes, her innumerable functions, are a mixture of physical, allegorical, and philosophical traditions respecting the fusion of the elements and the generation of beings. Hecate was the night; and by an extension of this idea, the primitive night, the primary cause or parent of all things. She was the moon; and hence were connected with her all those ideas which are grouped around the moon; she is the goddess that troubles the reason of men; the goddess that presides over nocturnal ceremonies, and consequently over magic; hence her identity with Diana for the Grecian mythology, and with Isis for the Egyptian; and hence also her cosmogonical attributes assigned to Isis in Egypt.

Dogs, lambs, and honey were generally offered to Hecate, especially in highways and cross-roads—hence she obtained the name of Trivia. Expiatory sacrifices were offered to her on the thirtieth of every month, in which eggs and young dogs were the principal objects. The remains of the offerings, together with a large quantity of all sorts of comestibles, were exposed in the cross-roads, and called the supper of Hecate. The poorer classes and cynics seized upon these viands with an eagerness that passed among the ancients as a mark of extreme indigence, or the lowest degree of baseness.

The Athenians also paid particular worship to Hecate, who was deemed the patroness of families and children. From this circumstance the statues of the goddess were erected before the doors of houses. Upon every new moon a supper was provided at the expense of the wealthy, and set in the streets, where the poorest of the citizens were allowed to feast upon it, while they reported that it was devoured by Hecate. This public supper was always held in a place where three ways met, in allusion to the triple nature of the goddess.

There were also expiatory offerings to supplicate the goddess to remove whatever evils might impend on the head of the public.

Her statues were in general dog-headed; and were set up at Athens and elsewhere in the market-places and cross roads. It is probable that the dog-headed form was the ancient and mystic one of Hecate, and that under which she was worshipped in the mysteries of Samothrace, where dogs were immolated in her honor. Her mysteries were also celebrated at Ægina, and their establishment was ascribed to Orpheus. Numerous statues of the goddess were to be seen in this island, one by Myron with a single face, others with two faces, attributed to the famous Alcamenes.

Hecate was generally represented as a woman with the head of a female, a horse, or a dog; and sometimes with three distinct bodies, having three different faces united in one neck.

ASTRÆOS. PALLAS. PERSES.

Crios and Eurybia (*Wide strength*), a daughter of Pontos, gave birth to the Titans, Astræos (*Starry*), Pallas (*Shaker*), and Perses (*Bright*).

Pallas married Styx, the daughter of Oceanos, who gave him powerful children; Zelos (*Zeal*), Nike (*Victory*), Kratos (*Power*), and Bia (*Strength*). In the war of the gods, Styx, by the advice of her father, went over with her children to Jupiter, and since that time the latter have their seat near the ruler of Heaven and Earth. Victory became one of the attendants of Jupiter.

IAPETOS.

Iapetos marries Clymene, Oceanos' daughter, and is the parent of the Titans, Atlas, Menœtius, Epimetheus, and Prometheus. Atlas married Pleïone, one of the Oceanides, and had twelve daughters called Atlantides. Seven of the daughters were changed into a constellation called Pleïades, and the rest into another called Hyades. Atlas was also the father of the fair nymph, Calypso, who so long detained Ulysses in her island in the distant west.

ATLAS.

The name of Atlas signifies the Endurer; and Homer calls him the *wise* or *deep thinking*, who knows all the depths of the sea, and keeps the long pillars which hold Heaven and Earth asunder.

It is hardly necessary to state, that the Atlas of Homer and Hesiod is not the personification of a mountain. In process of time, however, when the meaning of the earlier legend had become obscured or lost, Atlas, the keeper of the pillars that support the Heaven, became a mountain of Libya. It is remarkable, however, that in all the forms which the fable assumes, it is the god or man Atlas who is turned into, or gives name to the mountain. Thus, according to one mythologist, Atlas was a king of the remotest west, rich in flocks and herds, and master of the trees that bore the golden apples. An ancient prophecy delivered by Themis, had announced to him, that his precious trees would be plundered by a son of Jupiter. When therefore Perseus, on his return from slaying the Gorgon, arrived in the realms of Atlas, and seeking hospitality, announced himself to be a son of the king of the gods, the western monarch, calling to mind the prophecy, attempted to repel him from his doors. Perseus, inferior in strength, displayed the head of Medusa, and the inhospitable monarch was turned into the mountain which still bears his name.

According to another account, Atlas was a man of Libya, devoted to astronomy. Having ascended a lofty mountain, for the purpose of making observations, he fell into the sea, and both sea and mountain were named after him. His supporting the heavens was usually explained by making him an astronomer and the inventor of the sphere.

There is also another curious legend relating to Atlas, which forms part of the fables connected with the adventures of Hercules. When this hero in quest of the apples of the Hesperides, had come to the spot where Prometheus lay chained, moved by his entreaties, he shot the eagle that preyed upon his liver. Prometheus out of gratitude warned him not to go himself to take the golden apples, but to send Atlas for them, and in the mean time to support the Heaven in his stead. The hero did as desired, and at his request Atlas went to the Hesperides and obtained three apples from them; he then proposed to take them himself to Eurystheus, while Hercules remained to support the sky. At the suggestion of Prometheus, the hero feigned consent, but begged him to take hold of the heavens till he made a pad to put upon his head. Atlas threw down the apples and resumed his burden, and Hercules picked them up and went his way.

Various elucidations of the legend of Atlas have been given by the modern expounders of mythology. The best is that of Vollker. This writer, taking into consideration the meaning of his name, in connection with the position assigned him by Homer and Hesiod, and the species of knowledge ascribed to him, and also his being the father of two constellations, regards Atlas as a personification of navigation; the conquest of the sea by human skill, trade, and mercantile profit.

PROMETHEUS AND EPIMETHEUS.

The origin of men in these fictions is so subordinate, that they are represented as not even owing their existence to the reigning gods, but to a descendant of the Titans. Prometheus, a son of Iapetos, is said to have formed the first man out of clay. His three brothers, Atlas, Menœtius, and Epimetheus, were, as well as himself, hated by the gods. Iapetos, their father, was at the same time with the other Titans thrown into Tartarus. His powerful son, Menœtius, on account of his dangerous strength and haughty pride, was killed by Jupiter's lightnings; upon the shoulders of Atlas, Jupiter laid the whole burden of the weight of the skies; Prometheus was by his direction fastened to a rock, where a vulture perpetually gnawed at his liver; and Epimetheus was destined to bring woe and misery upon mankind. Thus odious to the gods was the family of Iapetos, from which man took his origin, and on whom all immeasurable sufferings were afterwards heaped together, by which he was made to atone for his grudged existence.

According to ancient fable, the formation of man was accomplished in the following manner:—Prometheus took a piece of earth, a portion of clay still impregnated with divine particles, moistened it with water, and formed man after the image of the gods; so that he alone raises his look to heaven. while all other creatures bend their eyes to the ground. This representation shows that Fancy could not ascribe even to the gods, a form superior to that of man. for there is, in universal nature (and nature is Fancy's great magazine), no being deserving this preference. The beams of the sun give light, but man sees; the thunder rolls and the waves of the sea roar, but the tongue of man utters distinct and intelligible sounds; the moon and stars glitter in light and beauty, but the human countenance is indicative of a superior illumination.

When Prometheus had succeeded in representing the divine form, he burned with desire to bring his work to perfection. He rose therefore to the chariot of Phœbus, in order to kindle the torch, from the fire of which he blew ethereal flames into the breasts of his creatures—thus giving them warmth and life. But the wrath of Jupiter was kindled against him, as a creator of divine formations, and he determined on the destruction of mankind. Prometheus, having sacrificed two bulls, wrapped the meat in one hide and the bones in the other, and then, in order to try

Jupiter, asked him which he would prefer as an offering. Jupiter designedly chose the worse part, that he might have a plausible pretext for anger against Prometheus, and of persecuting his creatures, and immediately deprived them of fire. He durst not give vent to his hatred against Prometheus himself. His first object was, to destroy his work; but in this he did not succeed. The noble son of Earth ascended a second time to the chariot of the sun, and again brought down the ethereal spark, hiding it in the stem of a reed. But when from afar, Jupiter descried the light of fire upon the earth, he formed the design of punishing men through their own folly. He therefore requested Vulcan to make a woman of clay, which he intended sending to Prometheus for a wife; he directed him to knead earth and water till it assumed the form of a virgin, like the immortal goddesses, and then to give it human voice and strength. Jupiter also desired Minerva to endow her with artist-knowledge, Venus to give her beauty, and Mercury to inspire her with an impudent and artful disposition. When formed, she was attired by the Seasons and Graces, and each of the deities having bestowed upon her the desired gifts, she was called Pandora (*All-gifted*).

Jupiter then gave her a beautiful box which she was ordered to present to the man who married her; and by the commission of the god, Mercury conducted her to Prometheus. In the box was enclosed the whole train of evils that threaten mankind. Prometheus, aware of the fraud, rejected the dangerous gift, and sent Pandora away without suffering himself to be captivated by her charms.

He continued to teach men every useful art, for which the employment of fire is necessary, and which was the greatest of his benefits; but deprived them of the view into futurity, lest they should anticipate unavoidable evils. Thus, notwithstanding the efforts of Jupiter, he went on to perfect the creation and formation of mankind, although well aware that he must atone for it in a horrible manner.

Jupiter, still more enraged by the failure of his cunning attempt, and burning with the desire of revenging himself upon Prometheus, now ordered him to be fastened to a rock, on Mount Caucasus, where a vulture fed all day upon his liver, which, growing again during the night, continued to be the means of his torments.

Meanwhile, the misfortunes appointed to men came upon them, in spite of the prudence of Prometheus. The inconsiderate Epimetheus, although warned by his brother, suffered himself to be captivated by the charms of Pandora; who, after he had married her, opened the pernicious box out of which all imaginable evils spread themselves over the whole earth, inflicting misery upon mankind. Pandora, perceiving the pernicious contents of the box, immediately closed it again. But, alas! it was too late. The evils had all escaped, and nothing remained in the box but Hope; who, according to Jupiter's decree, should in due time afford some consolation to mortals. And she alone has the wonderful power of easing the labors of man, and rendering the troubles and sorrows of life less painful.

Prometheus is represented as feeling deeply the sufferings of mankind. He may be considered as the never-ceasing disquietude, the restless, never satisfied desire of mortals; for the liver upon which the vulture preys never dies, and the liver was thought by the ancients to be the seat of desire. His inventive genius introduced fire, and the arts which result from it; and man, henceforth, became a prey to care and anxiety, the love of gain and other evil passions which torment him, and which are personified in the eagle that fed on the inconsumable liver of Prometheus.

According to the fable, the pains of Prometheus lasted until a mortal by his valor and invincible courage made himself a path to immortality, and thus, as it were, reconciled Jupiter to mankind. Hercules, son of Jupiter and Alcmene, killed the vulture with his father's consent, and delivered the sufferer from his long torments. As the mortal foe of the Titans, and the unrelenting persecutor of Prometheus, Jupiter strove to ruin the race of men. But as the quiet power that is superior to its own wrath, and in concord with fate, he at last calmly beheld the rising of new generations, that by sufferings, strength, and perseverance, became assimilated to the gods themselves.

OGYGES. DEUCALION.

After Prometheus retreats from the theatre and transactions of the world, those who take his place in the great cause of humanity, the new fathers of mankind, by whose assistance they rise as it were from oblivion, are Deucalion, Ogyges, Cecrops, and Inachos.

During the time of Ogyges, son of Terra, a deluge occurred which is anterior to that of Deucalion. The horizon of all history is closed by this Ogygian flood, and even the wide field of fable here finds its limits.

Ogyges reigned in Bœotia, which from him is sometimes called Ogygia; his power was also extended over Attica. It is supposed that he was of Egyptian or Phœnician extraction, but his origin as well as the age in which he lived, and the duration of his reign, are so obscure and unknown, that the epithet Ogygian is often applied to any thing of dark antiquity.

The Greek legend respecting the deluge of Deucalion is as follows:—Deucalion, son of Prometheus and Clymene, was married to Pyrrha, daughter of Epimetheus and Pandora. When Jupiter designed to destroy the brazen race of men on account of their impiety, Deucalion, by the advice of his father, made himself an ark, and putting provisions into it, entered it with his wife Pyrrha. Jupiter then poured rain from Heaven, and inundated a greater part of Greece, so that the people, except a few who escaped to the lofty mountains, perished in the waves. At the same time, the floods burst through the mountains of Thessaly, and all Greece without the Isthmus, as well as the Peloponnesus, was overflowed. Deucalion was carried along the sea in his ark for nine days and nights, until he reached mount Parnassus. By this time the rain had ceased; and leaving his ark, he sacrificed to Jupiter, who sent Mercury desiring him to ask what he would. His request was, to have the earth replenished with men. Thereupon, by the direction of Jupiter, he and his wife threw stones behind them, and those which Deucalion threw became men, and those thrown by Pyrrha, women.

Although Deucalion is called the renewer of the destroyed family of Prometheus, yet we see that other traditions, still more ancient, are connected with the fictions respecting him, and that they confine Deucalion's new creation, or formation of men, to a part of Greece.

Amphictyon, a son of Deucalion, first established a sacred association among the several tribes of Greece, who, by means of common consultations, were so closely united together as to form one nation. This sacred institution was called after the name of its founder, the Amphictyonic council.

Hellen, Deucalion's second son, from whose name the Greeks are called Hellenes, reigned in Thessaly, and was the father of Eolus, who became the ancestor of many heroes. The most renowned among them are Meleager, Bellerophon, and Iasion. Meleager killed the Caledonian boar, Bellerophon vanquished the monster Chimæra, and Iasion won the golden fleece.

These were considered as the most ancient of men, who existed before any other, and whose origin commenced beyond any record, a circumstance which fiction expressed in these words: "They were, ere the moon was." With this people, too, the original simplicity and innocence of manners degenerated into vice and depravity to such a degree, that Jupiter continued to hurl his thunderbolts upon the land of Arcadia, till at last even Earth stretched out her arms, imploring mercy.

KRONOS OR SATURN.

Kronos (*Time*) was the youngest of the Titans, and as the heavens measure out time to us, and earth is considered its beginning, he is said to be born of Uranos and Ge.

According to ancient fable, Kronos is married to Rhea (or *Succession*), and with them commence a new generation of gods, by whom the former, in future times, are to be deprived of their power. Lasting forms now gain the superiority; yet not without a long struggle against all-devouring Chaos, and all-destroying Time, of which Saturn himself is a symbol. He creates and destroys; therefore it is allegorically said, that he devours his own children, and even the stones, because he consumes the most durable substances.

Fable says, that his mother, Earth, had predicted to him that one of his sons would deprive him of his authority, and therefore he swallowed his own children as soon as they were born. Thus the crime which he had committed against his father was revenged. For as Uranos formerly dreaded, so Kronos now dreads seditious power. And while he reigned over his brothers, the Titans, he, in the same manner as his father had done, keeps the hundred armed giants and Cyclopes imprisoned in Tartaros. He fears ruin from his own children. The new-born creatures still rise against the source of creation that threatens to swallow them up again. Even as Ge formerly groaned on account of her children's imprisonment, so Rhea now laments the cruelty of her husband—the all-destroying power that spares not his own creations. When, therefore, the time came in which she was to become the mother of Jupiter, the future ruler of gods and men, she implored Earth and the starry Heaven, for the preservation of her child. But the ancient primitive deities were deprived of government, and the only influence left them was in prophecies and counsel. The supplicated parents, therefore, advised their daughter to conceal her son as soon as it should be born, in a fertile part of the island of Crete.

Wild, roving Fancy, now fixing herself upon a certain spot of earth, finds on this island, where the divine child is to be reared, her first resting-place.

By the advice of her mother, Rhea presented a stone to Kronos instead of her new-born child. The stratagem was successful; and by means of this stone so often mentioned by the ancients, bounds were set to destruction; the destroying power had, for the first time, taken death instead of life; and thus the latter gained time to rise, secretly, as it were, to light, in order to form and unfold itself. But it is not yet secure from the persecutions springing from the very source whence it derives its origin. Therefore the tutors of the child, the Curetes, whose nature as well as origin are enveloped in mysterious darkness, make a continual noise with their shields and spears, lest Kronos should hear the noise of the crying infant.

The education of Jupiter on the island of Crete forms one of the most attractive fictions of the imagination.

The goat Amalthea, which was afterwards placed among the stars, and whose horn became the symbol of plenty, suckles him with her milk. Doves bring him nourishment; golden-colored bees carry him honey; and the nymphs of the wood are his nurses. The physical, as well as intellectual powers of this future king of the gods and men, rapidly develope themselves. The old realm of Kronos approaches its end;—and, in addition to Jupiter, five more of his children are saved from destruction: viz. Vesta, Ceres, Neptune, Juno and Pluto.

United with them, Jupiter, after having delivered the Cyclopes out of prison, and received from them the thunderbolts, declares war against Kronos and the Titans. And now the modern gods, the descendants of Kronos and Rhea, separate themselves from the ancient deities or Titans, the children of Uranos and Ge.

The golden years of mortal men were placed by Fancy in those times when Jupiter did not yet rule with his thunder; under the reign of Saturn, imagination collected together all that is desirable to man but gone to return no more.

After having been deprived of his destructive power, Saturn escaped the fate of the other Titans, and

"Fled over Adria to the Hesperian fields."

There, in the plains of Latium, surrounded by high mountains, he concealed himself, and transferred thither the golden age, that happy period, when mankind lived in a state of perfect equality and all things were in common. He is said to have arrived in a ship at the Tiber, in the dominions of Janus, and in union with him to have reigned over men with wisdom and benignity.

This fiction is extremely beautiful and attractive, because of the unexpected transition from war and destruction, to peace and the quiet exercise of justice and benevolence. While Jupiter, still in danger of being deprived of his usurped authority, is hurling thunderbolts against his foes, Saturn, far from the scene of violence, has arrived in the quiet fields of Latium, where, under his reign, those happy times pass away which are celebrated in song, as a good that is passed and gone, and now sought for in vain.

Saturn's time was the grey time of yore; he swallowed his own children, buried in oblivion the fleeting years, and left no trace of bloody wars, destroyed cities, and crushed nations, which constitute the chief subjects of history ever since men began to record the events of the world. All that happy time, when liberty and equality, justice and virtue, were still reigning, men lived like the gods in perfect security, without pains and cares, and exempt from the burdens of old age. The soil of the earth gave them fruits without laborious cultivation; unacquainted with sickness, they died away as if overtaken with sweet slumber; and when the lap of earth received their dust, the souls of the deceased, enveloped in light air, remained as genii with the survivors.

In this manner the poets portray those golden times on which imagination, wearied with the scenes of the busy world, dwells with so much delight.

Saturnalia were festivals celebrated in honor of Saturn, and were instituted long before the foundation of Rome, in commemoration of the freedom and equality that existed among the inhabitants of the earth during the golden reign of Saturn.

This festival was celebrated in December, and at first lasted but one day (the 19th); it was then extended to three, and subsequently, by order of Caligula and Claudius, to seven. This celebration was remarkable for the liberty that universally prevailed during its continuance. Servants were then allowed freedom with their masters; slaves were at liberty to be unruly without fear of punishment; and until the expiration of the festival, wore a cap on the head as a badge of freedom and equality. Animosity ceased; no criminals were executed; nor was war ever declared during the Saturnalia, but every thing gave way to mirth and merriment. Schools were closed; the senate did not sit; and friends made presents to each other. It was also the custom to send wax tapers to friends as an expression of good feeling; for the Romans, as a particular respect to this deity, kept torches and tapers continually burning upon his altars.

Among the Romans, the priest always performed the sacrifices with his head uncovered, a custom never observed before any other god.

Fetters were hung on his statues in commemoration of the chains he had worn when imprisoned by Jupiter. From this circumstance, slaves who obtained their liberty, generally dedicated their fetters to him. During the celebration of the Saturnalia, the chains were taken from the statues, to intimate the freedom and independence that mankind enjoyed during the golden age.

In his temple, and under his protection, the Romans placed their treasury, and also laid up the rolls containing the names of their people, because, in his time, no one was defrauded, and no theft was ever committed.

Saturn is generally represented by the ancients, as an old man, bent with age and infirmity; he holds the sickle or scythe given him by his mother, and a serpent biting its own tail, which is an emblem of time and the revolution of the year: sometimes, he is leaning on his sickle and clothed in tattered garments; to these were added wings, and feet of wool, to express his fleet and silent course. Upon ancient gems, he is sometimes represented with a scythe in his hand, and leaning on the prow of a ship, on the side of which rises part of an edifice and a wall. This is probably in allusion to Saturn's having built the old city of Saturnia, near the Tiber, on the hills where Rome was afterwards founded. In this manner, Saturn sometimes appears as a symbol of all-destroying time, and sometimes, as a king who once reigned in Latium.

In the representations of the ancient deities, the imagination of the poet plays with grand images only. Its objects are the great spectacles which nature exhibits—the sky and the earth, the sea and the seditious elements, represented under the images of the Titans, the beaming sun and the shining moon; all which objects, being endowed with personality by a few striking features, afford better materials for poetry than for plastic art.

Out of the mist which envelopes these beings the more modern divine appearances spring forth in clear light, and distinct forms. Now, we behold Jove, the mighty god of thunder, with the eagle at his feet; Neptune, the shaker of the earth, with his trident; the majestic Juno, accompanied with her peacock; Apollo in eternal youth, with his silver bow; the blue-eyed Minerva, with helmet and spear; the chaste Diana, with her bow and arrow; Mars, the god of war; and Mercury, the swift messenger of the divinities; by means of plastic art, these modern deities gain distinct forms, and their individual power and majesty thus embodied, and placed in temples and sacred groves, became to mortals an object of religious veneration and worship.

But the pristine deities were, in a certain respect, the models for the modern. Fancy merely caused the sublime objects of religious veneration that already existed, to be regenerated in a new and youthful form; ascribing to them descent, name, and native place, in order to unite them more intimately with the ideas and fates of mortals. But in the productions of Fancy, she does not bind herself to a certain and fixed series of beings, therefore we sometimes find the same deity under different forms. For the ideas of divine, supernatural power always existed; but in the course of time, they became so blended with stories of human life, that in the magic mirror of the dark ages of antiquity, almost all divine images are repeated as in a magnifying reflector; in this contexture of several fables, the imagination found more ample scope; a circumstance by which the poets of all ages did not fail to profit.

Henceforth the history of the gods is mingled with that of men. The wars among the former having ceased, there is now nothing worthy their attention but the lives and fates of mortals, with which they seem to trifle; arbitrarily exalting the one, and depressing the other, yet at the same time assisting heroes of eminent virtue and valor, and raising them to immortality.

PART SECOND.

MODERN, SUPERIOR DEITIES

ZEUS OR JUPITER.

Hesiod, in his Theogonia, invokes the Muses who inhabit the heavenly mansions, and whose knowledge of generation and birth he had formerly sung.

"Tell, ye celestial powers," continues the poet, "how first the gods and world were made; the rivers, and the boundless sea with its raging surge. Also, the bright, shining stars, and wide stretched heaven above, and all the gods that sprang from them, givers of good things?"

The Muses answer, "First of all existed Chaos; next in order the broad-bosomed Earth; then Love appeared, the most beautiful of immortals. From Chaos, sprang Erebus and dusky Night, and from Night and Erebus, came Ether and smiling Day.

"But first the Earth produced the starry Heavens, commensurate to herself; and the barren Sea, without mutual love. Then, conjoined with Uranos, she produced the tremendous Titans; after whom, Time, crooked in counsel, was produced, the youngest, and most dreadful of her children. The Cyclops were next engendered; Brontes, Steropes, and Arges, and besides these, three other rueful sons were born to Heaven and Earth, Cottus, Briareus, and Gyes, with fifty heads and a hundred hands; haughty, hateful, and at enmity with their father from the day of their birth—for which cause, as soon as they appeared, he hid them in the grottoes and caves of the Earth, and never permitted them to see the light. Meanwhile, Oceanus married to Tethys, the eldest of the Titans, produced the rivers and fountains, with three thousand daughters, properties and productions of moisture. Heaven's usurping son, Time, marrying the second sister, Rhea, had three female children, Vesta, Ceres, and Juno, and as many males; Pluto, Neptune, and designing Jove, Father of gods and men.

"No sooner was this sovereign source of light brought forth, that is, disembarrassed of heterogeneous parts, than he seized the reins of the universe, that under him at last assumed a stable form. For associating with Metis (counsel, contrivance, thought), by her supreme direction he brought his inhuman parent's progeny to light, and settled his congenial powers, each in their respective dignity; Ceres to fructify the Earth; Juno to impregnate the air; Neptune to rule the sea; and Pluto to reign in the regions below; while Saturn's first-born, Vesta, remained unmoved, the coercive band of the immense machine.

"But in this settlement he met with cruel opposition. The Titan gods (properties of matter) combined against him, and in a long and furious war endeavored to drive him from the throne of Heaven, and reverse the recent dignities of the upstart Saturnian race. And now, the mighty frame had fallen into pristine Chaos, if, prompted by his all-wise associate, he had not first made his kindred gods partakers with himself of Nectar and Ambrosia (incense and immortality), and then released from darksome durance, the predominant igneous powers, sons of Heaven and Earth, Cottus, Briareus, and Gyes, whom he called up to light and made his allies in the war. By their irresistible strength, he at last vanquished the Titan gods, and confined them fast-bound in a prison waste and wild, as far under the Earth as Heaven is above it; a bulwark of brass, with three-fold night brooding over it, and its gates of adamant guarded by three enormous brothers, jailors of Almighty Jove."

Here are the seeds of all things, the roots of the opaque Earth, the barren sea, and the beginnings and bounds of the various orders of beings, all now shut up by the will of Jove, in the bottomless chasm, where darkness reigns and tempests howl, tremendous to the gods themselves. And Fable says, that things continued in this state until Honor and Reverence begot Majesty, who filled Heaven and Earth the day she was born; Awe and Dread sat down by her, and all three being defended by Jove's thunders from the attacks of the Titans, have ever since remained by the side of this god, who now rules supreme, having rightly arranged all the immortals, and allotted to each their respective dignity.

But after having subdued his greatest adversaries, new dangers arose to Jupiter from his own resolutions. He married Metis, daughter of Oceanus; and it was predicted by an oracle, that she would have a son who should be endowed with his mother's strength and his father's wisdom, and rule over all the gods. To prevent this, Jupiter, with flattering allurements, drew Metis over into his own person, and soon after brought forth Minerva, who, as a full-grown virgin in complete panoply, sprang from his head.

A similar danger threatened him when he wished to marry Thetis, who, according to another oracle, would have a son who should be more powerful than his father.

In this manner these fictions represent that a mighty being always dreads a still mightier; for with the idea of unlimited power, every fiction ceases, Fancy having no farther scope. But to have a just conception of Jove, let us first recollect Zeno's definition of nature—that it is a plastic fire ever generating by rule; and then obey the most philosophical of all poets, when he bids us

> "Look up, and view the immense expanse of Heaven,
> The boundless Ether in his genial arms
> Clasping the Earth. Him call thou
> God and Jove."

We can judge of the propriety of his claim to dominion upon reading what Zeno considers one of the highest steps in the scale of creation. " Ether," says he, " or pure, invisible fire, the most subtle and elastic of all bodies, seems to pervade and expand itself throughout the universe. If air is the immediate agent or instrument in the productions of nature, the pure, invisible fire is the first natural mover or spring whence the air derives its power. This mighty agent is every where at hand, ready to break forth into action, actuating and enlivening the whole visible mass, equally fitted to produce or to destroy; distinguishing the various stages of nature, keeping up the perpetual round of generation and corruption, pregnant with forms which it constantly sends forth and resorbs—so quick in its motion, so extensive in its effects, that it seems no other than the vegetative soul, or vital power of the world. This, then, is the true Zeus; the source of generation and principle of life—that heavenly, ethereal, that is, igneous nature, which spontaneously begets all things, the supposed parent of gods and men; and Fancy finding nothing in nature more pure and sublime than the Earth surrounding ether and sky, it was chosen by her as the archetype of the chief deity."

And what was his Hera? " The air," says the same author, " is the receptacle as well as source of all sublunary forms—the great mass or Chaos which imparts or receives them. The atmosphere that surrounds our earth contains a mixture of all the active, volatile parts of all vegetables minerals, fossils, and animals. Whatever corrupts or exhales, being acted on by solar heat produces within itself all sorts of chemical productions, dispersing again their salts and spirits in new generations. The air, therefore, is an active mass of numberless different principles; the general source of corruption and generation in which the seeds of all things seem to lie latent, ready to appear and produce their kind whenever they shall light on a proper matrix. The whole atmosphere seems alive—there is every where acid to corrode and seed to engender in this common receptacle of all vivifying principles; and here is the foundation of the marriage made by the poets between these kindred gods. And when we consider at what season of the year the air is impregnated with ethereal seed, when it is that all nature teems with life, we shall not wonder at the cuckoo's being the bird of Hera carved on the top of her sceptre at Argos, or at Zeus transforming himself into the spring's genial messenger when he first enjoyed his queen.

"Truth once lighted up shines on every thing around it, and the same thread of reflection will guide us through the labyrinth of a greater mystery; for this matron goddess and patroness of marriage, became once a year a pure, unspotted virgin, upon bathing herself in a sacred fountain in the Argive territory."

As the powerful and majestic goddess, Hera typifies the quick and rapidly moving energies of the productive principle that clothes the earth in the majestic garb of loveliness and beauty—and as the repelling and unattractive wife of Zeus, she typifies the cold frowns and chilling frosts of winter. Hence the physical allegories of their jealousies and quarrels.

Hera's chief archetype was the atmosphere which encompasses the earth, adhering in conjugal union to the ether that rests upon it; and this fiction of the marriage of Zeus and Hera is a representation of Fancy according to human notions and human relations; ridiculous, indeed, unless beheld with the poetical eye of imagination, that forms her gods after the images of men, and her men after the images of the gods. And here let us not pass an unjust judgment on times of old. Antiquity is not to be viewed and explained according to the ideas and customs of modern times, any more than the plays of childhood by the earnest pursuits of maturer life, or the follies of youth by the graver wisdom of old age. While we live, as it were, in the age of reason, the ancients lived in that of imagination; and the infinite and unlimited, being to Fancy a melancholy object, she gave life and animation to things formed and limited, in order to use them as models of her own creation. Therefore, to the boundless mass which surrounds man, the sky, earth, and sea, the ancients gave form and personality. They endeavored to unite the beauty and grace of formed objects, with the strength of the unformed and shapeless; and as in the tall and erect body of man the solidity of the oak is joined to the pliancy of the sapling, so their creative genius connected the power of the raging elements, and the majesty of the rolling thunder, with the majestic form, the eloquent lips, the frowning brows, and the speaking eye of man. And thus is formed the image of Jupiter Olympius; that being to whose hands imagination intrusted so much power, must be in harmony with the human form; because the capacity for thought could only be indicated in the expressive features of the human face, and the power to rule and reign could be represented only in the majestic form of man. And yet the god must be the superior; and to such a degree rose this power of embodying high conceptions in the art of the Greeks, inspired and consecrated as it was by its subjects, that they exhibited works similar indeed, but far superior to their models: for while excluding from their productions every thing contingent, they at the same time succeeded in uniting all that is essential to power, beauty, and sublimity.

In the character of their gods, the leading idea of the ancients was power; the expression of which predominates in their most sublime formations. The mighty head of Zeus, from which wisdom was created, bends forward, meditating and directing the changes of events, and producing their revolutions. Among all the celestials, the power of him who rules the thunder is the most unlimited, being restricted only by the invincible will of Fate, or the wiles of the cunning Hera.

Almost every nation had its Jupiter. Among the first was Jupiter Ammon, of Libya. His temple, the ruins of which are still to be seen, was in an oasis or island of verdure in the desert west of Egypt. Jupiter Serapis, worshipped in Egypt, was also very ancient Jupiter Belus, mentioned by Herodotus, was the Jupiter of the Assyrians. The Ethiopians called him Assabinus, the Gauls Taranus, and the inhabitants of the Lower Nile, Apis. The Romans considered him the protecting deity of their empire, and styled him Jupiter Capitolinus from his chief temple on the Capitoline Hill; Jupiter Tonans, or Thunderer; Jupiter Fulminans, or Fulgurator, scatterer of lightning.

The distinguishing characteristic in all representations of Jupiter, whether by artists or poets, is majesty; and every thing about him indicates dignity and authority. His look is sometimes intended to strike the beholder with terror, and sometimes with gratitude; and always to command respect and veneration. The fulmen in the hand of Jupiter was a sort of hieroglyphic, having three different meanings, according to the three ways in which it was represented. The first is a wreath of flame in a conical shape, like what we call the thunderbolt. This was adapted to Jupiter, when mild and calm, and was held down in his hand. The second is the same figure, with two transverse darts of lightning, and sometimes with wings on each side of it, to denote swiftness. This was given to Jupiter when he was represented as punishing.

Jupiter Pluvius is represented as seated in the clouds, holding up his right hand, from which pours a stream of rain and hail, while his fulmen is held down in his lap.

Jupiter Ammon was represented with the horns of a ram, which is accounted for by the following legend :— Bacchos being in the midst of the sands of Arabia, was seized with a thirst so burning, that he longed even for a drop of water. Jupiter then presented himself in the form of a ram, and striking the earth, caused the grateful liquid to spring forth in abundance. To commemorate the deed, Bacchos erected a temple in the deserts of Libya, giving it the name of Jupiter Ammon, *i. e. Sandy.*

The worship offered to Zeus was the most solemn of any paid to the heathen deities; it was greatly diversified among different nations, and the stories of his birth in a cave on the island of Crete, or at Thebes in Bœotia, or on a mountain in Arcadia, are but so many traditions of the several places where his worship became famous and was celebrated with the greatest pomp and ceremony. The reason of its having been so in Crete, is very evident; for these states were founded by Minos and Cadmos, two Attic princes, who introduced their national rites. But the Arcadians, whose lives were devoted to war or pasturage, in a rough, mountainous country, became afterwards a rude and fierce people in comparison to their neighbors, and yet they retained more traditions respecting the birth, education, and adventures of the gods, than the more civilized tribes of the Peloponnesus. This was owing probably to their early instruction; first by the descendants of Inachos, and then by the Danaides, in the religion and rites which each brought from their own country.

The victims most commonly offered, were a goat, a sheep, or a white bull with gilded horns; though not unfrequently the sacrifice consisted only of flour, salt, or incense.

At Olympia, every fifth year, the Olympic games were celebrated in honor of Zeus. This festival consisted of religious ceremonies, athletic contests and races, and was under the immediate superintendence of the Olympian Zeus. The exact interval at which they recurred was one of forty-nine and fifty lunar months alternately; so that the celebration sometimes fell in the month of July and sometimes in August.

The worship of Apollo was associated with that of Zeus, and the early tradition connects Hercules with the festival. This is another proof of the Dorian origin of the games, for Apollo and Hercules were two of the principal deities of the Doric race. There were altars at Olympia to other gods, which were said to have been erected by Hercules, and at which the victors sacrificed.

The festival itself may be divided into two parts, the

games or contests, and the festival rites connected with the sacrifices, with the processions, and with the public banquets in honor of the conquerors. The conquerors in the games and private individuals, as well as the theori or deputies from the various states, offered sacrifices to the different gods; but the chief sacrifices were offered by the Eleans in the name of the Elean state.

The contests consisted of various trials of strength and skill, which were increased in number from time to time. The earliest of these games was the foot race, and was the only contest during thirteen Olympiads. The space run was the length of the stadium in which the games were held, namely, about six hundred English feet.

In the 14th Olympiad wrestling was introduced B. C. 708. The wrestlers were matched in pairs by lot. When there was an odd number, the person who was left by the lot without an antagonist, wrestled last of all with him who had conquered the others. The athlete who gave his antagonist three throws, gained the victory. There was another kind of wrestling in which if the combatant who fell could drag down his antagonist with him, the struggle was continued on the ground, and the one who succeeded in getting uppermost and holding the other down, gained the victory.

In the same year was introduced the Pentathlon, which consisted of five exercises, viz. leaping, running, throwing the quoit, throwing the javelin, and wrestling. In leaping, they carried weights in their hands, or on their shoulders; and their object was to leap the greatest distance without regard to height. The Discus or quoit was a heavy weight of a circular or oval shape; neither this nor the javelin was aimed at a mark; but he who threw the furthest was the victor. In order to gain a victory in the Pentathlon, it was necessary to conquer in each of the five parts. Boxing was introduced in the 23d Olympiad (B. C. 688). The boxers had their hands and arms covered with thongs of leather called *cestus*, which served to defend them as well as to annoy their antagonists. The Pancratium consisted of boxing and wrestling combined. In this exercise, and in the cestus, the vanquished combatant acknowledged his defeat by some sign; and this is supposed to be the reason why the Spartans were forbidden by the laws of Lycurgus to practise them, as it would have been esteemed a disgrace to his country, that a Spartan should confess himself defeated.

The horse races were of two kinds, the chariot race and the horse race. The chariot race, generally with four horse chariots, was introduced in the 25th Olympiad (B. C. 680). The course had two goals in the middle, at the distance probably of two stadia from each other. The chariots started from one of these goals, passed round the other, and returned along the other side of the Hippodrome. This circuit was made twelve times; and the great art of the charioteer consisted in turning as close as possible to the goals, but without running against them or against the other chariots. The places at the starting post were assigned to the chariots by lot. There was another race between chariots with two horses, and a race between chariots drawn by mules was introduced in the 70th Olympiad and abolished in the 84th.

There were two sorts of races on horseback—one in which each competitor rode one horse throughout the course, and another, in which as the horse approached the goal, the rider leaped from his back and keeping hold of the bridle, finished the course on foot. In the 37th Olympiad (B. C. 632), running on foot and wrestling between boys was introduced. There were also contests in poetry and music at the Olympian festivals.

The Hellanodicæ, or judges in the Olympic games, were

chosen by lot from the whole body of the Eleans. Their office probably lasted only for one festival, during which time it was their duty to see that all the laws regulating the games were observed by the competitors and others, to determine the prizes, and to give them to the conquerors. An appeal lay from their decision to the Elean Senate. Their office was considered most honorable. Their dress was a purple robe, and in the stadium a special seat was appropriated to them. Under the direction of the Hellanodicæ was a certain number of deputies, who formed a kind of police, who carried into execution the commands of the Hellanodicæ.

All persons were admitted to a contest in the Olympic games who could prove that they were free men, that they were of genuine Hellenic blood, and that their characters were free from infamy and immorality. So great was the importance attached to the second of these particulars, that the kings of Macedon were obliged to prove their Hellenic descent before gaining admittance. The equestrian contests were necessarily confined to the wealthy, who displayed in them great magnificence; but the poorest citizens could contend in the athletic contests. The owners of the chariots and horses were not obliged to contend in person; and the wealthy vied with one another in the magnificence of the chariots and horses which they sent to the games. Alcibiades sent seven chariots to one festival, a greater number than had ever been sent by a private person; three of them obtained prizes. The only prize given to the conqueror was a garland of wild olive.*

The Greek kings in Sicily, Macedon, and other parts of the Hellenic world, contended with one another for the prize in the equestrian contests.

The Olympic games were celebrated with much splendor

---

* For a full account of Olympia, see large edition.

under the Roman Emperors, by many of whom great privileges were awarded to the conquerors.

In the sixteenth year of the reign of Theodosius, A. D. 394 (Ol. 293), the Olympic festival was for ever abolished.

The description of the Olympic games will, for the most part, serve also for the other three great festivals of Greece, viz. the Isthmian, Nemean, and Pythian games.

HERA OR JUNO.

By the poets, Hera is represented as the personification of sublime beauty united with power; and in her person is represented that high, commanding order of beauty which is superior to the delicacy of female charms and does not need them. She is called the reigning, the large-eyed, the white-armed; epithets which tend to inspire us with admiration rather than love. It is not the soft and tender eye that graces her image; it is greatness and majesty commanding awe and veneration; and of all the charms which constitute the reigning queen of heaven, poetry celebrates none but the powerful arm. And indeed, Hera acts a part in nearly all the violent events in heaven and on earth.

The raging elements in which the whole train of human passions is but a copy in miniature, are personated in her; for the violence of the elements is chiefly displayed in the lower atmosphere. Here they come in collision and interfere with each other; here they rob, and spoil, and breathe revenge; the rock groans in the furious sea; and under the blast of the storm the billows howl; here is a perpetual round of formation and destruction;—here is the theatre of insurrection and war; the seat of wrath, and mourning, and misery; here must Hecuba pull out her grey hairs, and Troy become a prey to the flames.

But above the atmosphere, in the pure ether, every thing is quiet, permanent, and regular;—there, the celestial globes complete their courses undisturbed, and nothing interrupts the music of the spheres;—the top of high Olympos rises above the clouds into the still ether, and thither imagination transfers the abodes of the blessed immortals, who, exempt from care and pain, sip the sweet nectar, while charmed with the sound of Apollo's lyre.

In this manner, Fancy always unites the human form of her deities with the heavenly archetype. The swan in the bosom of Leda, as the blue ether surrounds the earth; and the ether opens again to show the ruler of Olympos with his ambrosial locks, holding the nectar cup in his hand. Hera surrounds the globe with a transparent mist, which, pierced by the glittering rays of the sun, produces the rainbow, the archetype of Iris, Hera's swift messenger; who, standing in the clouds, announced to mankind the approach of the august queen of heaven; and the same Hera wanders on foot through this very mist to visit her foster-parents at the bounds of the earth. But Fancy, not choosing to dwell long on these objects, which she in a certain manner attempts to explain by her personifications, rather delights to roam among the beings to whom she has given personality; and represents Hera as opposing herself to the all-powerful Zeus, by whom she is suspended from Olympos on a chain into her own dominion, the atmosphere, with an anvil fastened to either foot. The heavenly and sublime is thus made to suffer the disgrace of being lowered down, and all celestials mourned at the sight; but Fancy, the earth-born daughter, delights in the sport.

The worship of Hera was solemn and universal in the heathen world. Young geese and the hawk as well as the peacock were sacred to her; and of plants, the dittany, the poppy, and the lily. The ancients offered on her altars a sow and a ewe lamb the first of every month.

Argos is the first place mentioned by Hera herself as among her favored and beloved cities. Urging Zeus to consent to the downfall of Troy, a city which she hated, together with Priam's family, because of the decision of Paris on Mount Ida, she endeavored to carry her point by a kind of barter; "There are three cities," said she, "which are dearest of all to me, Argos, Sparta, and Mycenæ; nevertheless, I willingly part with them, I abandon them entirely to thy will, if thou wilt consent to the downfall of Troy." (Il. iv. 50.)

The reason of this partiality to Argos, was the extraordinary veneration paid to her by its inhabitants. There, particular festivals were celebrated in her honor, which from her Greek name Hera, were called Heræa.

The games and contests of the Heræa took place in the stadium, near the temple. on the road to the Acropolis. A brazen shield was fixed in a place above the theatre, which was scarcely accessible to any one, and the young man who succeeded in displacing it, received a shield and a garland of myrtle as a prize.

The Argives always reckoned their year from her priesthood, as the Athenians from their Archons, and the Romans from their consuls.

Festivals were celebrated in honor of Hera in all the towns of Greece, where the worship of the divinity was introduced. At Ægina, the Heræa, or Hecatombæa, were celebrated in the same manner as those at Argos. The Heræa of Samos were derived from Argos, and were, perhaps, the most brilliant of all the festivals of this divinity. A magnificent procession consisting of maidens and married women in splendid attire and floating hair, together with men and youths in armor, went to the temple of Hera, and on arriving within the precincts, the men deposited their armor, and prayers and vows were offered to the goddess.

The Heræa of Elis were celebrated every fifth year, chiefly by maidens, conducted by sixteen matrons, who wove the sacred Peplus for the goddess. But before the commencement of these solemnities, the matrons sacrificed a pig, and purified themselves in the well of Peoria. One of the principal solemnities, was a race of the maidens in the stadium; for which purpose, they were divided into three classes according to their age; the youngest ran first, and the eldest last. The winner of the prize received a garland of olive boughs, together with part of a cow which was sacrificed to Hera. She was also allowed to dedicate her own painted likeness in the temple of the goddess. The sixteen matrons had each a female attendant, and performed two dances.

Juno, as well as Jupiter, appeared in a variety of characters. Among the Romans, the favorite one was that of Juno Matrona, dressed in a long robe; and thus their empresses were often represented. She was regarded as the protectress of married women, and was invoked by the Romans under the name of Juno Lucina.

She is generally represented by plastic art in her whole regal splendor, sitting upon a throne or on the eagle of Jupiter, holding in one hand a sceptre, and in the other a veil spangled with stars which flows round her head. Among earthly appearances, the tail of the peacock bears the strongest resemblance to the bright colors of the rainbow; therefore the chariot of Juno is represented as drawn through the air by those brilliant and majestic birds.

HESTIA OR VESTA.

Hestia was said to transfuse the earth with sacred warmth; and her archetype is the sacred flame of life, which invisibly pervades all animated beings. As an emblem of this animating and life-nourishing warmth in nature, as well as the pure flame that quickens the chaste bosom of the goddess, a perpetual fire was preserved in her temples. This fire signified that pure, unmixed, benign flame that quickens the chaste bosom of the goddess, and is so necessary to us, that human life cannot exist without it; for this latent heat being diffused through all parts of the human body, quickens, cherishes, refreshes, and preserves it; a flame really sacred and divine, moving and actuating the whole system of life, and expiring only with its last breath.

Poets say, that as it was by the assistance of Hestia, the enlivening, igneous principle, that Zeus obtained the government of the universe,— he allowed her to choose her own honors and privileges; being incapable of associating with any other element, she made choice of perpetual virginity, and the first share of every offering made to the other gods. Her priestesses, therefore, must be pure, unspotted virgins, and allowed the precedency at all feasts and sacrifices.

A pure feeling of gratitude led the ancients to acknowledge each benefit of nature by itself, under some significant emblem; and it was a particularly beautiful idea to cherish and preserve, as it were, this sacred flame, which serves man so beneficently, and to devote to its service immaculate virgins as its most sacred priestesses. A particular place of refuge was appointed to that element, which is so requisite to man, where it never was employed for human necessity, but always burned for its own sake, attracting the veneration of mortals.

Among the contemplative priests of the East, Hestia passed for the latent power of fire, or the internal texture and disposition of some sorts of matter that render it combustible, while others are little affected with heat. As such, she was the wife of Uranos and mother of Kronos— the sacred, eternal fire, worshipped with the greatest reverence and most pompous ceremonies by all the eastern nations. But among the less speculative Europeans, who received the knowledge of this goddess at second hand, she was considered only as Saturn's daughter, and a national tutelary deity. Numa, the pious Sabine, priest and king, made her the guardian of the infant state, though, generally speaking, she was worshipped as a domestic deity and protectress of the family seat all over Italy, and long before in Greece.

This goddess, then, the pure, eternal Hestia, appears in a double capacity; either as the grand, enlivening genius of the terrestrial globe, worshipped with solemn ceremonies, and honored by annual processions, under the name of Orosmades by the Persians, and that of Serapis by the Egyptians; or, as the permanent, immovable seat of gods and men, the Earth itself;—and by an easy transition, the native soil of a nation, or the fixed habitation of a family. Ovid, in his Fasti, hints at them both; but Plato confines them to the latter; when describing the movement of the universe, he says that the supreme god, the beneficent Zeus, driving a winged chariot through the heavens, marches first, directing and inspecting all things; after whom the whole host of deities and dæmons, ranged in twelve bands, follow in order, but that Hestia alone remains at home.

The very ancient worship of Vesta spread its influence over domestic life, contributing to render it pure and happy. She was the genius of the fireside; and every beneficial influence of the fire that tends towards physical preservation, or moral improvement, was considered as her gift. And as the surrounding all of nature itself which she animated with tender glow, was, as it were, her temple, so Vesta is said to have caused man to surround his dwelling by a covering for shelter; teaching him to secure himself against the severe influence of the elements, and to assemble together and dwell in union with his family around the domestic hearth. For this reason, she was one of the household gods to whom the Romans daily sacrificed. Her statue was placed at the entrance of every dwelling, which was therefore sacred to Vesta, and called Vestibulum.

In the ancient Roman house, the hearth was the central part, and around it the inmates daily assembled for their common meal. Every meal thus taken was a fresh bond of union among the members of the family, and at the same time an act of worship to Vesta, combined with a sacrifice to her and the Penates. Every dwelling was therefore, in some sense, a temple of Vesta, but a public sanctuary united all the citizens of the state into one family. This sanctuary stood in the Forum, between the Capitoline and Palatine hills, and not far from the temple of the Penates.

The mysteries and worship of Vesta were first brought into Italy by Æneias from Phrygia; where they were originally received from the East. Numa Pompilius built her a temple at Rome, into which no males were allowed to enter; he also instituted those celebrated priestesses who bore the name of Vestals, or Vestal virgins; and who were, as their name indicates, consecrated to Vesta. Their existence at Alba Longa is connected with the earliest Roman traditions; for Silvia, the mother of Romulus, was a member of the sisterhood.

Their establishment in the city, in common with almost all matters connected with religion, is generally ascribed to Numa, who first appointed four ; to which Tarquin added two more. They were originally chosen by the monarchs; but during the republic and empire, this duty was intrusted to the Pontifex Maximus.* The virgins chosen for this service were between six and ten years of age; and if a sufficient number did not voluntarily present themselves as candidates for the office, twenty virgins were selected for a choice, and those among the number upon whom the lot fell, were obliged to become priestesses. Plebeians, as well as Patricians, were eligible to the office, but the choice fell on those who were born of good families, and whose persons were free from blemish or deformity.

The time of their consecration to this service lasted thirty years. During the first ten years, the priestess was engaged in learning her mysterious duties; the ten follow-

---

* The institution of that high order of priests called *pontifices*, was attributed to Numa. The *pontifex maximus*, chief of these priests, was interpreter of all sacred rites, or rather a superintendent of religion; having the care, not only of public sacrifices, but even of private rites and offerings, forbidding the people to depart from stated ceremonies, and teaching them how to honor and propitiate the gods.

ing were employed in discharging them with fidelity and sanctity; and the ten last, in the instruction of those who had entered the novitiate; while thus employed, she was bound by a solemn vow of chastity; but after the time specified was completed, she was at liberty to throw aside the emblems of her office, return to the world, and even enter the marriage state. Few, however, availed themselves of these privileges; those who did so were said to have lived in sorrow and remorse; hence such a proceeding was considered ominous, and priestesses generally died as they had lived, in the service of the goddess.

The chief employment of the Vestals was, to maintain the sacred fire which burned in honor of Vesta. If it ever happened to expire, all Rome was in consternation, as it was considered a direful presage, and was made the occasion of a general mourning; and public spectacles were forbidden until the crime was expiated by a severe punishment inflicted on the offender, to whose carelessness the calamity was to be attributed. The fire was again rekindled by friction.

Another sacred charge of the Vestals was, to preserve a sacred pledge on which was supposed to depend the very existence of Rome, which, according to some authorities, was the Palladium of Troy, and others, the mysteries of the god of Samothrace. Their other ordinary duties consisted in presenting offerings to the goddess at stated times, and in sprinkling and purifying the shrine every morning with water; which, according to the institution of Numa, was to be drawn from the Egerian fount, although in later times it was considered lawful to use any water from a living spring or running stream; but not such as had passed through pipes. When used for sacrificial purposes it was mixed with salt which had been pounded in a mortar, then placed in an earthen jar, and dried in an oven.

They also assisted at all the great public, holy rites,

such as the festivals of the Bona Dea, and the consecration of temples; they were invited to the public banquets; and we are told that they were present at the solemn appeal made to the gods by Cicero during the conspiracy of Catiline.

If a Vestal violated her vows of chastity, nothing could save her from a violent death. Numa ordered such to be stoned; but a more cruel torture was devised by Tarquinius Priscus, and inflicted from that time till the abolishment of the order by Theodosius the Great. When condemned by the college of Pontifices, she was stripped of her vittæ and other badges of office, scourged, attired like a corpse, placed in a close litter, and borne through the forum, attended by her weeping friends with all the ceremonies of a real funeral, to a rising ground called the Campus Sceleratus, just within the city walls, close to the Colline gate. There, a small vault was prepared under ground, containing a couch, a lamp, and a table with a little food. The Pontifex Maximus, having lifted up his hands to heaven and uttered a secret prayer, opened the litter, led forth the culprit, and placing her on the steps of the ladder which gave access to the subterranean cell, delivered her over to the common executioner and his assistants, who conducted her down, drew up the ladder, and having filled the pit with earth until it was level with the surrounding ground, left her to perish, deprived of all the tributes of respect usually paid to the departed.

The labors of the Vestals were unremitting, and the rules of the order rigidly enforced; but as a compensation for their privations, extraordinary honors and privileges were granted them. They were maintained at the public cost, and from sums of money and land bequeathed from time to time to the corporation. From the moment of their consecration, they became, as it were, the property of the goddess alone, and were completely released from all parental authority without going through the forms of emancipation. They had a right to make a will, and to give evidence in a court of justice without taking an oath; distinctions first conceded by a Horatian law to a certain Caia Tarratia, or Tufetia, and afterwards communicated to all belonging to the order.

From the time of the triumviri, each was preceded by a lictor when she went abroad, and so great was the deference paid them by the magistrates, as well as the people, that the consuls themselves made way for them, bowing their *fasces** as they passed. Augustus granted to them all the rights of matrons who had borne three children, and assigned them a conspicuous place in the theatre; a privilege they had previously enjoyed at gladiatorial shows. Great weight was attached to their intercession in behalf of those who were in danger and difficulty, of which we have a remarkable example in the entreaties which they addressed to Sulla on behalf of Julius Cæsar, and if they chanced to meet a criminal as he was led to punishment, they had a right to demand his release, provided it could be proved that the encounter was accidental. Wills, even those of emperors, were committed to their charge, for when in such keeping they were considered inviolable; and in like manner very solemn treaties, such as that of the triumvirs with Sextus Pompeius, were placed in their hands. If any one died in office, her remains were interred within the walls of the city; an honor seldom granted by the Romans.

---

* *Fasces* were rods bound in the form of a bundle, and containing an axe in the middle, the iron of which projected. These rods were carried by the *lictors*, or public officers, who attended the superior magistrates at Rome. From the representations of the *fasces*, they appear to have been usually made of birch, but sometimes also of the twigs of the elm. They are said to have been derived from Vetalonia, a city of Etruria.

To offer insult to the Vestals was a capital crime, and if any one attempted to violate their chastity, he was publicly scourged to death in the Forum.

The dress of the Vestals was a *stola*,* over which was an upper vestment made of linen; on the head they wore a close covering called infula, from which hung ribbons or vittæ; and in addition to this, they wore, when sacrificing, a peculiar head-dress called suffibulum, consisting of a piece of white cloth bordered with purple, oblong in shape, and secured by a clasp. In dress and general deportment, they were required to observe the utmost simplicity and decorum; as any fanciful ornaments in the one, or levity in the other, were always regarded with disgust and suspicion. From a passage in Pliny, we infer that their hair was cut off, probably at the period of their consecration; whether this was repeated from time to time, does not appear; but they are never represented with flowing locks.

Annual festivals were celebrated by the Romans, in honor of Vesta, on the 9th of June, and were called Vestalia. Banquets were then prepared before the houses, and plates of meat were sent to the Vestals to be offered up to the goddess. Mill-stones were turned by asses, decked with garlands, as they were led in procession around the city; ladies followed bare-footed to the temple of the goddess, where an altar was erected to Jupiter, surnamed Pistor.

By the poets, Mercury and Vesta are made intimate friends: they are the beneficent teachers and keepers of men, in whose songs they are united, and represented as

---

* A dress worn over the tunic, which came as low as the ankles or feet. It was fastened round the body by a girdle, and over the shoulder by a clasp. It usually had sleeves, but not always.

The *stola* was the characteristic dress of the Roman matrons, as the *toga* was of the men.

dwelling in friendly concord, and teaching the useful arts.

Whenever ancient art ventured to represent Vesta, the goddess bore a flambeau in her hand; but a mystical veil always covers her chaste form.

Vesta, represented with the torch, is sometimes thought to be the ancient Vesta, who probably was the same as Terra. In the fictions of the ancients, the earlier and later deities are often confounded, and, as it were, lost in one another; and since Earth, one of the pristine deities, no longer makes a distinct appearance among the moderns, she seemed to be renewed in Vesta, as Helios in Apollo.

CYBELE.

The Greeks renewed the fiction of Terra in Cybele, and considered her as the mother of all creatures, gods as well as men. The archetype of Cybele was likewise the great productive power that gives rise to all formations. She was conceived to be the ruler of the elements and the beginning of time; the highest goddess of the heavens, as well as the queen of the lower world; and even the representative of every deity, keeping the female character, because of her ever-producing power.

Although this goddess is represented sitting in a chariot drawn by lions, and bearing a mural or tower crown upon her head, to indicate her all-subduing power, together with her sovereignty of the earth overspread with cities, yet this representation is merely an external cover for her incomprehensible formless character.

In the temple of the great mother of life, at Pessinus in

Galatia, a small stone of a blackish color, and rough, irregular surface, represented the Alma Mater. It was also the idea of this mysterious being which was hidden in the Egyptian Isis, whose temple bore this inscription, "I am all that is, that was, and that will be, and no mortal has lifted my veil."

POSEIDON OR NEPTUNE.

In the great division of the universe by Zeus, the empire of the sea was committed to Poseidon, who rises in imperial majesty as Pontos, Oceanos, and Nereus retreat to the shade. He was made the ruler of the waters; his supreme command raised the stormy waves, and his mighty trident calmed the seditious floods. Not only the ocean, rivers, and fountains were subjected to him, but he also caused earthquakes at his pleasure, and raised islands from the depths of the sea, by a blow of his trident Homer represents him as rising from the depths of the sea, and in three steps crossing the whole horizon. "The mountains and the forests," says the poet, "trembled as he walked; all the hosts of the sea rose to hail their king, and the waves fell back in awful respect."

As god of the sea, Poseidon was entitled to more power than any other deity except Zeus; but though descended from the same father as the Thunderer, Poseidon, like the element in which he reigns, is but a subordinate power.

Polyphemos was deprived of his only eye by Ulysses; and this injury done to his beloved son, by mortal hands, Poseidon left not unavenged, but severely punished the daring Ulysses, by rendering vain, as long as possible, all attempts made by the unfortunate traveller to regain his home. He made him endure all dangers and hardships that can befall a seafaring man; and when, by the will of Fate, he must at last reach his native island, Poseidon avenged himself by transforming into a rock the innocent ship of the hospitable Phæacians, which had brought him thither. Thus dangerous was it, even to the favorite of Minerva, to offend the dreadful power of the resistless element.

When the Muses were entertaining themselves in the Aönian mountain with song, and play on the lyre, in so gay a manner that all the environs participated in their joy, and Helicon itself leaped under their feet, falling into a passion, Poseidon sent up Pegasos charging him to set limits to the mirth and noisy merriment of those revellers. On arriving at the top of the mount, Pegasos had only to paw the ground, to bring all to its quiet, proper course; and from beneath his foot arose that well-known fountain, from which the poets sip their inspiration, and which from its origin is called Hippocrene.

The archetype of Poseidon is the vast sea, which being, as it were, angry at all that is prominent, strives to reduce every thing to its own level. Therefore, when, during the siege of Troy, the Greeks were building a wall around their ships, to serve as a bulwark against their enemies, Poseidon was angry; and hastening to Zeus, gave vent to the bitterness of his wrath in these words: "The renown of this wall will spread over the earth; yet my own wall, which with the assistance of Apollo I built around Troy for Laomedon, will be forgotten." To which Zeus replied, "Illustrious shaker of the earth, if another god, less powerful than thou, should care for such a work as that, I should not wonder; but thy glory already reaches as far as the sun; and thou wilt, I trust, as soon as the Greeks have departed, sink that wall into the sea, and cover the shores with sand, that no traces of its existence may remain." With such words Zeus upbraided him for his envy, as well as his regard for the works of mortal men. (Il. vii. 546.)

All that moves rapidly onward affords pleasure to the ruler of the waves. He bends over his spirited steeds, to encourage them, and the swiftly flying ship is his delight. Poets tell us, that the horse owes to him its existence, saying that he produced that animal by striking the ground with his trident. Hence he is called Hippias or Hippodromus, and is esteemed the president of the horse race. They also make him the father of the winged Pegasos, and of Arion, the noblest steed that ever bore kings or heroes. Endowed with the swiftness of the wind, he threw off his rider in one of the Grecian games, to win the prize for himself.

To the Egyptians, who hated the sea, and seldom left their own country, Poseidon was scarcely known; but with all maritime nations he was a favorite deity. As the god of ships and all marine affairs, altars were consecrated and temples erected to his honor.

The Libyans in particular held him in great veneration; esteeming him above all other gods. His most celebrated temples were at the Corinthian Isthmus, at Onchestos, Helice, and Trœzene.

Some writers suppose that the Romans worshipped Neptune as Consus, the god of counsel; and as such, counsel being generally given in private, his altar was under ground, or in an obscure and private place, where sacrifices were offered to him.

The Consualia, at Rome, were festivals instituted in honor of Consus. It was during one of these festivals that Romulus carried away the Sabine women, who had assembled as spectators of the games.

The animals offered to him in sacrifice, were a black bull, rams, and a boar-pig; and the Roman soothsayers always offered to him the gall of their victims, which in taste resembles the bitterness of sea water.

Neptune was generally represented sitting in a chariot made of a scollop shell, and drawn by sea horses, or dolphins, but sometimes standing, holding his trident, guiding winged horses as his chariot flies over the sea. These sea horses had the tails of fishes, with only two feet, which were the fore-feet of a horse, according to the description given in Statius:

> "Good Neptune's steeds to rest are set up here
> In the Ægean gulf; whose fore-parts harness bear;
> Their hinder parts fish-shaped."

In the grim aspect of Neptune is depicted the raging element over which he presides. He is often represented as holding in his right hand the trident, or the three-pointed sceptre, the symbol of his power, and in his left, the reins by which he guides his proud coursers, and his garment waving in the tempest.

The Isthmian games, one of the four great national festivals of the Greeks, derived their name from the Corinthian Isthmus, where they were celebrated. At the narrowest part of the Isthmus, between the coast of the Saronic and the western foot of the Œnian hills, was the temple of Poseidon; and near it was a stadium and a theatre of white marble. The entrance to the temple was adorned with statues of the victors in the Isthmian games, and with groves of pine trees.

These games were said originally to have been instituted in honor of Melicertes, who was also called Palæmon. Their original mode of celebration, as Plutarch remarks, partook more of the character of mysteries than of a great national assembly with its various amusements, and was performed at night. Subsequent to the age of Theseus, the Isthmian games were celebrated in honor of Poseidon; this innovation is ascribed to Theseus himself, who, according to some legends, was the son of Poseidon, and who, in the institution of the games, or Isthmian solemnities, is said to have imitated Hercules, the founder of the Olympian games.

The season of the Isthmian solemnities was, like that of all the great, national festivals, distinguished by general rejoicing and feasting. The contests and games were the same as those of Olympia; and embraced all the varieties of athletic performances, such as wrestling, the pancratium, together with horse and chariot racing. Musical and poetical contests were likewise carried on; and in the latter, women were allowed to take part, as we must infer from Plutarch, who, on the authority of Polemo, states that in the treasury of Sicyon, there was a golden book which had been presented to it by Aristomache, the poetess, after she had gained the victory at the Isthmia. At a late period of the Roman Empire, the character of the games at the Isthmia appears greatly altered; for in the letter of the Emperor Julian, above referred to, it is stated that the Corinthians purchased bears and panthers for the purpose of exhibiting their fights at the Isthmia; and it is not improbable that the custom of introducing fights of animals on this occasion commenced soon after the time of Cæsar.

The prize of a victor at the Isthmian games consisted at first of a garland of pine leaves and afterwards of a wreath of ivy; but in the end, the ivy was again superseded by a pine garland. Simple as such a reward was, a victor in these games gained the greatest distinction and honor among his countrymen; and the victory not only rendered the individual who obtained it a subject of admiration, but shed lustre over his family and the whole town or community to which he belonged.

Hence Solon established by a law that every Athenian who gained a victory at the Isthmian games, should receive from the public treasury a reward of one hundred drachmæ. His victory was generally celebrated in lofty odes, of which we still possess some beautiful specimens among the Odes of Pindar.

HADES OR PLUTO.

Hades was the god of Hell, of riches, and funeral obsequies. His name, Hades, or Aides, signifies the invisible or unknown; a name indicating of itself a gloom which no mortal could penetrate. He was also called the subterranean or Stygian Jupiter, and plastic art represented him like imperial Jove, but with gloomy, rather than benignant features. His

Latin name was Dis, signifying wealth—so called because wealth comes from the bowels of the earth; and because, as Cicero observes, all things proceed from the earth, and return to it again under his direction.

He is sometimes represented as having on his head an ancient corn measure, the emblem of Earth's fertility. At others with a helmet, which renders the wearer invisible, and which is supposed to indicate the safety that men find in the grave; or with his garment drawn over his head to intimate the god concealed.

Hades was much renowned among the Egyptians, who had frequent representations of funeral ceremonies. In their representations of him. a radiant crown surrounds the head, and a serpent is twined round his body, sometimes accompanied with the signs of the zodiac. According to some mythologists, Hades, as well as many other gods of the Egyptians, was originally worshipped as the sun; and Zeus, Poseidon, and Hades are considered as the symbols of one solar year, diversified according to the changes of the seasons.

Tartaros, or Erebos, was the abode of night, where, at the remotest boundary of the Earth, the sun was supposed to sink into the sea. There, too, was the mansion of Hades, beneath which, in a dark prison, the Titans bemoaned their fate.

Fable says, that the residence of Pluto was so obscure and gloomy that all the goddesses refused to marry him, and he therefore determined to obtain a wife by force, and that, after a violent earthquake, he visited the island of Sicily, where he saw Persephone, the daughter of Ceres, gathering flowers in the plains of Enna, surrounded by her female attendants, and immediately carried her away in his chariot, concealing his retreat by opening a passage for himself with a blow of his trident.

As wife of Pluto, and queen of hell, Proserpina presided over the death of mankind; and according to the opinion of the ancients, no one could die if the goddess herself, or Atropos, the minister, did not cut off one of the hairs from the head. From this superstitious belief, it was customary to strew some of the hair of the deceased at the door of the house as an offering to Proserpina.

The Sicilians were very exact in their worship of Proserpina; and as they believed that the fountain Cyane had risen from the earth at the very place where Pluto had opened himself a passage, they annually sacrificed there a bull, the blood of which was suffered to flow into the water. Her worship was universal, and she was known by the different names of Theogamia, Libitina, Hecate, Juno Inferna, etc, etc.

Hades is represented as sitting on a throne, surrounded by the most gloomy darkness; his countenance severe and frowning. holding in his hand a two-pointed sceptre, and also a key, which signifies that when once the dead are received into his kingdom, the gates are locked against them, and thence there is no regress.

Hades was considered as inexorable, and for that reason no temples were erected to him as to the rest of the superior gods. Sacrifices of black sheep and a bull were offered to him in the night. Their blood was not sprinkled upon altars, or received into vessels, as at other sacrifices, but was permitted to run into the earth, as if it could penetrate the realms of the god. Among plants, the cypress and maiden-hair were sacred to him, as well as every thing deemed inauspicious, particularly the number two. According to some of the ancient writers, Hades sat on a throne of sulphur, from which issued the rivers Lethe, Cocytus, Phlegethon, and Acheron. The triple-headed dog Cerberos, watched at his feet; the Harpies hovered around him; Persephone sat on his left hand, and near her the Erinnyes, their heads wreathed with snakes, while the Parcæ, each holding the symbol of her office, completed the group. According to others, the gates to his dominions were watched by the triple-headed dog Cerberos; and before they can be reached, four rivers must be crossed, the very names of which fill the soul with terror. The first is Acheron, the sighing river, a son of Earth. He was born in a cave, and having an unconquerable aversion to light, ran down into Orcus, where he was changed into the river which still retains his name. Styx, terrible above all, is a lake rather than a river, and has already been mentioned among the ancient deities. The third river, Cocytus, flows out of the river Styx, and the murmur of its waters, the sound of which imitates the howlings of the damned, is inexpressibly dismal; Phlegethon, the fourth river, rolls slowly along its waves of fire.

The entrance to the infernal regions, called Avernus, is described as having around it a host of dreadful forms; Disease, Old Age, Terror, Hunger, Death, War, Discord, and the Furies, the avengers of guilt, with snaky hair, and whips of scorpions. Near this dismal cavern is the road to the river Acheron, whither resort the departed spirits, in order to obtain a passage over. Charon, the aged, surly boatman, receives them into his boat, if they have been honored with funeral rites, but inexorably rejects those who have not. On the other side of the river is the gate leading to the palace of Hades the sovereign of those dreary realms, guarded by the triple-headed Cerberos, which is always on the watch.

Within this seat of horror, are first seen the souls of infants who expired as soon as born. Then those who destroyed themselves, or were put to death unjustly. Beyond them, wandering in myrtle groves, are the victims to love and despair. Then succeed the abodes of heroes

Not far from them, is seen the dread tribunal, where Minos Æacos, and Rhadamthys administer strict justice, and pass the irrevocable sentence. Then Tartaros, the tremendous prison, surrounded by three massy walls, having three gates of solid brass, round which the flaming Phlegethon rolls its waves of fire, and Cocytus extends its stagnant marsh. Here, likewise, is the river Styx, by which the gods swear their inviolable oath; and Lethe, whose waters produced forgetfulness of past events to those who drank them. In Tartaros, according to Virgil, those were punished who had been disobedient to parents; traitors, faithless ministers, and such as had undertaken unjust or cruel wars; or had betrayed their friends for the sake of gain. According to Ovid, it was the place where the Danaïdes, Tantalos, Sisyphos, and others were punished.

The Elysian fields are represented as adorned with all the beauties of nature which can soothe and delight the mind, and was the abode of the heroic and virtuous. Hills, covered with fragrant shrubs, delightful valleys, flowery plains, shady groves, lucid streams, mild and balmy air, and gentle and unclouded sunshine, all conspire to render the Elysian fields the seat of happiness and tranquillity. It was the habitation of the blessed; particularly of the souls of those who had lived in the golden age, before man was stained with guilt. Here the souls of the just, freed from the passions and prejudices of mortality, ranged from grove to grove, enjoying the pleasures of friendship and contemplation, until, at the command of Zeus, they drank of the waters of Lethe, and the oblivious draught caused them instantly to lose all remembrance of the past. They then returned again in human form to the earth, where, forgetful of the joys of Elysium, they patiently endured the cares and sorrows of humanity, until the close of a well-spent life again restored them to the mansions of the just.

This fiction of the Greeks and Romans is borrowed from the funeral rites of the Egyptians. Near the Egyptian towns was a certain tract of ground appropriated as a common burying-place, and Diodorus Siculus gives an exact description of the customs practised at Memphis. According to him, their burying-place was on the other side of the Lake Acherusia, on the shore of which sat a tribunal of forty three judges, who inquired into the merits of the deceased person; and if he had been disobedient to the laws, he was refused the rites of interment. When no accuser appeared, or he who deposed against the deceased was convicted of falsehood, their lamentations for him ceased, and they commended his excellent education, his respect for religion, his equity, chastity, and other virtues. All the attendants applauded these praises, and congratulated the deceased upon being prepared to enter the eternal abode of the virtuous.

On the shore of the lake was a severe and incorruptible boatman, who, by order of the judges, and never upon any other terms, received the deceased into his boat. The kings of Egypt were treated with the same rigor, and never admitted into the boat without the permission of the judges. The other side of the lake to which they were conveyed, was a plain embellished with meadows, brooks, and groves. This place was called Elizout, or the Elysian fields—that is, a habitation of repose or of joy. At the entrance of the abode was the figure of a dog, with three pair of jaws, called Cerberos. This symbol was expressive of their affection for the departed; the dog being, of all animals, the emblem of attachment. To the figure of the dog they gave three heads or throats, to express the three cries made over the friend's grave, according to the custom which granted that honor to none but good men. Therefore, the placing this figure over the head of a newly-buried person, signified his having been honored with the lamentations of his family, and the cries which friends never fail to utter over the graves of those whom they have loved and valued for their good qualities.

These practices among the Egyptians were instructions addressed to the people, who were given to understand by such ceremonies and symbols, that death was followed by an account which must be given before an inflexible tribunal; but that what was so dreadful to the wicked, was to the good only a passage to a state of happiness and bliss.

The whole fiction of Pluto, or Hades, alludes to the grave, whose narrow bounds imagination enlarged into a world of shades. The kingdom of Hades is therefore represented as a desolate empire, and his palace a narrow mansion. There is the same allusion to decay in the old and leaky boat of Charon, which only creeps, as it were, across the rivers, taking up much slime in its crevices. The dead themselves are represented like a world of dreams; the empty shades appearing and disappearing in a moment, yet sensible of what they had formerly been, and of what they had possessed; and still strive to accomplish those pursuits in which they had been engaged when living in the upper world, like a man who works and fatigues himself during a dream without attaining his object.

When Ulysses, by the command of Circe, went down into the lower world, the souls of all the departed whom he had known during his life-time assembled round the ditch into which he shed the blood of his victims. His mother presented herself to him; but when he wished to embrace her, the empty shade retreated, telling him, that after the body was destroyed, the souls evaded every touch, like a dream. The shade of Agamemnon stretched forth its arms towards his friend and counsellor, but had not the power to embrace him. Ulysses also addressed the shade of Achilles, congratulating him on the renown he had enjoyed while living, and for his being now esteemed among the dead. To which Achilles replied, that were it possible, he would return to life and serve as a poor day-laborer for scanty wages, rather than reign in his present abode over all the departed. The shade of Heracles too appeared to Ulysses, although he himself had his seat among the celestials.

DEMETER OR CERES.

Of the three august daughters of Kronos and Rhea, Hera alone is the reigning queen of Heaven : while Hestia and Demeter exercise their beneficent influence upon the earth; the one impregnating it with sacred, fertilizing warmth, and the other calling forth the nourishing ear of corn.

Demeter, the mother of Persephone, was evidently a goddess of the earth, whom some ancient system married to Zeus, the god of the Heavens. In Homer, she is but slightly mentioned, and she does not appear among the deities of Olympus. She seems to have been early distinguished from the goddess called Earth, and to have been regarded as the protectress of the growing corn, and of agriculture in general.

Demeter was the happy mother of Persephone ; to whom, however, the sweet light of day was granted but a short time; youth and beauty in her soon becoming a prey of inexorable Orcus.

Persephone, sang the Homerid, was in the Nysian plain with the ocean-nymphs gathering flowers. She plucked the rose, the violet, the crocus, the hyacinth, when she beheld a Narcissus of surprising beauty, an object of amazement to "all immortal gods and mortal men," for one hundred flowers grew from one root,

"And with its fragrant smell wide heaven above
And all earth laugh'd, and the sea's briny flood."

Unconscious of danger, the maiden stretched forth her hand to seize the wondrous flower, when, suddenly, the wide earth gaped; Aïdoneus in his golden chariot rose, and catching the terrified goddess, carried her off in it, shrieking to her father for aid, unheard and unseen by gods or mortals, save only by Hecate, the daughter of Persæos, who heard her as she sat in her cave, and by king Helios, whose eye nothing on earth escapes.

So long as Persephone beheld the earth and the starry heaven, the fishy sea, and beams of the sun, so long she hoped to see her mother and the tribes of the gods; and the tops of the mountains and the depths of the sea resounded with her voice. At length her mother heard; she tore her head attire with grief, cast a dark robe around her, and like a bird hurried over moist and dry. Of all she inquired tidings of her lost daughter; but neither gods, nor men, nor birds could give her intelligence. Nine days she wandered over the earth with flaming torches in her hand; she tasted not of nectar nor ambrosia, and never once entered the bath. On the tenth morning Hecate met her; but she could not tell who had carried away Persephone. Together they proceeded to Helios; they stand at the head of his horses, and Demeter entreats that he will say who is the ravisher. The god of the Sun gives the required information, telling her that it was Aïdoneus, who, by the permission of her sire, had carried Persephone away to be his queen; he then exhorts the goddess to patience, by dwelling on the rank and dignity of the ravisher.

Helios urges on his steeds; the goddess, incensed at the conduct of Zeus, abandoned the society of the gods, and came and dwelt among men. But she now was heedless of her person and no one recognized her. Under the guise of an old woman—"such," says the poet, "as are the nurses of law-dispensing king's children, and house-keepers, in resounding houses," she came to Eleusis and sat down by a well, beneath the shade of an olive. The three beautiful daughters of Keleos, a prince of that place, coming to the well to draw water, and seeing the goddess, inquired who she was, and why she did not go into the town. Demeter told them that her name was Dos, and that she had been carried off by the pirates from Crete, but that when they got on shore at Thoricos, she had contrived to make her escape, and wandered thither. She entreats them to tell her where she is; and wishing them young husbands and as many children as they may desire, begs that they will endeavor to procure her a service in a respectable family.

The princess Callidice tells the goddess the names of the five princes, who with her father governed Eleusis, each of whose wives would, she was sure, be most happy to receive into her family a person who looked so god-like: but she prays her not to be precipitate, but to wait till she had consulted her mother, Metaneira, who had a young son in the cradle, of whom, if the stranger could have the nursing, she would obtain a large recompense.

The goddess bowed her thanks, and the princesses took up their pitchers and went home. As soon as they had related their adventure to their mother, she agreed to hire the nurse at large wages:

> And they as fawns or heifers in spring-time
> Bound on the mead when satiate with food;
> So they, the folds fast-holding of their robes
> Lovely, along the hollow cartway ran;
> Their locks upon their shoulders flying wide,
> Like unto yellow flowers.

The goddess rose and accompanied them. As she entered the house a divine splendor shone all around. Metaneira, filled with awe, offered the goddess her own seat, which, however, she declined. Iambe, the serving-maid, then prepared one for her, where she sat in silence, thinking of her "deep-bosomed" daughter, till Iambe, by her tricks, contrived to make her smile and even laugh. Metaneira offered her a cup of wine, which she declined, and would only drink the *kykeon,* or mixture of flour and water. She undertook the task of rearing the babe, who was named Demophoön, and beneath her care " he throve like a god." He ate no food; but Demeter breathed on him as he lay in her bosom, and anointed him with ambrosia, and every night she hid him "like a torch within the strength of fire," unknown to his parents, who marvelled at his growth.

It was the design of Demeter to make him immortal; but the curiosity and folly of Metaneira deprived him of the intended gift. She watched one night, and seeing what the nurse was about, shrieked with affright and horror. The goddess threw the infant on the ground, declaring what he had lost by the inconsiderateness of his mother, but announcing that he would be great and honored, since he had " sat in her lap, and slept in her arms." She then tells who she is, and directs that the people of Eleusis should raise an altar and temple to her without the town on the hill Callichoros.

> Thus having said, the goddess changed her size
> And form, old age off-flinging, and around
> Beauty respired; from her fragrant robes
> A lovely scent was scattered, and afar
> Shone light emitted from her skin divine:
> And yellow locks upon her shoulders waved;
> While, as from lightning, all the house was filled
> With splendor.

She left the house, and the maidens waking at the noise found their infant brother lying on the ground. They took him up, and kindling a fire, prepared to wash him; but he cried bitterly, finding himself in the hands of such unskil ful nurses.

In the morning the wonders of the night were narrated

to Keleos, who laid the matter before the people, and the temple was speedily raised. The mourning goddess took up her abode in it, but a dismal year came upon mankind; and the earth yielded no produce. In vain the oxen drew the curved ploughs in the fields; in vain was the seed of barley cast in the ground; "well-garlanded Demeter" would suffer no increase. The whole race of man ran the risk of perishing, and the dwellers of Olympos of losing gifts and sacrifices, had not Zeus discovered the danger and thought on a remedy.

He despatches "gold-winged Iris" to Eleusis to invite Demeter back to Olympos, but the dissatisfied goddess will not comply with the call. All the other gods are sent on the same errand, and to as little purpose. Gifts and honors are proffered in vain; she will not ascend to Olympos, or suffer the earth to bring forth, until she shall have seen her daughter.

Finding there was no other remedy, Zeus sends "gold-rodded Argos-slayer" to Erebos, to endeavor to prevail on Hades to suffer Persephone to see the light. Hermes obeyed, quickly reached the "secret places of earth," and found the king at home seated on a couch with his wife, who was mourning for her mother. On making known to Aïdoneus the wish of Zeus, "the King of the Subterraneans smiled with his brows" and yielded compliance. He kindly addressed Persephone, granting her permission to return to her mother. The goddess instantly sprang up with joy, and heedlessly swallowed a pomegranate which Hades presented to her.

> Then many-ruling Aïdoneus yoked
> His steeds immortal to the golden car:
> She mounts the chariot, and beside her mounts
> Strong Argos-slayer, holding in his hands
> The reins and whip: forth from the house he rushed,
> And not unwillingly the coursers flew.

> Quickly the long road they have gone; not sea,
> Nor streams of water, nor the grassy dales,
> Nor hills retard the immortal coursers' speed,
> But o'er them going, they cut the air profound.

Hermes conducted his fair charge safe to Eleusis: Demeter, on seeing her, "rushed to her like a Mænas on the wood-shaded hill," and Persephone sprang from the car "like a bird," and kissed her mother's hands and head.

When their joy had a little subsided, Demeter anxiously inquired if her daughter had tasted any thing while below; for if she had not, she would be free to spend her whole time with her mother; whereas, if but one morsel had passed her lips, nothing could save her from spending one third of the year with her husband; and the other two she could pass with her and the gods:

> And when in spring-time with sweet smelling flowers
> Of various kinds the earth doth bloom, thou'lt come
> From gloomy darkness back—a mighty joy
> To gods and mortal men.

Persephone ingenuously confesses the swallowing of the grain of pomegranate, and then relates to her mother the story of her adventures. They pass the day in delightful converse:

> And joy they mutually received and gave.

"Bright-veiled Hecate" arrives to congratulate Persephone, and henceforward becomes her attendant. Zeus sends Rhea to invite them back to Heaven. Demeter now complies,

> And instant, from the deep-soiled cornfields fruit
> Sent up; with leaves and flowers the whole wide earth
> Was laden.

She taught "Triptolemus, horse-lashing Diocles, the strength of Eumolpos, and Kelcos the leader of the people," the mode of performing her sacred rites. The goddess then returned to Olympos. "But come," cries the Homerid,

> But come, thou goddess who dost keep the land
> Of odorous Eleusis, and round-flowed
> Paros, and rocky Anthron, Deo queen,
> Mistress, bright-giver, season-bringer, come;
> Thyself and child, Persephoneia fair,
> Grant freely, for my song, the means of life.
> But I will think of thee and other songs.

Throughout the whole of this attractive fiction, may be traced the idea of the mysterious development of the grain hidden in the lap of the earth, and of the inward, secret-life of nature. There is no other object found in nature, in which to appearance life and death border so closely together, as in the grain of seed buried in the earth, never again to re-appear to the eye of man; but, at the moment when life seems entirely extinct, a fuller and richer existence begins anew. Demeter, who is said first to have bestowed the blessing of grain upon mortal man, is in the chain of divine beings, that one, who, through the medium of her person, carries the blessed influence of the sky down to the dark dominions of Hades. Hades, who is called the subterranean or Stygian Jupiter, is married to the beautiful daughter of Jupiter Olympius, and in this manner the opposite ideas of life and death being united in the person of Persephone, she connects with a mysterious band the high and the deep—Olympos and Orcus.

Upon ancient marble coffins, the ravishment of Persephone is often met with; and in the mysterious festivals which were celebrated in honor of Demeter and her daughter, it seems as if the close connection of the terrible and beautiful had been intended to fill the minds of the initiated with astonishment and awe; and at last, all that appeared opposite and contrary in the beginning, melted away, and was lost in harmony and beauty.

Demeter is represented as one of the most placid and meek among the heathen deities; yet she made Erisicthon, who violated one of her groves, sensible of her power by afflicting him with perpetual hunger. At another time, during her search for her daughter, she entered a cottage to slake her burning thirst, and was scoffed at by a rude boy, because of her eagerness in drinking.

Indignant at the ignominy, she bespattered the offender with water, by which he was immediately transformed into a spotted lizard, and in this shape, bore witness to the power of the formidable goddess.

Demeter is commonly represented as holding a sickle in her right hand, and in her left, the torch which she lighted at Mount Ætna. At her feet are coiled the dragons which drew her chariot; a wreath of wheaten ears confines her golden tresses, and a cornucopia is generally placed near her, to indicate the plenty produced by agriculture. She is also represented with a garland of corn upon her head; in one hand holding a poppy, and in the other a lighted torch. Again she appears as a countrywoman, on the back of an ox, carrying a basket on her left arm, and holding a hoe; and sometimes riding in a chariot drawn by winged horses. In the Vatican, are some fine antique statues of this goddess; one of them is nearly nine feet high, and was for nearly three centuries the principal ornament of the theatre of Pompey at Rome. Another of these is smaller, not above three feet six inches high.

The Romans paid great adoration to Ceres, and her festivals were celebrated yearly by the Roman matrons, during eight days in the month of April. These matrons abstained for several days from wine, and every carnal enjoyment; and at the festivals, bore lighted torches in commemoration of the goddess; and whoever attended them without a previous initiation, was punished with death. These festivals were called Cerealia, and were the same as the Thesmophoria of the Greeks.

Sicily was supposed to be the favorite retreat of Ceres, and Diodorus says that she and her daughter first made their appearance to mankind in Sicily, which Pluto received as a nuptial dowry from Jupiter. The Sicilians made a yearly sacrifice to Ceres, every man according to his ability; and the fountain of Cyane, through which Pluto opened himself a passage when conveying away Proserpina, was publicly honored with an offering of bulls, and the blood of the victims was shed in the waters of the fountain. Besides these, other ceremonies were observed in honor of the goddess who had so peculiarly favored the island. The commemoration of Proserpina's disappearance was celebrated about the beginning of harvest, and the search of Ceres, about the time that the corn is sown in the earth. The latter festivals continued six successive days.

Attica, which has been so eminently distinguished by the goddess, greatly remembered her favors in the celebration of the Eleusinian mysteries.

This great festival was celebrated every fourth year by the Celeans and Philiasians, as also by the Lacedemonians, Parrhasians, and Cretans; but more particularly by the Atticans at Eleusis, where it was introduced by Eumolpos

B. C. 1356, and was the most celebrated of all the religious ceremonies of Greece.

Each of the gods had, besides the public and open, a secret worship paid to him, to which none were admitted who had not previously been through the preparatory ceremonies of initiation. This secret worship was termed *the mysteries*, and was the most sacred part of the pagan religion.

The first original mysteries of which we have any account, were those of Osiris or Isis in Egypt, from whence they were derived by the Greeks. They were observed in various places, and always with the same object, viz. to inculcate the doctrine of a future state of rewards and punishments; but those celebrated at Athens in honor of Ceres, were termed, by way of eminence, *The Mysteries;* and were so superstitiously observed, that if any one ever revealed them, it was supposed he would be followed by divine vengeance.

In cultivating the doctrine of a future life, it was taught that the initiated would be happier after death than other mortals; that while the souls of the profane stuck fast to mire and filth, and remained in darkness, the souls of the initiated wing their way to the islands of bliss and the habitations of the gods. But lest it should be mistaken that any other means than a virtuous life should entitle men to future happiness, the restoration of the soul to its original purity was openly proclaimed as the object of the mysteries. "It was the end and design of initiation," says Plato, "to restore the soul to that state from whence it fell, as from its entire native seat of perfection." They contrived that every thing should tend to show the necessity of virtue, as appears from Epictetus. "Thus the mysteries became useful; thus we see the true spirit of them, when we begin to apprehend that every thing therein was instituted by the ancients for the amendment of life." Porphyry gives us some of those moral precepts which were enforced in the mysteries; as to honor parents, to offer up fruits to the gods, and to forbear cruelty to animals. It was required that the aspirant to the mysteries should be of a pure and unblemished character, and free even from the suspicion of any notorious crime; and to ascertain the truth on these requisitions, he was severely interrogated by the priests, or hierophantes, who impressed him with the same sense of his obligation to conceal nothing, as is now done at the Roman confessional.

During the celebration of the mysteries, the greatest purity and elevation of mind was enjoined upon the votaries. "When you sacrifice or pray," says Epictetus to Arrian, "go with a prepared purity of mind, and with dispositions so previously disposed, as are required of you when you approach the ancient rites and mysteries." And Proclus tells us, that "the mysteries and the initiation drew the souls of men from a material, sensual, and merely human life, and joined them in communion with the gods." Nor was a less degree of purity required of the initiated for their future conduct. They were obliged by solemn engagements to commence a new life of strict piety and virtue, which was done by a severe course of penance. According to Gregory Nazianzen, no one could be initiated into the mysteries of Mithras, until he had undergone all sorts of mortifying trials, and approved himself holy and impassible. Under this discipline and these promises, the initiated were esteemed the only happy men; and the advantages conferred by the ceremonies of initiation, both here and hereafter, made its subjects an object of universal regard. Persons of all ages and sexes were initiated, and it was considered so serious a crime to neglect that part of the religion, that the accusation of it contributed to the death of Socrates.

The chief minister who officiated at these festivals was

called a hierophantes or mystagogos, the revealer of sacred things. He was a citizen of Athens, and held his office during life; though, among the Celeans and Philiasians, it was limited to the period of four years. The priest was obliged to devote himself wholly to the deities, and his life must be chaste and single. The Hierophant had three attendants; the first was a torch bearer, and was permitted to marry; the second was a sacred Herald; and the third administered at the altar. Besides these, there were other inferior officers, who took particular care to see that every thing was done according to custom. The first was one of the archons, whose duty was to offer prayers and sacrifices, and to see that there was no indecency or irregularity during the celebration. Four others were elected by the people called curators, or Epimeletes; one from the sacred family of the Eumolpids;* another was one of the Ceryces, and the rest from among the citizens. This celebration, sacred to Ceres and Proserpina, lasted for nine successive days from the 10th to the 20th of September. These days were consecrated to the ceremonies of preparation and purification, the particulars of which were founded upon the story of Ceres' adventures in search of Proserpina. The singing of sacred hymns, in honor of the goddess, always formed a part of the service.

The first day of celebration was called the assembly, as the worshippers then met together; the second day they were commanded to purify themselves by bathing in the sea;—on the third day sacrifices were offered; chiefly a mullet, and also barley from the field of Eleusis. These oblations were considered so sacred, that the priests were not permitted to partake of them, as at other sacrifices. On the fourth day they made a solemn procession, while

---

* The Eumolpids were the priests of Demeter, at the celebration of her mysteries.

on every side the people shouted, Hail, Ceres! Women followed carrying baskets, in which were sesamum, carded wool, grains of salt, a serpent, pomegranates, etc., etc. The night of the fifth day they ran about with torches; the sixth day the statue of Inachus, holding a torch, was carried in solemn procession from Ceranicus to Eleusis; the statue, as well as those who accompanied it, was crowned with myrtle, and nothing was heard but singing and noisy merriment. The way through which they issued from the city was called the Sacred Way; on the bridge over the Cephissus they derided those that passed by; and after passing this bridge, they entered Eleusis, by a place called the mystical entrance. On the seventh day were sports in which the victors were rewarded with a measure of barley, as that grain was first sown in Eleusis. On the eighth day the mysteries were celebrated a second time, when those who had not been initiated were admitted by a repetition of the lesser mysteries. The ninth and last day of the festival, two vessels were filled with wine, one of which was placed towards the east, and the other towards the west; after the repetition of some mystical words, they were both thrown down, and the wine being spilt on the ground, was offered as an oblation to the goddess.

The fifth day of the sacred festival was distinguished by a magnificent procession of the initiated, who were clad in purple robes, and bore on their heads crowns of myrtle; the priests led the way into the interior of the temple through the southern portico, which has been described. The worshippers followed in pairs, each bearing a torch, and in solemn silence. But the evening of the tenth day of this august pageant was the most remarkable. It brought with it the consummation of the mystic ceremonies. On it, the initiated were admitted for the first time to a full enjoyment of the privileges which the mysteries conferred. Having gone through the previous rites of fast ing and purification, they were clad in the sacred fawn skin, and led at eventide into the vestibule of the temple. The doors of the building itself were as yet closed. Then the profane were commanded by the priests with a loud voice to retire. The worshippers remained alone. Presently strange sounds were heard; dreadful apparitions, as of dying men, were seen; lightnings flashed through the thick darkness in which they were enveloped, and thunders rolled around them; light and gloom succeeded each other with rapid interchange. After these preliminaries, at length the doors of the temple were thrown open. Its interior shone with one blaze of light. The votaries were then led to the feet of the statue of the goddess, who was clad in the most gorgeous attire; in her presence their temples were encircled by the priests with the sacred wreath of myrtle, which was intended to direct their thoughts to the myrtle groves of the blessed in those happy isles to which they would be carried after death; their eyes were dazzled with the most vivid and beautiful colors, and their ears charmed with the most melodious sounds, both rendered more enchanting by their contrast with those fearful and ghastly objects which just before had been offered to their senses. They were now admitted to behold visions of the creation of the universe, to see the workings of the divine agency by which the machine of the world was regulated and controlled, to contemplate the state of society which prevailed upon the earth before the visit of Ceres to Attica, and to witness the introduction of agriculture, of sound laws, and of gentle manners, which followed the steps of that goddess; to recognize the immortality of the soul, as typified by the concealment of corn sown in the earth, by its revival in the green blade, and by its full ripeness in the golden harvest; or, as the same idea was otherwise expressed, by the abduction of Proserpina, the daughter of Ceres, to the region of darkness, in order that she might pass six months beneath the earth, and then arise again to spend an equal time in the realms of light and joy. Above all, they were invited to view the spectacle of that happy state in which they themselves, the initiated, were to exist hereafter. These revelations contained the greatest happiness to which man could aspire in this life, and assured him of such a bliss as nothing could exceed or diminish in the next.

Besides the various rites and ceremonies described above, several others are mentioned, but it is not known to which day they belonged; the Eleusinian games, which Mersius assigns to the seventh day, are said to have been the most ancient in Greece. In these contests, the prize of the victors consisted of ears of barley. It was considered the greatest profanation of the Eleusinia, for any to come as a supplicant to the temple with an olive branch, and whoever did so, was put to death without trial, or fined one thousand drachmæ. At other festivals, as well as at Eleusis, no man could be seized or arrested for any offence during the celebration. The garments in which the votaries were initiated, were held sacred, and considered as efficacious in averting evils, charms, and incautations.

The Eleusinian mysteries lasted about eighteen hundred years; long surviving the independence of Greece. Attempts to suppress them were made by the Emperor Valentinian, but he met with strong opposition; and they were finally abolished by Theodosius the Great.

Respecting the nature and end of these mysteries, various opinions have been entertained by modern scholars. The following are some of the results of inquiries made by the learned and judicious Lobeck.

In the very early ages of Greece and Italy, and probably of most countries, the inhabitants of the various independent districts into which they were divided, had very little communication with each other; and a stranger was regarded as little better than an enemy. Each state had its favorite deities, under whose special protection it was supposed to be, and each deity was propitiated by sacrifices and ceremonies which were different in different places. It is further to be recollected that the Greeks believed their gods to be very little superior in moral qualities to themselves, and they feared that if promises of more splendid and abundant sacrifices and offerings were made to them they might not be able to resist the temptation. As the best mode of escaping the calamity of being deserted by their patrons, they adopted the expedient of concealing their names, and excluding strangers from their worship. Private families in like manner excluded their fellow-citizens from their family sacrifices; and in those states where ancient aërolites and the like were preserved as ancient Palladia, the sight of them was restricted to the magistrates and the principal persons in the state.

The worship of Ceres and Proserpina was the national and secret religion of the Eleusinians, from which the Athenians were of course excluded, as well as the other Greeks; but when Eleusis was conquered, and the two states coalesced, the Athenians became participators in the worship of these deities. Gradually, with the advance of knowledge, and the decline of superstition and national illiberality, admission to witness the solemn rites celebrated each year at Eleusis, was extended to all Greeks of either sex and of every rank, provided they came at the proper time, had committed no inexpiable offence, had performed the requisite previous ceremonies, and were introduced by an Athenian citizen. These mysteries, as they were termed, were performed with some splendor at the expense of the state, and under the superintendence of the magistrates; hence it follows, as a necessary consequence, that the rites could have contained nothing that was grossly immoral.

PHŒBOS-APOLLO.

The Grecian Apollo is one of those divine representations that are completely finished to the finest strokes and features. Fancy, adorning him with the charms of eternal youth, calls him the far-shooting god, who bends the silver bow; and the father of poetry, who plays on the golden harp. But since Apollo cannot fulfil the various tasks of being on earth the divine patron and teacher of poesy and music—of delighting the gods on Olympos with his lyre and song, and at the same time driving the chariot of the sun, the imagination of the poets seems to have blended the two persons of Helios and Apollo merely for the sake of unity, while in fact they recognized two different beings; the one going up and down the sky as the shining sun, the other wandering on the earth, a new born, immortal youth, with golden locks, charming the hearts of gods and men with play and song.

The chief archetype of Apollo is the sun's rays, in eternal and youthful splendor. It assumes human form, and with it, rises to perfect beauty, in which the very expression of destructive power melts away in the harmony of the youthful features. As in the rays of the sun, that are both beneficent and destructive, fertilizing and producing decay, creation and destruction are united, so the divine form of which those rays are the archetype, unites in itself both terror and mildness. For the god of beauty and youth, who delights in lyre and song, carries at the same time the quiver upon his shoulder, draws the silver bow, and in wrath sends his arrows among men to cause by their means contagious sickness; or he kills them with his soft weapons.

The twins of Latona, Apollo and Diana, are the twins

deities of death, who divide the human race between them. Apollo takes man for his aim, and Diana, woman; and thus they kill with mild arrow, those who are overcome with old age;—like the leaves of verdant trees, that keep themselves in a state of sempiternal bloom and fresh color, merely by successively falling to decay, or like those sacred doves of Jupiter, which, flying by the dangerous Scylla, always lose one of their company, which is instantly replaced by the father of the gods, lest the number be impaired. Thus one generation of men imperceptibly makes room for another; and whoever falls asleep overpowered by age and infirmity, is said, in the language of poetry, to have been killed by a soothing weapon, either from the hand of Apollo or Diana.

That this was the way of thinking among the ancients, appears from the manner in which they express themselves. "The small, happy island where I was born," relates the swineherd Eumæus to Ulysses, "is situated beneath a healthy and benevolent sky; there men are not swept away by odious sickness; but when old age comes over them, Diana or Apollo appears with silver bow, and kills them with arrows that give no pain." (Od. xv. 402.) And when Ulysses, in the lower world, asks the shade of his mother in what manner she had died, he receives the answer, "Not Diana's soft arrow has killed me, nor has sickness taken me away; but the longing after thee, my son, and my grief for thy fate, deprived me of sweet life." (Od. xi. 196.)

Neither Apollo nor Diana, however, has always this pleasing and beneficent appearance. From time to time, the god of the silver bow is seen angry at the inhabitants of the earth; and then he walks forth like a black cloud, or the dark night itself, and the quiver rings on his back as he moves on with hasty anger. "Then he sends his arrows into the camp of the Greeks, there to produce con tagious sickness, which sweeps away man by man, and suffers not the flames of the funeral piles to be extinguished." (Il. i. 44.) And in the same manner the wrath of Diana brings destruction upon Actæon and the children of Niobe.

Still, serenity, benevolence, and loveliness constitute the chief character of Apollo; and he whose arrow wounds, heals again. Not only is he venerated under the name of the Healing, but he is also the father and teacher of Æsculapius, who is acquainted with the means of soothing every pain, and knows a medicine for every sickness, and who, by his art, can save even from death itself.

With reference to this turn of character, an ancient poet, endeavoring to fill the mind with serenity and joy, suggests the following consolation: " If thou art afflicted now, and mourning, it will not always be thus; for not always does Apollo bend his bow; soon will he awaken again the silent Muse to play and song." (Horace, Lib. ii. Od. x.)

In all these fictions, the image of Helios is to be recognized: it is the animating sunbeam which awakens the heart to gaiety and song. It is also the all-seeing, the all-discovering sunbeam, that assumed a form in the prophesying Apollo, as well as in Apollo the herdsman; for those flocks that graze without herdsmen and shepherds, are, as fiction asserts, watched by the all-seeing sun. Yet, all these grand features are embodied in the more tender form of that Apollo whose parents were Jupiter and Latona. He is the shepherd of king Admetos' flocks; he inspires the divining Pythia; he leads the choruses of the Muses.

Fable says that on the isle of Delos he awoke to life; and soon after his birth, the divine power that dwelt in him speedily developed itself. The august goddesses, Themis, Rhea, Dione, and Aphrodite, were present at his birth, and wrapped him in soft habiliments. Thetis gave him nectar and ambrosia; and when he had tasted the divine food, his swathing bands no longer confined him; the divine boy stood on his feet, and even his tongue was loosed. "The golden lyre," cried he, "shall be my joy; the carved bow my pleasure; and in oracles will I reveal the events of futurity." And when he had thus spoken, now a blooming youth, he walked forth majestically over mountains and islands. He came to Pytho, with its craggy summits, and there arose, as swift as thought, into the assembly of the celestials. There then at once reigned lyre and song; the Graces tenderly embracing their friends and companions, the Horæ, joined with them in the Olympian dance; while the Muses, with harmonious voice, sang the joy of the blessed immortals; the grief of mortal men, who know no means of escaping old age and death.

When Apollo afterwards descended from the Olympian seat, he killed, on the very spot from which his oracles were to spread over the earth, the dragon Python, and the beams of the sun caused the slain monster to decay. There, in the deep, rocky valley of Parnassus, stood the famous temple of Apollo, and over the cleft of a cavern, the tripod was placed on which the priestess sat, through whose mouth the god revealed the future.

The tradition of the birth of Apollo on the floating island of Delos, is taken from the Egyptian mythology, which asserts that the son of Vulcan, supposed to be Orus, was saved by his mother Isis from the persecution of Typhon, and intrusted to the care of Latona, in the island of Chemnis. The ancient origin of the god is clearly shown, even in his very name; and a very striking analogy exists between the Apollo of the Greeks and the Crishna of the Hindoos. Both are inventors of the flute; Crishna is deceived by the nymph Tulasi, as Apollo is by Daphne; and the two maidens are each changed into trees, of which the Tulasi is sacred to Crishna, and the Bay tree to Apollo. The victory of Crishna over the serpent Calyanaga, on the borders of Yamuna, recalls to mind that of Apollo over the serpent Python; and it is worthy of remark, that the vanquished reptiles respectively participate in the homage that is rendered to the victors.

It appears that the ancient Egyptians, after having ascertained the great benefit of the inundation, changed the name of their evil genius, the water monster, from Ob to Python, which had reference to the deadly effects of the miasmata, arising from the steam of the mud which the deluge had left upon the earth; and in this, he is plainly making an allusion to Typhon, which, by a simple transposition, is the same name. In making Python spring from the slime of the deluge, does not the poet intend to point out the noxious vapors that rise in Egypt after the Nile has subsided? And when he says that Apollo slew him with his arrows, does he not conceal, under this emblem, the victory of Orus over Typhon, or, at least, the triumphs of the sunbeams over the vapors of the Nile? Python, says Bailey, is derived from Putho to putrify, and the serpent Python being slain by Apollo, is thus interpreted: by Python is understood the ruin of the waters; Apollo slew this serpent with his arrows; that is, the beams of the sun dispersed the noxious vapors, which destroyed man like a devouring serpent.

A very strong affinity exists between the religious systems of Egypt and Greece. We find the same animal, the wolf, which, by its oblique course, typified the path of the star of day, consecrated to the sun, both at Licopolis and Delphi. This emblem transfers to the Greek traditions, the fables relative to the combats of Osiris. The Egyptian comes to the aid of his son Horus under the figure of a wolf; and Latona, the mother of Apollo, disguises herself in the same form when she quits the Hyperborean region to take refuge in Delos

In the festival of the Daphnephoria, celebrated every ninth year, in honor of Apollo, it is impossible not to see an astronomical character. It took its name from the laurel, or bay tree, which the finest youths of the city carried in solemn procession, and which was adorned with flowers and branches of olives. To an olive tree, decorated in its turn with branches of laurel and flowers intertwined, and the lowest part covered with a veil of purple, were suspended brazen globes of different sizes, types of the sun and planets, and ornamented with purple garlands, the number of which (three hundred and sixty-five) was the symbol of the solar year. On the altar, too, burned a flame, the agitation, color, and crackling of which served to reveal the future; a species of divination peculiar to the sacerdotal order, and which prevailed also at Olympia in Elis, the centre of most of the sacerdotal usages of the day.

At the head of the procession walked a youth, whose father and mother must be living. This youth was, according to Pausanias, chosen priest of Apollo every year, and called Bay-Bearer. He was always strong, of a handsome figure, and selected from the most distinguished families of Thebes. Immediately before this youthful priest, walked his nearest kinsman, who bore the adorned olive wood. The priest followed, bearing in his hand a bay-branch; his hair dishevelled and floating, wearing a golden crown, and a magnificent robe, which reached down to his feet, and a kind of shoe which was introduced by Iphicrates; behind the priest followed a choir of maidens, with boughs in their hands, and singing hymns. In this manner the procession went to the temple of Apollo Ismenius. It would seem from Pausanias, that all the boys of the town wore laurel garlands on this occasion, and that it was customary for the sons of wealthy parents to dedicate to the god brazen tripods; a considerable number of which were seen by Pausanias himself. Among them was one which was said to have been dedicated by Amphitryon at the time when Hercules was Daphnephoros. This last circumstance shows that the Daphnephoria, whatever changes may have been subsequently introduced, was a very ancient festival.

There was a great similarity between this festival and a solemn rite observed by the Delphians, who every ninth year sent a sacred boy to Tempe. This boy went on the sacred road and returned home as Bay-Bearer, amid the joyful songs and choruses of maidens. This solemnity was observed in commemoration of the purification of Apollo at the altar in Tempe, whither he fled after killing the Python.

The Athenians seem likewise to have celebrated a festival of the same nature; but the only mention we have of it is in Proclus, who says that the Athenians honored the seventh day as sacred to Apollo; that they carried bay-boughs, and the basket containing what appertained to the sacrifice, adorned with garlands, and sang hymns.

The worship of Apollo was universal, and his power acknowledged in every country; but more particularly in Egypt, Greece, and Italy, where temples and statues were erected to his honor. His most famous temple was at Delphi; his statue, which stood upon mount Action, was particularly famous. It was seen from a great distance at sea, and was a mark to mariners in navigating that dangerous coast. Before the battle of Actium, Augustus addressed himself to it for victory. He had a famous colossus at Rhodes which was one of the seven wonders of the world.*

This colossus, or brazen statue of the sun, was placed

---

* The following enumeration is generally given of the Seven Wonders of the World: The Colossus of Rhodes, the Temple of Diana at Ephesus, the statue of Jupiter Olympius, the gardens of Babylon supported on pillars, the Walls of Babylon, the Pyramids of Egypt, and the tomb of Mausoleus.

across the mouth of the harbor ; and its legs stretched to such a distance, that a large ship under sail might easily pass between them. It was seventy cubits high, or a hundred English feet; its fingers were as long as ordinary statues ; and few men could with both arms grasp one of its thumbs. Scarcely sixty years had elapsed before this work of art was thrown down by an earthquake, which broke it off at the knees, where it remained till the conquest of Rhodes by the Saracens (A. D. 684), when it was beaten to pieces, and sold to a Jew merchant, who loaded nine hundred camels with its spoils.

Apollo is generally represented with long hair, and the Romans were fond of imitating his figure ; therefore, their youth were remarkable for fine hair, which was not cut short until the age of seventeen or eighteen. He is always represented in the perfection of united manly strength and beauty; holding in his hand either a bow or a lyre, and his head generally surrounded with rays of light.

Among the poetical fictions of the ancients, that of Apollo is one of the most sublime and lovely, because it dissolves the idea of a destructive power in that of youth and beauty; thus harmoniously combining two ideas entirely opposite. It seems owing to this circumstance, too, that plastic art in the most beautiful representation of Apollo, which, as a sacred bequest of antiquity, was spared by all-destroying time, had attained to a degree of perfection comprising all that is truly beautiful, the sight of which fills the soul with admiration, because of the harmonious multiplicity it expresses. The Apollo Belvidere is esteemed the most excellent and sublime of all the ancient productions. It was found about twelve leagues from Rome, in the ruins of ancient Antium, and purchased by Pope Julius II. when a cardinal ; he removed it to the Belvidere of the Vatican from whence it takes its name.

Apollo Musagetes is another celebrated statue which takes its name from his occupation as Musagetes or conductor of the songs of the Muses.

The animals and birds consecrated to Apollo were the wolf and hawk, as symbols of his piercing eye; the crow and raven, from their supposed faculty of presiding over the future; the cock, which announces the dawn, and foretells the rising of the sun; the swan, because from Apollo it is supposed to have a faculty of divination, and foreseeing happiness in death, dies singing; the grasshopper, from its tuneful powers, and hence the custom among the Athenians of fastening golden grasshoppers in their hair in honor of Apollo.

As the natural enemies of the flocks over which he presided, wolves and hawks were offered in sacrifice to him; also bullocks and lambs. The olive tree was sacred to him, as its fruits cannot ripen without his influence; and the laurel, always flourishing, ever young, and conducing to divination, furnished the leaves with which he was often crowned.

The first discovery of the oracle at Delphi is said to have been occasioned by some goats, who were feeding on Mount Parnassos, near a deep and large cavern with a narrow mouth. These goats were observed by a goatherd (called by Plutarch, Ceretas) to leap and frisk strangely, and as they approached the cavern, to utter unusual sounds; his curiosity excited him to examine it, when he found himself seized with a like fit of madness, skipping, dancing, and foretelling things to come.

At the news of this discovery, multitudes flocked thither; and the place was soon covered with a kind of chapel, originally made of laurel boughs, but finally converted into a temple of great magnitude and splendor. Such indeed was its reputation, and so great the multitude that came

APOLLO MUSAGETES.

from all parts to consult the oracle, that the riches brought into the temple and city became comparable to that of the Persian kings.

At first, the whole mystery requisite for obtaining the prophetic gift, was, to approach the cavern and inhale the vapor issuing therefrom; but at length, several enthusiasts having in the excess of their frenzy cast themselves headlong into the chasm, it was thought expedient, by way of prevention, to place over the hole whence the vapor issued, a machine which they called a tripod, because it stood upon three feet. Upon this a woman was seated, when she imbibed the vapor without danger, as the tripod stood firmly upon the rock. This priestess was named Pythia, the Greek etymology of which word is to *inquire*.

The Pythia, before placing herself upon the tripod, bathed in the waters of the fountain Castalis, at the foot of Parnassos, and also crowned herself with the leaves of a laurel tree that grew near the place. While seated upon the tripod she was closely surrounded by the priests of the temple. The sanctuary itself was entirely covered with bay-branches: in addition to this, the burning incense overclouded every thing as if with mysterious night, which no profane curiosity ventured to investigate.

The priestess was originally a virgin; but the institution was changed when Echecrates, a Thessalian, had offered violence to one of them, and none but women above the age of fifty were permitted to enter upon that sacred office. They always appeared dressed in the garments of virgins to intimate their purity and modesty, and they were solemnly bound to observe the strictest laws of temperance and chastity, that neither fantastical dresses nor lascivious behavior might bring the religion or sanctity of the place into contempt.

There was originally but one Pythia, besides subordinate priests; afterwards two were chosen, and sometimes more. The most celebrated priestess was Phemonoë, supposed to be the first that gave oracles at Delphi. They were said to have been agitated by strange and ghastly contortions on ascending the tripod, which resulted no doubt from the anguish of convulsed and shattered nerves. At times they attempted to escape from the priests, who detained them by force. At length, yielding to the impulse of the god, they gave forth some unconnected words, which were put into wretched verse by the poets who attended, giving occasion to the raillery, that Apollo, though prince of the Muses, was the worst of poets. This oracle, like all others, was obscure and ambiguous, and not inaccessible to the temptation of corruption.

The oracle could be consulted only on certain days; and excepting on these, the priestess was forbidden on pain of death to enter the sanctuary of Apollo. Alexander, before his expedition into Asia, came to Delphi on one of those forbidden days, and entreated Pythia to mount the tripod, which she steadily refused to do. The impetuous prince, not brooking opposition, drew her by force from her cell; on their way to the temple, she exclaimed, "My son, thou art invincible!" As soon as these words were pronounced, Alexander declared himself satisfied, and would have no other oracle. It was always required that those who consulted the oracle should make large presents to Apollo; and hence arose the opulence, splendor, and magnificence of the temple at Delphi.

The Pythian games celebrated in honor of Apollo near the temple at Delphi, were, according to the most received opinion, first instituted by Apollo himself, in commemoration of his victory over the serpent Python. They were originally celebrated once in nine years, and afterwards every fifth year. According to some authors the gods were among the combatants, and the first prizes won by

Pollux in boxing, Castor in the horse race, Hercules in the Pancratium, Zetes in fighting with armor, Telamon in wrestling, and Peleus in throwing the quoit. These illustrious conquerors are said to have been rewarded by Apollo himself, who was present with crowns and laurels. Others say, that it was merely a musical contest, in which he who best sang the praises of Apollo obtained the prize, which was presents of gold or silver, and afterwards changed to a garland of the palm tree. The songs which were sung were called the Pythian, and were divided into five parts, containing a representation of the victory of Apollo over the serpent Python. A dance was also introduced; and in the 48th Olympiad, the Amphictyons, who presided over the games, increased the number of musical instruments by the addition of the flute; but as that instrument was more particularly used in funeral songs and lamentations, it was soon rejected as unfit for merriment, and the festivals which represented the triumph of Apollo over the conquered serpent.

Pausanias states, that the most ancient temple of Apollo at Delphi was formed with branches of laurel; and that the branches were cut from the tree that was at Tempe. The form of the temple resembled a cottage. After mentioning a second and a third, the one raised, as the Delphians said, by bees, from wax and wings, and sent by Apollo to the Hyperboreans, and the other built of brass, he adds, that to this succeeded a fourth and more stately edifice of stone. Here were deposited the numerous presents of Gyges and Midas, Alyattes and Crœsus, as well as those of the Sybarites, Spinatæ, and Siceliots; each prince and nation having their separate chapel or treasury for the reception of those offerings, with an inscription attesting the name of the donor, and the occasion of the gift.

ARTEMIS OR DIANA.

Artemis, the daughter of Zeus and Leto, or Latona, and twin sister of Apollo, was the goddess of chastity, of the chase and the woods. As a celestial deity, she was Luna or the moon; as a terrestrial goddess, Artemis or Dictyna; and in the infernal regions, Hecate, or Persephone. She was supposed to enlighten heaven by her rays, to restrain wild animals by her bow and dart on earth, and to keep in awe the multitude of ghosts in the regions below.

Her father, Zeus, at her earnest entreaties, granted her the sempiternal state of a virgin; she then took up her bow and arrows, kindled her flambeau at Zeus' lightning, and accompanied by her nymphs went forth through the dark forests and woody mountains. Bending her silver bow, she sends forth the fatal shafts on every side; the tops of the mountains tremble, and the forests resound with the panting of the wounded deer.

Yet, even in the tumult of the chase, the goddess does not forget her divine brother, whom, of all immortals, she loves most. After having enjoyed herself in the sylvan sport in which she delighted—speeding over the hills, followed by a train of nymphs, in pursuit of the flying game, she unbends her bow, hastens to Delphi, the residence of the shining Apollo, suspends there her weapon, and leads the choruses of the Muses and Graces, who chant forth the praises of the heavenly Leto because she was the mother of such children.

Diana shines brightest as the sister of Phœbos-Apollo, who sheds upon her his own glorious splendor. United with him, she with terrible arrows kills the children of Niobe; in union with him, she directs her soothing weapons against the families of men, who, like withering leaves, are to make room for generations to come. She is said to have prepared herself for this, by trying her arrows first on trees, then on animals, and lastly on a lawless city, annoying its inhabitants with pernicious shafts that carried sickness and plagues along with them.

The archetype of Diana is the shining moon; who, cold and chaste, scatters her modest, silver light over mountain-tops and forest glades. The chasteness of Diana is a fearful trait in her character, as witnessed in the fate of Actæon, the hunter, who surprised her when bathing. He fell a victim to her offended, virgin modesty, for she immediately changed him into a stag, and suffered his own dogs to devour him.

Another example of her severity is afforded in that unfortunate priestess of hers who profaned her sanctuary by receiving into it the youth whom she loved. The offended goddess punished the whole country with plagues and pestilence, until the guilty couple were sacrificed upon her altar. Virgins making the vow of chastity devoted themselves to Diana, who, with dreadful punishments avenged the violation of this vow. Whenever therefore, one of the virgins who by sacred promises had become a devoted priestess of Diana, changing her resolution, wished to marry, she trembled at the thought of the vengeance of her goddess, and endeavored to reconcile her by supplications and sacrifices.

During the Trojan war, Diana ventured to challenge the stronger Juno; but she had reason to repent of her forward boldness when made to feel the powerful arm of Jupiter's spouse. "The deer of the mountain thou canst kill, but not fight against those who are stronger than thou." Thus saying, Juno, with her left hand laid hold of both Diana's, took off with her right the quiver from the shoulder of the poor prisoner, and struck her with it on either cheek, so that the arrows were scattered upon the ground. Like a timid dove escaped from the claws of a hawk, so fled Diana, weeping, and leaving her quiver, which, together with the scattered shafts, were taken up and restored to her by Latona. (Il. xi. 480.)

Although these divine persons act in the manner of human beings, the fiction itself, if viewed as a whole, is not destitute of beauty. The same dreadful quiver from which deadly arrows spread over the race of mortals, is an easy toy in the hands of the august Juno, who uses it as an instrument wherewith to chastise the forward insolence of the less powerful Diana; and the latter, whose blushing cheeks feel the blows of that quiver inflicted by a stronger hand, accoutred with which she is accustomed to walk forth in majestic pride, affords a striking picture of female power deeply humbled.

The wiser Apollo, when challenged by Neptune, on the same occasion, returns his antagonist this answer: " Why should I fight with thee for the sake of miserable mortals, who, like the leaves of trees, last but a short time, and then wither away? Let us refrain from fighting, and let them carry on the war among themselves." (Il. xi. 461.)

Diana was supposed to be the same as the Isis of the Egyptians, whose worship was introduced into Greece, with that of Osiris, under the name of Apollo. In the previous article we have spoken of the change produced by Grecian ideas on the attributes and worship of that Deity, and a change no less remarkable took place in that of Diana.

At Delos she is evidently a cosmogonical power; for there she is the mother of Eros, who, in the Theogonies, is always taken for the creative force. With the Scythians, she is a ferocious goddess, of a frightful form, and eager after the blood of men. As such she first appeared to the Spartans; since, at the very sight of her, they were seized with fright bordering on delirium. In Colchis, she has so little of the Grecian character as to defend the golden fleece against the attempts of the Argonauts. Her hounds guard the seven doors of the enclosure which contains the precious treasure, and her voice issues commands to monsters that recall the fictions of India. At Ephesus, the slightest inspection of her figure betrays the sacerdotal imprint. But how different a being is she in the Grecian mythology! And yet, on a closer inspection, we shall find that even here none of her attributes are completely lost. Diana is the goddess of the chase; and Isis, accompanied by her faithful hounds and the dog-headed Anubis, searched for the body of her husband; and the companions of Isis become the pack of Diana. Diana guides in the heavens the silvery globe that dissipates the obscurity of the night, and her bow is adorned with the splendors of the crescent; Isis is also the moon, and the crescent appears among the ornaments of the goddess at Ephesus. Diana is the cause of the infirmities of women, strikes them with delirium, and sometimes with death; Isis was once the Tithrambo of Egypt, or the moon viewed with reference to its unhealthy influence.

In the same manner, Diana becomes Hecate, slain by Hercules and resuscitated by Phorcys. And yet, so great is the repugnance of the Greeks to admit any thing into their religious system which may have a reference to science, that as they separate Apollo and Helios, so they make two distinct deities of Diana and Selene; and thus render the goddess of the chase more free, more independent, and possessed of more individuality.

A chaste virgin, she defies the power of love, and punishes with severity the errors of her attendant nymphs. This notion of virginity, prevalent even in the worship of the savage nations, is an idea natural to man, and which sacerdotal influence seeks to record and prolong. With the Greeks, however, over whom none of this influence was exercised, such an attribute becomes an object of secondary importance, and is considered the effect of caprice, or of the modesty of a young female; and the poets at one time throw doubts on its reality, and at another upon its duration. Yet, virgin as she is, Diana presides over the birth of children, a combination in which no one can mistake the union of the power which destroys with that which creates. We see, then, how incoherent are the traces of sacerdotal ideas, which survive this strange metamorphosis. The Hertha of Scythia, the Bendis of Thrace, the Isis of Egypt, the Diana of Ephesus, that motionless, enigmatical, and fettered mummy, become, beneath Grecian skies, a young and active huntress, who, in her course as rapid as the winds, pursues on the mountain tops the timid inhabitants of the woods.

Diana is always represented as taller by the head than her attendants; her face somewhat manly, her legs bare, well shaped and strong, her feet sometimes bare, and sometimes covered with the cothurnus* or buskin of the ancient hunters. By poets and artists, she is represented as armed with bow and arrows, and has threescore nymphs in her train. She is also represented with a quiver and attended by dogs, and sometimes drawn in a chariot by two white stags or her nymphs. Again, she appears with wings, holding a lion with one hand and a panther in the other; or in a chariot drawn by two horses, one white and one black.

The representations of this goddess are generally known by the crescent on her head, by the dogs which attend

---

* *Cothurnus* was a kind of boot or buskin worn by the hunters, and also by actors of tragedy, when they represented the characters of gods or heroes. They differed from the *sandal*, which was a mere sole tied about the toes and ancles with thongs and straps of leather, while the *cothurnus* covered the foot and leg as high as the calf, and was ornamented with gold, gems, and ivory.

her, and by her hunting habit. As the celestial Diana, she is described by Statius as of majestic stature; and, in the council of the gods, appears with the bow and quiver on her shoulders.

The Diana Triformis, also called Hecate, and Trivia by Ovid, Horace, and Virgil, when her statues stood where three roads met, is represented by these poets as having three heads,  and sometimes with three bodies. She was frequently invoked in enchantments, as being the infernal Diana, and then appears more like a Fury than a celestial goddess.

In antique sculpture, Diana is frequently represented as descending with her head veiled to a shepherd who is sleeping. This fable might have originated from an eclipse of the moon; if so, her veil would be the most significant and characteristic part of her costume. The ancients represented death under the symbol of the sleeping Endymion, and upon marble coffins, enclosing the ashes of youths who had fallen early into the tomb, Diana is to be seen descending from on high to the lips of the happy slumberer.

The inhabitants of Taurica were particularly attached to

the worship of this goddess, and cruelly offered on her altars all strangers who were shipwrecked on their coasts. In Asia her temple was served by a priest who had always murdered his predecessor, and the Lacedæmonians yearly offered her victims till the age of Lycurgos, who changed this barbarous custom to that of flagellation. Her most famous temple was that at Ephesus.

ARES OR MARS.

Ares, the son of Zeus and Hera, and the god of war, presided over gladiators, and whatever exercises and amusements were manly and warlike.

From his name the hill at Athens, the assembling place of that court of judicature so renowned for its justice, was called Areiopagos; and also the hill of Ares, because he was said to have been tried there for the murder of Hallirrothios, son of Poseidon.

Ares is generally represented in the figure of a man, armed with a helmet, pike, and shield, or in a chariot drawn by furious horses, called by the poets Flight and Terror. Sometimes Discord precedes him in tattered garments, while Clamor and Anger follow behind.

His companion, Bellona, daughter of Phorcys and Keto, was called Enyo by the Greeks. She was anciently called Duelliona, and according to some was the sister of Ares, or to others, his daughter, or wife, and was often confounded with Athena, the goddess of war. She prepared the chariot of Ares for battle, drove the horses, and also appeared in battles with dishevelled hair, a torch in her left hand, and the right armed with a whip which she used to animate the combatants.

Thus we see that to the dreadful and terrible, even to destructive war, the imagination of the ancients ascribed personality. Thus they tempered the idea of that wild, impetuous power that rages like a tempest through the host engaged in the bloody strife, that breaks helmets, dashes weapons to pieces, and crushes chariots; that throws alike to the ground the valiant and the faint-hearted in the whirling storm of the battle, triumphing over its wasting destruction. The human form in which this terrible appearance was embodied by imagination, and associated in the assembly of the gods, presented a model to the warrior, the majesty of which he partly appropriated to himself by bold and valorous deeds.

That the human form of Ares should be dissolved from time to time in the idea of the fighting army itself, lies in the nature of poetical representations. Thus, when in a combat before Troy, he was wounded by the valiant Diomedes, aided by Athena, he roared, as the poet tells us, like ten thousand men, so that on hearing the voice of the brazen god of war, terror seized both Greeks and Trojans. Enveloped in clouds, he immediately ascended to Olympos, appearing to Diomedes as the nightly gloom that precedes a tempest. On arriving at the abode of the immortal gods, he complained to Zeus of the audacity of men. But Zeus reproved him with angry words: "Trouble me not with thy complaints, inconstant! Thou art to me the most odious of all the gods that dwell in Olympos; for thou knowest no other pleasure than strife, war, and contest. In thee dwells the whole character of thy mother, and hadst thou been the son of another god, and not my own, thou wouldst long ago have lain deeper than the sons of Uranos." (Il. v. 850.)

The inconstancy of Mars, with which he is reproached, not only by his father, but also by Minerva, who calls him a deserter, that now sides with one enemy now with another, implies the idea of war itself, represented by poetry as something that exists, as it were, for its own sake, not caring if the bustle and tumult of the battle are continued, who are the conquered, and who the conquerors.

Although the violent and inconstant Mars was often reproved and upbraided by Jupiter and Minerva, the more gentle and meek deities, and for this very reason the more powerful, he still held his seat among the celestials; and on earth, temples and altars were erected to his honor. Indeed, by his youthful impetuosity, he even contrived to win the love of the tender Venus, who, unmindful of her duty towards her husband, maintained a secret intercourse with the god of war. From this disguised connection between the tender and the violent, Harmonia was produced; who afterwards became the wife of Cadmos, the founder of Thebes.

In the same manner as Venus binds the impetuous god of war by her tenderness, Minerva restrains his violence by her wisdom For when on a certain occasion, the threatening injunction of Jupiter prohibited the gods from taking any part in the contests between the Greeks and Trojans, and Mars had been apprised that in one of their fights, Ascalaphus was slain, immediately commanded his servants, Fear and Terror, to put his horses to his chariot; then taking up his glittering arms he thus addressed the inhabitants of Olympos: "Be not angry with me, celestials, because I go to avenge the death of my son Ascalaphus; my paternal heart will not suffer me to remain tranquil, even though Jupiter should hurl his lightnings upon me." Minerva sprang from her seat, and pulling his brazen spear out of his hand, tore the helmet from his head, and the shield from his shoulder. "Madman," she cried, "thou wilt bring ruin upon us all, if Jove's wrath be excited to the utmost! Refrain from thy anger, for many lie slain who were stronger than thy son, and many stronger than he will yet fall. Who can save mortals from death?" Thus spoke the goddess of wisdom, and brought the furious Mars back to his seat. (Il. xv. 115.)

In all these human representations of the gods, who

does not perceive the display of great images and sublime ideas, which give beauty and dignity to the fictions themselves? Wild destruction, tender sublimity, high charms of beauty, and guiding wisdom, are variously mingled and concealed, under the guise of human forms.

Mars, according to his profession as a warrior, is represented in complete armor, bearing shield and spear. An antique gem preserved in one of the German Museums, shows him as descending from the cloud-capt Olympos, supporting himself by his right hand upon the cliffs of mountains, and carrying on his left arm a buckler and spear.

Among the ancients, the worship of Mars was not very universal; his temples in Greece were not numerous, but in Rome he received the most unbounded honors. The warlike Romans were proud of paying homage to a deity, whom they esteemed the patron of their city, and the father of the first of their monarchs. His most celebrated temple at Rome was built by Augustus, after the battle of Philippi, and dedicated to Mars Ultor, or the Avenger. Among the Romans it was usual for the consul, before entering on an expedition, to visit the temple of Mars, where he offered his prayers, and in a solemn manner, shook the spear which was in the hand of the statue of the god, at the same time exclaiming, "*Mars, Vigila!* God of War, watch over the welfare and safety of the city."

His priests among the Romans were called Salii; they were first instituted by Numa, and their chief office was, to guard the sacred ancile, which was supposed to have fallen from heaven. The oracle was consulted respecting it, and declared that the empire of the world was destined for the city that should preserve that shield. Numa Pompilius, second king of Rome, caused several to be made so exactly like it, that it was almost impossible to distinguish the original. The form was oval.

His altars were frequently stained with the blood of the horse and the wolf—the former for his warlike spirit, and the latter for his ferocity; the dog was consecrated to him for his vigilance in the pursuit of his prey; the raven because he follows the march of armies; and the magpie and vulture for their greediness and voracity. The Scythians generally offered him asses, and the people of Caria, dogs. The weed called dog-grass was sacred to him, because it is supposed to grow in places which are fit for fields of battle, or where the ground has been stained by the effusion of human blood.

The Romans paid great adoration to Bellóna; but she was held in still greater veneration by the Cappadocians, where she had above three thousand priests.

Her temple at Rome, in which the senators gave audience to foreign ambassadors, and to generals returned from war, was without the city, in the Porta Carmentalis. At the gate was a small column, called the column of war, against which a spear was thrown whenever war was declared against an enemy.

The priests of the goddess were called Bellonarii; they consecrated themselves by making large incisions, particularly in the thigh, and receiving the blood in their hands to offer as a sacrifice to the goddess. Lactantius described them as cutting themselves most furiously in her worship; and Tertullian adds, that having collected the blood that flows from these gashes, they pledged the neophytes who were initiated into their mysteries, and then, in their wild enthusiasm, predicted bloodshed and wars, the defeat of enemies, and the besieging of towns.

ATHENA OR MINERVA.

When the blue-eyed Athena sprang forth from the immortal head of Zeus, Olympos shook and trembled; and the charioteer of the sun stopped his snorting steeds, until the new-born goddess took off her radiant armor.

Athena was immediately admitted to the assembly of the gods, and had great power awarded to her. She could prolong the life of men, bestow the gift of prophecy, and indeed was the only divinity whose authority and consequence were equal to those of her father.

Not being the offspring of a mother, her bosom was as cold as the steel with which it was covered. Her nature approached to manly greatness; tenderness and female affection dwelt not in her heart. By this disposition, equally adapted to quiet, unprejudiced musing on art and science, and to undaunted participation in warlike occupations, her two-fold character, as Goddess of Wisdom and as Heroine, is at once explained and justified; for in a female, the want of tender feelings is always connected with a desire of destruction, which constantly gains strength. It is the tender-hearted, affectionate Aphrodite, who, merely out of love to Adonis, and not on her own account, pursues with him the roes and fawns of the forest; but the colder Artemis delights in chase and destruction itself, only forgetting it for a moment, when, with secret fondness, she steals a look at the slumbering Endymion.

Athena, the cold and chaste virgin, being destitute of every feeling of tenderness and languishing passion, finds her pleasure, like the stern god of battle, in warlike tumult, and delights in the sight of destroyed cities. There is, however, this difference; she at the same time patronising the peaceful arts, does not share with him the impetuosity and violence of character by which he is distinguished. Repulsive coldness is the chief feature that characterizes her, and renders her equally capable of being the directress of just wars, and of practising the laborious task of weaving; of inventing useful arts, and guiding the wrathful minds of heroes. When Achilles was about to draw his sword against Agamemnon, his king and chief, the blue-eyed goddess suddenly stood behind him with terrible look, invisible to every one but himself, seized his yellow hair, and assuaged the wrath of the young hero with prudent advice. He withdrew his mighty fist from the silver handle, and the sword dropped back into its scabbard. Thus Pallas-Athene, even in the midst of war, appears as a mediator and peace-maker; nor is she by any means to be confounded with Bellona, who, with terrific countenance, and dishevelled hair, brandishes a bloody whip in her right hand, while the other shakes the heavy lance, and drives the chariot of the God of War. Bellona is a subordinate being, who, even by her appearance and deportment, betrays her inferior standing. In her wild aspect, no quiet look discloses the divine spark of inward wisdom or inventive genius. Her glaring eye darts rage and fury; her figure is not graced with that majestic air, in which the just ruler of battles and the august guide of heroes is to be recognized; her headlong impetuosity, her cruel desire of murder and devastation, discover the worthy companion of Discord, as well as the ferocious driver of Ares' snorting coursers.

In the divine person of Athena, warlike disposition was tempered partly by her female sex; yet more so by those faculties which rendered her the benefactress of mankind in bestowing upon them the peaceful arts. For the same goddess who delighted in the din of battle and the shouts of fighting heroes, taught mankind the art of weaving, of building ships, and of pressing oil from olives. When she was engaged in the contest with Poseidon as to the right of giving a name to the capital of Cecropia, than which none more advanced in the arts and sciences has ever adorned the earth, it was agreed in the council of the gods, that the honor of naming it should belong to whichever of the claimants should bestow the most useful present upon its inhabitants. Poseidon, upon this, struck the ground with his trident, and immediately a horse issued from the earth. Minerva produced the olive, and obtained the victory by the unanimous voice of the gods, who observed that the olive, as the emblem of peace, is far preferable to the horse, the symbol of war and bloodshed. The victorious deity called the capital Athenæ, and became the tutelar goddess of the place.

The opposition of apparently quite different and incongruous features in the character of Minerva, is by no means prejudicial to the beauty of her fictitious person. On the contrary, fiction becomes thereby, as it were, a sublimer language, which summons together a number of dispersed ideas into tuneful harmony; as is the case in the representation of Apollo. It is true, that such diversified ideas are seldom united in the microcosm of the thinking mind; yet a single glance into the immense world of nature, must convince us that their prototypes are connected in sisterly union, all apparent differences and contradictions of creation and destruction being dissolved, and life and death combined in the most perfect and beautiful harmony.

Nor can it be justly asserted, that the unity and harmony of the whole in Minerva's character is distorted by the seeming contradiction of its single features. They all refer to the cold, reflecting wisdom, which, guarded by the want of feeling, and a sort of forbidding callousness, never hears the voice of passion. The petrifying head of Medusa threatens from the shield that covers Minerva's breast; and over her head hovers the gloomy, melancholy bird of night. She is the faithful friend of the enduring, persevering, cold, and cunning Ulysses, as well as the admonisher, who recalls the enraged heroes to presence of mind.

The deep sense which lies concealed in all the fictions of the ancients, betrays itself also in the power of Minerva, being represented as superior to that of Mars. The warlike spirit that keeps possession of itself, that looks with quiet eye over the field of battle, and at the same time sufficiently comprehensive to attend to the arts and sciences of peace, gets advantage of the impetuous one who is always ready to fight. When, during the war with Troy, the gods themselves had engaged in the combats, either to aid the Greeks or assist the Trojans, and had challenged each other, the turbulent god of war, rushing on the more tender Pallas, furiously thrust his spear against her shield; but, against that, even Jupiter's lightnings are of no avail. The goddess, however, falling back a little, takes up in her strong hand an immense field stone, and hurls it upon the forehead of Mars, so that he is precipitated to the Earth, covering with his body seven acres of ground.

Notwithstanding the strong, manly features, with which the picture of Minerva is drawn by poetry, she still continues a woman, who shares the foibles common to her sex. She is said to have invented the flute; but seeing in a fountain the distortion of her face while playing on this instrument, she threw it away, to the great misfortune of Marsyas, who found it, and challenged Apollo to a trial of skill in music. Like Juno she was jealous, too, and like her, could not rest until Troy stood in flames and Priam's race was destroyed, because Paris had denied her as well as Juno the prize of beauty, awarding it to the soft charms of Venus. The actions of Minerva are numerous, as well as the kindnesses by which she endeared herself to man. She and Neptune disputed as to which would give a name to the city of Cecropia. Fabulous as the narratives of that period confessedly are, and prone as the inhabitants of Attica were to enhance their national glory, by adorning its annals with fictitious embellishments, yet it is not difficult to trace some footsteps of truth in those legendary records which they have handed down to us, of the most distant ages of their own history.

The earliest monarch of this country whose name is preserved, was Cecrops. Backward, beyond him, historical tradition did not go. He was therefore an Autochthon or Indigenous—the offspring of the earth. In his days, it is said, the gods began to choose favorite spots among the dwellings of men for their own residence; or, as the expression seems to mean, particular deities were worshipped with especial homage in particular cities. It was at this time, then, that Minerva and Neptune strove for the possession of Attica. The question was to be determined by the natural principle of priority of occupation. Cecrops, the king of the country at that period, was called upon to arbitrate between them in the controversy. It was asserted by Neptune, that he had appropriated the territory to himself, by planting his trident on the rock of the Acropolis at Athens, before the land had been claimed by Minerva. He pointed to it, there standing erect, and to the salt spring which had then issued, and was flowing from the fissure of the cliff which had opened for the reception of the trident.

On the other hand, Minerva alleged that she had taken possession of the country at a still earlier period than had been done by the rival deity. She appealed, in support of her claim, to the Olive, which had sprung at her command from the soil, and which was growing near the fountain produced by the hand of Neptune from the same place.

Cecrops was required to attest the truth of her assertion. He had been witness to the act; and he therefore decided in favor of Minerva, who then became the tutelary deity of Athens.

It is not difficult to perceive that, in this tradition, a record is preserved of the rivalry (which may be considered the natural production of the soil, the form and the situation of Attica itself) between the two classes of its population—the one devoted to maritime pursuits, and aiming at commercial eminence—the other contented with its own domestic resources, and preferring the tranquil occupations of agricultural and pastoral life, which were typified by the emblematical symbol of peace. The victory of Minerva which it commemorates, is a true and significant expression of the condition of this country, and of the habits of its people, from the days of Cecrops to those of Themistocles.

Athena was invoked by all artists, particularly such as worked in wool, embroidery, painting, and sculpture, and it was considered the duty of every member of society to invoke the assistance of a deity who presided over industry, taste, and wisdom. Her worship was universal, and she had magnificent temples in Egypt, Phœnicia, and all parts of Greece, Italy, Gaul, and Sicily.

The Panathenæa, the greatest of the Athenian festivals, was celebrated in honor of Athena as the guardian deity of the city of Athens. It is said to have been instituted by Erichthonios, and to have been called originally Athenæa; but in the time of Theseus, it obtained the name of Panathenæa, in consequence of his uniting into one state the different independent communities into which Attica had been previously divided.

There were two Athenian festivals which had the name of Panathenæa; one called the Great and the other the Less. The former was celebrated once in every five years, with great magnificence, and attracted spectators from all parts of Greece. The latter was celebrated every year in the Piræus. In both the Panathenæa there were gymnastic contests, among which the torch race seems to have been very popular. In the time of Socrates a torch race on horseback was introduced at the Less Panathenæa. At the Great Panathenæa there was also a musical contest, and a recitation of the Homeric poems by rhapsodists; in these contests the victors were rewarded with vessels of sacred oil. The most celebrated part of the grand Panathenaic festival, was the solemn procession of the Peplos, or sacred robe of Athena. This Peplos was covered with embroidery, the work of maidens belonging to the noblest families of Athens, representing the battles of the Gods and the Giants, especially the exploits of Zeus and Athena, and also the achievements of the heroes in the Attic mythology; hence, Aristophanes speaks of men worthy of this land and the Peplos.

At the celebration of the festival, the Peplos was brought down from the Acropolis where it was wrought, suspended like a sail upon a ship, and then drawn through the principal parts of the city to the Parthenon, and there placed before the statue of the goddess within. The old men carried olive branches, the young men wore armor, and the young women carried baskets on their heads, and were called Canephores. On this occasion, the sacrifices were very numerous, and during the supremacy of Athens, every subject state was obliged to furnish an ox for the festival. It was made a season of joy, and even prisoners were liberated that they might take part in the general rejoicing.

The Minerva of the Romans corresponded in some measure with the Pallas-Athene of the Greeks. She was the patroness of arts and industry, and the mental powers were considered as under her peculiar care. She was the deity of schools: her statue was always placed in them, and the five days of the festival called Quinquatria, celebrated in the month of March, were holidays to the scholars. At their expiration, they presented their master with a gift called Minerval. According to Varro, Minerva was also the protecting goddess of olive grounds; but it may be doubted whether this was not a transference of one of the attributes of Pallas-Athene.

The festivals of Minerva were named Minervalia, or Quinquatria. They were two in number; the former, called the Greater, were celebrated in March, the time when, according to the Tuscan discipline, Minerva cast her lightnings. It was named Quinquatrus as being on the fifth day after the Ides; the ignorance of the Romans made them extend the festival to five days; it was followed by the Tubilustrum. The Lesser was in the Ides of June, and was celebrated by the flute players. As both the trumpet and flute came to the Romans from Etruria, this proves Minerva to have been introduced there from that country. Therefore, no derivation of her name can be given, as it does not seem to be a translation.

Athena is represented as a beauty of the severer kind, and without the grace and delicacy which for instance distinguished Aphrodite. Dignity, and a becoming air, firmness and composure, with regular features, and a certain masculine sternness, form the peculiar characteristics of her face and figure. Hence the heads of her are so like Alexander the Great, that they have been occasionally mistaken for his. Her dress and attributes are adapted to her character. She has a helmet upon her head, and a plume nodding formidably in the air. In her right hand she holds a spear, and in her left grasps a shield with the head of the dying Medusa upon it. The same figure, with all its terrors and beauties, is also on her breast-plate; and sometimes she is represented with serpents about her shoulders. An owl, the bird sacred to her, is sometimes seen hovering over her helmet.

In most of her statues, Athena is represented as seated, and sometimes holds in her hand a distaff instead of a spear. When she was depicted as the goddess of the liberal arts, she was arrayed in a variegated veil. Sometimes her helmet was covered with the figure of a cock, which, on account of its great courage, was appropriated to the deity of war. Some of her statues represented her helmet with a sphinx in the middle, supported on either side by griffins;* and on some medals a chariot drawn by four horses; and in others a dragon or serpent appears with winding spires at the tops of her helmet.

The shield or corselet with the Gorgon's head is supposed by some to represent the full-orbed moon; by others it is regarded as the emblem of divine wisdom.

---

* *Griffin*—A fabulous animal, said to be generated between the Lion and the Eagle. It is described as having the head and paws of the lion, the ears of the horse, the wings of the eagle, and a crest formed like the dorsal fins of a fish.

Pallas-Athene is in Homer, and in the general, popular system, the goddess of wisdom and skill. In war she is opposed to Ares, the wild war-god, as the patroness and teacher of just and scientific warfare. Therefore she is on the side of the Greeks, and he on that of the Trojans. But on the shield of Achilleus, where the people of the besieged town were represented as going forth to lie in ambush, they are led by Ares and Athena together; possibly to denote the union and skill required for that service. Every prudent chief was supposed to be under the patronage of Athena; therefore, Odysseus (or Ulysses) was her special favorite, whom she relieved from all perils, and whose son Telemachos she also took under her protection, assuming a human form to be his guide and director. In like manner Cadmos, Heracles, Perseus, and other heroes, were favored by this goddess.

As the patroness of arts and industry in general, Pallas-Athene was regarded as the inspirer and teacher of all able artists. Thus she taught Epios to form the wooden horse, by means of which Troy was taken; and she also superintended the building of the ship Argo. She was expert in female accomplishments, having woven her own robe and that of Hera, which last she is said to have embroidered very richly. When Pandora was made for the ruin of man, she was attired by Pallas-Athene; and when Iason was setting forth in quest of the golden fleece, she gave him a mantle wrought by herself. She is said to have taught this art to mortal females, who had won her affection.

By the Homerid. Athena and Hephæstos are united as the civilizers and benefactors of mankind by means of the arts which they taught them, and we find them in intimate union in the mythic systems of Attica.

The ægis or shield of Zeus and Athena was supposed to

THE ÆGIS OR SHIELD.

have been made originally of the skin of a goat, and afterwards by Hephæstos of brass, and rendered terrible by a Gorgon's head being sculptured upon it. Lactantius says, that it was made of the skin of the goat which suckled Jupiter, and that he first used it against the Titans. Ægis is also used for the pieces of goat-skin with which the warriors  covered their breasts and shoulders as a guard against the weapons of their enemies. A variety of ancient monuments attest the antiquity of this practice.

Homer gives to the ægis of Zeus the power of being both offensive and defensive, as all his deities, with whatever circumstances they are endued in common with mortals, are made to possess some peculiar and supernatural power. The blood which issues from their wounds is *ichor;* their drink is *nectar;* and their food is *ambrosia.* This poet always personifies the effects which the arms of his gods and heroes, and the charms of his gods and goddesses, have over mortals; placing in the girdle of Aphrodite the most attractive charms of love, which influence in secret the hearts of the wisest. He who on the buckler of Agamemnon has placed Fear and Terror, naturally added to the ægis of Zeus, Force and Discord; and to add more honor to the arms of this most powerful god, he places the head of the terrible Gorgon with its intertwined serpents in the middle of his breast-plate. These are the arms which gave to Jupiter the name of *Ægiochus,* the holder of the Ægis.

The ægis of Athena, with which she descended into the camp of the Greeks, to excite them to battle and dissuade them from the disgraceful intentions they had conceived of abandoning Troy and returning home, is described by

Homer, as precious, indestructible, and eternal, fringed with a border composed of a hundred tufts of gold, each valued at a hundred oxen.*

The ferocious custom of cutting off the heads of their enemies, or scalping them, as practised by barbarous nations, and which is undoubtedly the origin of the ægis, is sometimes found even among the Greeks; as in the Iliad we find Diomedes cutting off the head of Dolon. Among ancient nations, the head or scalp of an enemy was carried as a mark of triumph on their shields; and in later times they imitated it in metal for the centre and ornament of their bucklers. On one of the vases in Sir W. Hamilton's collection, now in the British Museum, is represented a large buckler, bearing in the middle a human head which has nothing in common with the Gorgon. In more modern times, a head was placed on the cuirass. Homer, in describing the ægis, does not mention its being covered with scales, but only a skin, in the middle of which is. a Gorgon's head encircled with snakes. The scales appear to be a posterior addition, and give an idea of greater resistance. Virgil has not omitted the scales in describing the ægis forged by the Cyclops in the depths of Ætna.

As Athena typifies the mind or wisdom of Zeus, there is a peculiar propriety in her wielding the same ægis with her great parent. But this armor was not peculiar to Zeus and Athena, although generally appropriated to them by the poets. In the fifteenth book of the Iliad, Apollo marches at the head of the Greeks, conducting to combat the people who followed the mighty, terrific, shagged, dazzling ægis which the artist Hephæstos had given to Zeus. In the temple of Zeus at Olympia, there was a statue of Victory which had a golden buckler, on which were the

---

* Theseus gave to his money the impression of an ox. Hence the expression, worth ten or a hundred oxen.

ægis and Gorgon, probably because victory proceeded from Jupiter; and Rome, for a similar reason, namely, being under the special protection of Jupiter and Minerva, was personified on a beautiful medallion, as a female warrior armed with the ægis.

The ægis at length descended from deities to heroes, warriors and emperors. On a fine cameo, in the royal library at Paris, Ulysses is covered with the ægis, as a symbol of the protection of Minerva. This allegory of the protection which the gods offered to men, became a species of amulet; and above all, the Gorgon, or Medusa's head, was conceived by the ancients to have the virtue of averting witchcraft, or enchantment; for which reason the Roman emperors, without bearing what is more properly the ægis, have a Gorgon's head sculptured in the middle of their breasts on the *lorica* or brigantine. The only instance generally known, of the ægis being fixed on the arm, is on an intaglio in the cabinet of the Emperor of Russia, representing Jupiter Axur, or the Beardless. Jupiter is generally represented with the ægis on the left shoulder, as in the beautiful cameo of the royal cabinet at Paris, which represents Jupiter Ægiochus. The ægis on the knees, as in the figure of Tiberius, on the grand cameo of the same cabinet, indicates peace and repose to the world.

The Palladium, a celebrated statue of the goddess Pallas-Athene, was about three cubits high, and represented her as in a sitting posture, holding a pike in her right hand and a distaff and spindle in her left.

The Palladium is said to have fallen from heaven near the tent of Ilus, at the time when that prince was employed in building the citadel of Ilion or Troy; and Apollo, by an oracle, declared that the city should never be taken whilst the Palladium was contained within its walls. Hence, the assailants of Troy became exceedingly anxious to get possession of this treasure; and Ulysses, accompanied by Diomedes. undertook to purloin it. Having entered the citadel at night by stealth, they stole the Palladium away; the consequence of which act was the fall of Troy.

The Parthenon, or chief temple of Athena, the virgin goddess, and patroness of Athens, stood on the summit of the Acropolis. This celebrated structure is now reduced to the last stages of ruin and decay; little remains of what formerly constituted one of the most elegant, if not the most spacious monuments of heathen superstition, but this little is venerable for its age and history; and highly interesting for the evidences which it still affords of Grecian skill in architecture. Its beautiful proportions are, indeed, now lost in the surrounding mass of miserable huts; its glittering whiteness dimmed by the corroding hand of time, and its towering columns shattered and cast down by the merciless engines of modern warfare; but yet, while a vestige is to be found of such excellence, it will not cease to be inestimable to the scientific traveller, and the philosophical inquirer into the state of society in former ages.*

HEPHÆSTOS OR VULCAN.

Hephæstos, the Olympian artist, is in Homer the son of Zeus and Hera. According to Hesiod, he is the son of Hera alone, who in this wished not to be outdone by Zeus, who had produced Athena from his own brain.

Hephæstos is the god of fire, especially as a power of a physical nature, that manifests itself in volcanic districts, and as the indispensable means in arts and manufactures. Hence fire is called the breath of Hephæstos, and the name of the god is used by the Greek and Roman poets as synonymous with it. As a flame arises from a little spark,

---

* For a full description see large edition.

so the god of fire was delicate and weakly from his birth, for which reason he was so disliked by his mother, that she flung him from Olympos. He was received by Thetis and Eurynome, and dwelt with them for nine years in a grotto, surrounded by Oceanos, and there made for them a variety of ornaments.

According to later writers, Hephæstos was educated with the rest of the gods in heaven, and was expelled from Olympos by Zeus. Hera raised a storm, which drove Heracles out of his course at sea; Zeus then tied her hands and feet together, and suspended her between heaven and earth. Hephæstos attempted to free his mother, and, for this act, was kicked down from heaven by Zeus. The island of Lemnos is said to have received the god.

In this island, where earthquakes and eruptions of volcanoes were frequently experienced, and also in the smoking of Ætna, in Sicily, from whose bowels the fire which found no vent often produced a subterranean thundering, imagination has discovered suitable places for the workshops of Hephæstos, in which the mighty hammers of the Cyclopes resounded.

On Olympos, he is said also to have had his own palace, imperishable and shining like stars. It contained his work-shop, with the anvil, and twenty bellows which worked spontaneously at his bidding, and there he made his beautiful and marvellous works. All the habitations of the gods were of his workmanship, as were their chariots and arms. He made armor for Achilleus and other mortal heroes. The fatal collar of Harmonia was the work of his hands. The brass-footed, brass-throated, fire-breathing bulls of Æetes, the king of Colchis, were the gift of Hephæstos; and he made for Alcinoös, king of the Phæacians, the gold and silver dogs which guarded his house. For himself he formed the golden maidens, who waited on him, and whom he endowed with reason and speech. He gave to Minos, king of Crete, the brazen man Talos, who each day compassed his island three times, to guard it from the invasion of strangers. The brazen cup in which the sun-god and his horses and chariot are carried round the earth every night, was also the work of this god.

The first work of Hephæstos is said to have been a throne of gold, which he presented to his mother, to avenge himself for her want of affection towards him—upon which Hera was no sooner seated than she found herself unable to move. The gods attempted to set her at liberty by breaking the chains with which she was confined; but to no purpose, as Hephæstos alone had the power to unloose them.

It is worthy of remark that the only instances we meet of Hephæstos working in any other substance than metal are in Hesiod, where, at the command of Zeus, he forms Pandora of earth and water, and where he uses gypsum and ivory in the formation of the shield which he makes for Heracles. That framed by him for Achilleus, in the Iliad, is all of metal.

He was celebrated by the ancient poets for his ingenious works. By their imagination, painful and wearisome labor, in a work-shop filled with steam and smoke, joined to the idea of sublime art, that works there indefatigably with productive genius, was wrought up into this divine being, whose entire strength was concentrated in the mighty arm that managed the weighty hammer upon the anvil, while the lamed feet were enfeebled and tottering.

He was hurled from heaven, for smoke and black steam, together with half-smothered flame, do not agree with pure ether; they are in contradiction to the idea of serenity, beauty, and divine dignity. Nevertheless, Fancy contrived to usher even this personage into the splendid theatre of high, divine Olympos, securing to him a place among the celestials, by bestowing upon him the comical part on the heavenly stage. The gods raise peals of laughter when they behold Hephæstos in the place of Ganymedes, making the round in the assembly of the immortals, reaching them the nectar cup, and jesting himself at his own bodily defects.

Yet the bold imagination of the ancients, which we can not help admiring, found means on the other hand to shroud again this comical character in divine power and sublimity by connecting with it a dignity superior to every thing human. Her grand picture of the supernatural world, far from being degraded by a figure like that of Hephæstos, becomes, on the contrary, more variously shaded, and gains new charms. The halting son of Hera, on account of his deformity, was thrown from Olympos, and after his re-admission into the community of the gods, ministered the nectar cup in the place of the graceful Ganymedes in so awkward a manner, as to excite the shouting mirth of the immortals. The same Hephæstos is the inimitable artist, with whose assistance even they themselves cannot dispense.

At his work-shop, the limping feet are not prejudicial to him; he needs only his arms. And with strong arm, indeed, manages he the stithy! Air and fire are at his command. At his nod the bellows blow and kindle the flames, producing a greater or gentler heat, according to his wants. Every one of his ideas is instantaneously carried into effect with divine genius, and from beneath his skilful hands, the work springs forth majestically. It is also an easy matter to him to infuse life and motion into his creations. He forges twenty tripods rolling upon wheels, which, at his command, enter the assembly of the gods, and return to him again. He formed for himself female servants of gold, that support him when he is walking. When he leaves his stithy, he arrays himself in royal attire and bears a sceptre.

Though a deformed cripple, he has the most beautiful being that dwells on Olympos for his wife. Thus plastic art, although in its appearance poor and uncomely, is, in the representation of Hephæstos, married to beauty itself. By this marriage between Aphrodite and the god of fire, the comical turn of his character gains the highest charm; the conjugal unanimity of the divine couple being disturbed by the jealousy of Hephæstos. The story of the artificial net, which the offended husband contrived to throw over Ares and Aphrodite, while he called together all the celestials to show them the disgraceful spectacle, and to complain of his misfortune, is, in ancient poetry, a source of amusement, both among gods and men.

Especially in the person of Hephæstos do we find that endeavor to unite opposite and seemingly contradictory features into one character, which is peculiar to the fictions of the ancients. With regard to what is external, he, the ugliest of all the celestials, is married to the loveliest being that Fancy ever created; in his character, the ridiculous is united with dignity; and in his body, feebleness is connected with strength; the strong and skilful arm compensating for the limping feet. We are by no means to consider this apparent inconsistency in the poetical productions of the ancients as a defect, originating, perhaps, in the heedless play of humor; on the contrary, we are rather to admire the ingenuity and boldness of Imagination, who shrinks not from seeming difficulties, and succeeds in adjusting the variety of materials, collected together for the picture of her celestial world, into so happy and concordant a composition

The fiction of Hephæstos also shows us the high estimation in which the ancients held the art of working metals; it is, of all the arts, the peculiar business of a god.

Although Hephæstos first appears in a clear and distinct form among the modern gods, yet his person may be faintly recognized through the clouds in which the ancient deities are shrouded. The Curetes, or Corybantes, were, according to an old tradition, his descendants. He was likewise one of the most ancient Egyptian deities, or perhaps the most ancient of them. The Curetes made a noise with their weapons, which, as tradition relates, were of iron. The Cyclopes, before the reign of Zeus, had prepared thunder and lightning in the caverns of the earth; and Earth herself had already forged the sickle with which Saturn was maimed. According to another tradition, the Cabeiri, a kind of mysterious beings, who, in the remotest times of antiquity, were venerated in Egypt and Samothrace, were sons or descendants of Hephæstos. His person itself, however, is always hidden in darkness.

That mythology represents the fine arts as assisting each other, is a fine and significant intimation. When Prometheus was occupied in forming his men, both Athena and Hephæstos lent him their aid; and when the latter was afterwards, at the command of Zeus, obliged to fasten the father of mankind to the fatal rock, he, not daring to resist the will of the thunderer, complied with it, amid tears and lamentations.

Vulcan, the male artist among the celestials, had a desire to marry Minerva, the female one; but she withstood his entreaties as well as threats. His son Erichthonios, the earth-born, is said, however, to have been always a favorite with Minerva. She appointed him king of her beloved city of Athens, where the desire of hiding his mis-shapen feet, both of which were those of a dragon,* led him to the invention of the covered four-wheel carriage.

The God of Fire, represented by Homer, on occasion of Thetis coming to his dwelling to see him and his wife, and to order at the same time a new suit of armor for her son Achilles, is entirely human. No sooner had he heard of the august Thetis, the old friend of his house, than, in order to appear with decency in the presence of the goddess, he before leaving his work-shop, washed his face, breast, neck and hands, with a wet sponge, lest his visitor should be offended at beholding him covered with dust, to which his occupation necessarily exposed him.

The worship of Vulcan was well established, particularly in Egypt, at Athens, and at Rome. In the sacrifices that were offered to him, it was usual to burn the whole victim, and not to reserve a part as in immolations to other gods. A calf and a boar-pig were the principal victims offered.

Vulcan was sometimes represented as lame and deformed, holding a hammer in the air, ready to strike; while with the other hand he turns, with his pincers, a thunderbolt upon his anvil. He appears in some monuments with a long beard, dishevelled hair, his figure partially covered, and a small, round cap on his head, and holding in his

---

* It is worthy of observation, that, in the mythological fictions of the ancients, to almost every being sprung from the earth, or related to it, dragon form, or dragon feet are ascribed.

hand the pincers and hammer. The Egyptians represented him under the figure of a monkey.

Upon antique gems, he is commonly represented as an artist, occupied in his work-shop with forging arrows for Cupid.

APHRODITE OR VENUS.

Aphrodite, the perfection of creation, the Goddess of Love and Beauty, who presided over the propagation of every species of being, was, according to Homer, the daughter of Zeus and the blooming Dione, the youngest of the Titan sisters.

Besides the numberless local divinities of this name, the first mythologists acknowledged two original powers—the eldest a child of Uranos and last production of Heaven, and therefore of the Titan race, who bore her part in the productions of the universe; and the youngest, the daughter of Zeus and Dione—the power arising from the vivifying, ethereal spirit, acting upon the plenitude of matter. According to Orpheus, the former brought forth the world and all it contains. "All things are of thee," says he; 'thou cementest the universe, thou swayest the three-fold Fates; thou generatest whatever is in the heavens above, or the teeming earth below, or in the unfathomed depths of the sea." Euripides makes Aphrodite the daughter of Kronos and Eunomia (*Time and Good Order*).

The Grecian Aphrodite arose from the foam of the sea, was received by the Horæ, who dressed her in divine attire, placed a golden crown upon her head, and adorned her neck, arms, and ears with golden ornaments. Zeus gave her the Graces for companions, Cupids attended upon her, and her chariot was drawn by doves. Every stroke in this picture breathes tenderness; yet, the son of the goddess is armed with bow and arrows, indicating the power of his heavenly mother, the all-subduing deity.

The dominion of Aphrodite over the heart was assisted and supported by a famous girdle, called *zone* by the Greeks, and *cestus* by the Latins. This mysterious cincture gave beauty and grace to the wearer, even when deformed, and possessed the power of inspiring love. When Hera wished to inspire Zeus with this affection, she borrowed the magic girdle from Aphrodite.

In this lovely goddess, those charms of grace and beauty are venerated which allude to matrimonial union; but as the beneficent impulse of love, if not carefully guarded by reason and morality, may prove pernicious, bringing destruction on individuals, as well as war and mischief upon whole nations, the Goddess of Love is represented as a dreadful being.

Having promised Paris the fairest wife on earth, because he adjudged the prize of beauty to her in preference to all the other goddesses, she incited him to deprive Menelaos, king of Sparta, of his lawful spouse, the god-like Helena—at the same time instilling into the bosom of this woman inconstancy and unfaithfulness. Thus the goddess kept her word, not caring for the misery and ruin in which it might result; and at all times, and in every danger, she proves a zealous friend to Paris. During the siege of Troy, the offended Menelaos was about to kill Paris in single combat, when Aphrodite suddenly covered him with nightly darkness, and led him safely to his perfumed closet.

Should this deity unite in herself the cold wisdom of Athena, or the awful earnestness of Themis, then indeed she would be incapable of the injustice of gratifying the wishes of one favorite at the expense of a whole city; nay, of a whole country, laid waste on his account. But then she would likewise cease to be exclusively the goddess of Love, or a product of Fancy; in whose person is represented the influence of the passion, indifferent to the consequences; not caring whether it leaves the traces of bloody wars, or ages exhibiting the bliss of peace, together with generations rejoicing in their own existence.

In the productions of Fancy, it is the very want of completeness, the very appearance of defect, in the features of the person represented, by which alone imagination is enabled to create and people a whole world with supernatural beings, each distinguished by its own characteristics. The august Hera is destitute of placid loveliness, and is obliged to borrow the girdle of Aphrodite; the mighty god of war is deficient in reflection and prudence, and his impetuosity is restrained by Athena.

Aphrodite is possessed of the highest charms imaginable; but Athena, destitute of female delicacy, is far superior to her in power. In one of the battles fought before Troy, in which the gods themselves at last challenged each other, Aphrodite being on the side of the Trojans, received from the strong hand of Athena (who assisted the Greeks) such a blow as made her knees sink under her.

"Would to Heaven," exclaimed Athena, triumphantly, "that all the Trojans might equal the heroism and valor of Aphrodite!" (Il. xii. 428.) And at another time, Aphrodite, when wounded in her snow-white hand by the cold Diomedes, came to Olympos, complaining to her mother Dione of the daring of mortal men. Athena railed at her in terms like these: "Aphrodite, forsooth, was persuading a handsomely dressed Grecian lady to follow along with her beloved Trojans; and, in caressing the fondling, she scratched her delicate hand with the golden clasp which fastened the robe of her favorite." Then the father of the gods and men smiled, and said, "Warlike work, my love, is not thy business; it is thy sweet care to prepare the joys of the wedding feast; the care of war's wild tumult leave to Ares and Athena." (Il. v. 42.)

Thus the imagination of the ancients sportively trifles with the deities whom she created after the image of man, yet always choosing such natural prototypes as are both grand and sublime.

The worship of Aphrodite was universally established. Statues and temples were erected to her in every kingdom; and the ancients delighted in paying homage to a divinity by whose influence alone mankind was supposed to exist. She was chiefly worshipped at Cythera and Cyprus; and fable says, that it was to the shores of the latter island that the waves of the sea gently carried the Goddess of Love as she arose from its foam. On this charming island, whole cities, together with groves, temples, and altars, were consecrated to Aphrodite. Her favorite residence, however, was Paphos, where offerings and vows were presented in her temple, from every quarter of the earth. And from the veneration with which all nations here rendered homage to the Goddess of Beauty, she was called queen of Paphos. From two other places on Cyprus, Amathus and Idalion, she received the poetical appellations, Idalia and Amathusia; and from the island itself, she had the name of Cypria.

From the remotest countries pilgrims came to Cnidos, there also to pay homage to the love-inspiring goddess, whom skilful art had endowed with human form, and thus rendered her visible to the eyes of men. There, the image of Aphrodite stood in an open temple, unveiled to the view of mortals. It was the Aphrodite of Praxiteles, a worthy object of admiration.

The most ancient temple of Aphrodite in Greece, stood on the island of Cythera; and the idea of the goddess herself was so intimately connected with the place of her residence, that both names became one, and in poetical language, the Goddess of Love was called Cytheræa.

In the more ancient temples of this goddess in Cyprus, she was represented under the form of a rude conical stone;

but the Grecian sculptors and painters. Praxiteles and Apelles, vied with each other in forming her image the ideal of female beauty and attraction. She appears sometimes rising out of the sea and wringing her locks; sometimes drawn in a conch by Tritons, or riding on some marine animal; and sometimes drawn in a car by doves.

The birds sacred to Aphrodite were swans, doves, and sparrows. Horace places her in a chariot drawn by swans, and Sappho gives her sparrows. In one of the odes ascribed to Anacreon, a dove announces herself as a present from the goddess to the bard. The bird called Iynx or Fritillus, of which so much use was made in amatory magic, was also sacred to this goddess; as was likewise the swallow, the herald of Spring, the season of love. Her favorite plants were the rose and the myrtle.

The husband assigned to this goddess is the lame artist Hephæstos; and she is fabled to have loved Anchises, the father of Æneias.

Adonis, son of Cyniras and Myrrha, was famed for his beauty, and became a favorite of Venus. The tender goddess, not able to live without him, partly laid aside her softness for his sake, following him to the chase of the deer. She accompanied him like his faithful genius, warning him to spare his precious life, whenever his daring spirit instigated him to pursue the tracks of fierce and dangerous beasts. But, disregarding the entreaties and warnings of the goddess, he soon ran to destruction. Meeting with a fierce boar, he hurled his dart at him; but, not being mortally wounded, the beast plunged his white tusks into the side of the handsome youth. He sank, the blood gushing in abundance from his wound, and when Aphrodite sought her beloved Adonis, she found him in the agony of death.

In vain did she endeavor to recall him to life, and with

bitter complaints accused the cruelty of his fate. Distracted, the goddess ran barefoot through the woods and lawns; her delicate skin was pierced by thorns; and her blood, dropping upon the rose, changed it from white to red. By degrees, her despair changed to softer mourning; she sprinkled with nectar the ground that received the blood of her beloved Adonis, and gave him a kind of immortality by raising from it the flower Anemone, which, by its soon withering, expresses the brief period of life allotted to the beautiful son of Myrrha.

A festival in honor of Adonis was annually celebrated at Byblos by the Phœnician women during two days; the first of which was spent in grief and lamentation at his death, and the second in joy and triumph at the fabled resurrection of Adonis from the dead. During this festival the priests of Babylon shaved their heads, in imitation of the priests of Isis in Egypt.

In Greece, whither these rites were transplanted, the festival was prolonged to eight days. It is uncertain when the Adoneia was first celebrated in that country; but we find Plato alluding to the gardens of Adonis, as pots and boxes of flowers used in them were called, and the ill-fortune of the Athenian expedition to Sicily was in part ascribed to the circumstance of the fleet having sailed during that festival.

In Greece it was celebrated in the same manner as in Phœnicia. On the first day the citizens put themselves in mourning, and coffins were placed at every door; the statues of Venus and Adonis were borne in procession, with the gardens of Adonis. At the conclusion of the ceremony, they were thrown into the sea or some river, where they soon perished, and thus became emblems of the premature death of Adonis, who, like a young plant, was cut off in the flower of life.

This tale of Adonis is evidently an Eastern myth. His

own name and those of his parents refer to that part of the world. He appears to be the same with the Thammuz mentioned by the prophet Ezekiel (ch. viii., v. 14),

> Whose annual wound in Lebanon allured
> The Syrian damsels to lament his fate,
> While smooth Adonis from his native rock
> Ran purple to the sea, supposed with blood
> Of Thammuz yearly wounded;

and to be a Phœnician personification of the sun, who, during a part of the year is absent, with the goddess of the under world, and during the remainder with Astarte the queen of Heaven. The legend says, that Aphrodite committed Adonis to the care of Persephone, who afterwards refused to part with him; the matter being referred to Zeus, he decreed that Adonis should have one-third of the year to himself, be another third with Aphrodite, and the remaining third with Persephone.

Adonis was an oriental title of the sun signifying Lord; and the loss of this mighty lord was lamented in all countries where the Assyrian and the Phœnician traditions were received; and his return to impregnate the world with his genial vigor, was welcomed with the highest demonstrations of joy. The boar supposed to have killed him, was the emblem of winter; during which, the productive powers of nature being suspended, Aphrodite, who went hand in hand with spring, was said to lament the loss of Adonis until he was again restored to life; hence the Syrian and Argive women annually mourned his death, and celebrated his renovation to life. The mysteries of Adonis and Aphrodite, at Byblos in Syria, were held in similar estimation with those of Demeter and Dionysos at Eleusis, and of Isis and Osiris in Egypt.

There is none of the Olympians of whom the foreign origin is so probable as that of Aphrodite. She is generally regarded as being the same with the Astarte of the Phœnicians. There can be little doubt of the identification of Astarte with the Grecian Aphrodite, for the tale of Adonis sufficiently proves it; and that this took place at a very early period, is evinced by Homer's so frequently giving Aphrodite the name of Cypris. Still we look on Aphrodite to be, as her name seems to denote, an originally Grecian deity; at first, probably, merely cosmogonic, but gradually adopted into the system of the Olympians, and endowed with some of the attributes of Hera (who was also identified with Astarte), and thus became the patroness of marriage. It was probably on account of her being esteemed the same with Astarte, the moon goddess and queen of Heaven, that Aphrodite was so frequently styled the heavenly (Urania). It is very important to observe that she was so named at her temple in Cythera, which was regarded as the holiest and most ancient of her fanes in Greece. Her antique wooden statue in this temple was armed; as it was also in Corinth and Sparta. In this last city, she was styled Urania, and her worship there was eminently Asiatic in character.

HERMES OR MERCURY.

While Hera was sleeping, Zeus went to see Maia, the graceful daughter of Atlas, in a shady cave; and to this secret visit Hermes is said to have owed his existence. Being born in the morning, he at noon played on the lute invented by himself, and in the evening he stole Apollo's oxen.

The lute was invented by him in the following manner. Secretly leaving his cradle at noon, on the first day of his life, and stepping over the threshold, he met a tortoise, whose shell appeared to him a fit instrument for giving musical tones when furnished with strings: "Now thou art dumb," said he, " but after thy death, thy song will be heard." Thus addressing the animal, he immediately killed it, and furnished the shell with seven concordant strings, which he touched with a small stick. As soon as he had tuned the newly-invented instrument with skilful ear, he could not forbear singing to it, and chanted forth the praise of every thing that met his eye, even the tripods and vessels in his mother's house; till at last, his song, passing into a higher strain, found a worthier subject, in the love of Zeus and Maia, his divine parents.

When evening came on, and the sun had descended into the ocean, Hermes found himself upon the Pierian mountains, where the herds of the immortal gods were feeding. From these he stole fifty oxen belonging to Apollo, and devising many a crafty trick to avoid detection, as he drove them onward through valleys and over mountains, he would have escaped discovery but for an old man, who, digging in the field, saw the boy with the oxen, and afterwards betrayed him to Apollo. On the shores of the river Alpheus, Hermes killed two of the stolen oxen, making a sacrifice of them to himself. Having done this, he carefully extinguished the fire, hid the ashes in the ground, and threw the remainder of the killed animals into the river, together with the shoes he had made of twigs and put upon the feet of the oxen, in order to conceal their tracks, or render them undiscernible. All this he performed by moonlight. Before the break of day he gently stole back into his mother's dwelling, and lay down again in his cradle, pulling the clothes around him, and holding the lute, his dearest plaything, in his hand.

Apollo, angry at the theft committed on his oxen, appeared to call Hermes to account, and to recover his property. The thief feigned a deep sleep, having the lute lying under his arm. Apollo threatened to precipitate him into Tartaros, if he would not immediately point out the place where the oxen were hidden. Then the cunning boy, twinkling his eyes, answered him, "How cruelly, son of Leto, dost thou address a little boy who was not born until yesterday, and who cares for things very different from driving oxen; who is longing for sweet slumber and his mother's breast, and whose feet are too tender and feeble to tread long and rough paths. Nay, I will swear by Zeus, my father's head, that neither I myself have stolen the oxen, nor do I know who committed the deed."

Upon this, it was agreed between them, that both should appear before the father of the gods on Olympos, that he might reconcile their difference. Apollo stated his complaint, while Hermes stood by in his swathing-clothes, in order to refute the charge by the appearance of his tender age. "Have I then indeed," said he, "the appearance of a strong man, able to drive away oxen? Certainly, father, thou shalt hear nothing but the truth from me. Whilst the oxen were stolen, I was lying in sweet slumber, and did not pass the threshold of my mother's dwelling. Thou knowest thyself, too, that I am innocent; yet I am ready to protest my innocence with a solemn oath, and I shall one day reward the cruel word of that false one. But thou, father, be the protector of the younger." Thus spoke Hermes, with twinkling eyes, and Zeus smiled at the boy because he was prudent enough to deny so finely the charge brought against him. But at the same time he commanded him to tell where the oxen were hidden, and when Hermes obeyed the injunction, accompanying Apollo to the hiding-place, a reconciliation took place between them, of which the invented lute was the pledge.

For when the sweet sound of the instrument had touched the ear of the god of harmony, he was enraptured; and caressing the inventor, "Truly," said he, "this invention is worth fifty oxen." Upon this, Hermes made him a present of the lute, and Apollo became transported with joy, at the thought of possessing so inestimable a treasure

In order, however, to secure it to himself, he requested Hermes to swear by the Styx never to steal the sweetly-sounding lute from its present possessor. In return for his lute, Apollo gave him the golden wand, which had the power of settling all differences; and these two, now closely united, ascended hand in hand to Olympos. It was art that wove the band that united them, and Zeus rejoiced in the concord

Hermes became afterwards the messenger of the immortals He is the swift, the rapidly moving power among the celestials, who, as if firmly established in their own majesty, send the fleet, inventive idea from heaven to earth, re-admitting it into their divine council as soon as its task is accomplished.

His archetype is speech. Speech, the tender breath of air, must, as it were, steal into the effective connection of things, in order to make up by thought and prudence for the deficiency of power and strength. The word of speech is winged, because it is only to be heard when accompanied by the swift breath of the lungs, and flies like a bird let loose, that cannot be recalled. For this reason, the beautiful expression of the ancients, "The word wants its wings."

According to a poetical representation, a golden chain hangs down from his mouth, reaching from Olympos to the listening ears of the dwellers on the earth, who, in this manner, are persuaded by the irresistible charms of the sweet melody that flows from his lips.

Irresistible also is his art to settle differences, to reconcile enemies—in short, to dissolve all dissonant objects in harmonious union. Once, in his boyhood, he found two serpents in his way engaged in furious strife; he struck between them with his golden wand, and behold! the reptiles instantly forget their fury, and twine themselves in gentle coil round the wand, at the top of which their heads meet in eternal concord. There is no emblem to be found more expressive of reconciliation and peace, as well as harmonious connection of what is opposed and contending, than this wand surrounded with coiling serpents, which, in the hand of the divine herald, thenceforward constituted a token of his authority.

Nothing is more charming and attractive in the fictions of the ancients, than their description of the rapid development of divine power in these supernatural beings —a power, which, as if having existed long ago, and being only new born in a particular form, does not suffer itself to be long restrained by swathing-clothes and cradle.

In this light, airy representation, the imagination of the ancients embodied the ideas of quick, inventive faculty, and cunning activity, which displayed itself alike in deceptive persuasion, and easily accomplished sportive theft, at which even the pilfered himself, hearing the adventurous roguishness, was forced to smile. Jocularity and cunning being here clothed with divinity and immortality, present a new figure in the great picture of the divine assembly; fitter, upon the whole, to charm our eyes by its variety of composition and splendid colors, than to improve our hearts by its moral exhibitions.

In the human breast, the voice of an invisible, supernatural power speaks intelligibly, bidding man lift up his eyes from the earth to a higher world. The ancients, too, heard this voice; but misapprehending it, they formed to themselves a supernatural world, after the pattern which nature and human life presented to them. Therefore, nothing appeared to them mean or unholy, that rose from the general, uncreating influence of nature, and contained, although noxious in itself, the germ of beauty or utility.

Fancy assigns to her divine beings no bounds with regard to actions; on the contrary, she gives to the inward impulse the fullest scope; suffering them to stray even to the extreme limits of mischief, because in her fictions the great contrasts, together with the huge masses of light and shade, which otherwise we perceive merely as scattered and single, are concentrated in a small compass, and because every one of her beings comprises, as it were, in its own person, the substance of all things considered from some sublime point of view.

In this respect, the fiction of Hermes is one of the most beautiful and comprehensive. He is the swift herald of the immortals; the god of speech; the tutelary genius of the roads; in him the winged word is renewed when repeated from his lips, in delivering the commands of the gods; with his golden wand he leads the dead to the world of shadows; he is likewise the author of all prudent and cunning designs, plots, and artifices; the patron of thieves, the teacher of men in the art of wrestling, or of conquering strength by agility, and the president over trade and gain.

As messenger of Zeus, he was intrusted with all his secrets; and as the ambassador and plenipotentiary of the Gods, was concerned in all alliances and treaties. In the wars of the giants, he showed himself brave, spirited, and active. He delivered Ares from his long confinement which he suffered from the superior powers of the Aloeids; he purified the Danaïdes from the murder of their husbands; he tied Ixion to his wheel in the infernal regions; he destroyed the hundred-eyed Argos; he sold Heracles to Omphale, queen of Lydia; he conducted Priamos to the tent of Achilleus to redeem the body of his son Hector; and he carried the infant Dionysos to the nymphs of Nysa. He gave many proofs of his thievish propensity, and increased his fame by robbing Poseidon of his trident, Aphrodite of her girdle, Ares of his sword, Zeus of his sceptre, and Hephæstos of his mechanical instruments.

Mythologists are pretty well agreed in recognizing a telluric power in the Hermes of the Pelasgian system. The simplest derivation of his name is from a Greek word, signifying *earth*, and by the name of his mother, Maia, is probably meant Mother Earth.

He seems to have been the deity of productiveness in general; but he came gradually to be regarded as presiding more particularly over flocks and herds. From this last view some of his Hellenic attributes may be simply deduced. Thus the god of shepherds was naturally regarded as the inventor of music; the lyre is ascribed to Hermes, as the pipes are to Pan, music having always been a recreation of shepherds in the warm regions of the south. In like manner, as the shepherd lads amuse themselves with wrestling and other feats of strength and activity, their tutelar god easily became the president of the *palæstra*. So also trade, having consisted chiefly in the exchange of cattle, Hermes, the herdsman's god, was held to be the god of commerce; and the skill and eloquence employed in commercial dealings, made him to be the god of eloquence, artifice, and ingenuity, and even of cheating. As herdsmen are the best guides in the country, it may be thence that Hermes was thought to protect wayfarers, and thence to be a protector in general. For this cause it may have been, that god-sends or treasure-trove were ascribed to him.

The rural deity, when thus become active, sly and eloquent, was well adapted for the office which was assigned him of agent and messenger of the gods, to whom we also find him officiating as cup-bearer. As a being whose operations extended into the interior of the earth, Hermes would seem to have been in some points of view identified with Hades. In Pindar, this latter deity himself performs the office generally assigned to Hermes, that of conducting the departed to Erebos. Possibly it may have been on this account, that Solon directed the Athenians to swear by Zeus, Poseidon, and Hermes.

The Grecian spirit completely modified the Egyptian Hermes, to produce the Hermes or Mercury of the Grecian mythology; where he is quite a different being. In Egypt he presides over the sciences, writing, medicine, and astronomy, and composes many divine works, containing the elements of these several departments of knowledge; in Greece he is the god of shepherds and merchandise. The interpreter of the gods in Egypt, he becomes in Greece only their messenger; and it is by virtue of this latter title that he preserves his wings, which were among the Egyptians merely an astronomical symbol.

The god is usually represented with a *chlamys*, his *petasus* or winged cap, and his *talaria* or winged sandals, and the *caduceus* or wand presented to him by Apollo, which had the power of settling all differences, of putting any one to sleep, and of waking them again, and also of bringing souls out of Hell. The petasus and talaria were gifts from Zeus.

The ancient statues of Hermes were merely wooden posts with a rude head and pointed beard carved on them. They were what is termed ithyphallic, and were set up on the roads and foot-paths, also in the fields and gardens. From this representation he became with the Romans the god

Terminus; but when they were made acquainted with the twelve great deities of the Athenians, they adopted the Grecian Hermes under the name of *Mercurius.* In honor of this deity, the Romans celebrated an annual festival in a temple near the Circus Maximus, when sacrifices and prayers were offered to him.

An ancient gem exhibits the following accurate representation of Mercury: As god of the roads, he stands before an altar, over which rises an antique milestone, which he touches with his wand. Upon the altar lies a staff, as an intimation of travellers dedicating their walking staves to Mercury, after having accomplished a journey. As a sign of the safety of the roads, an olive branch is entwined around the stone. The god bears on his head the winged cap; as he is standing, the winged sandals are not fastened to his feet.

The Council of Jupiter, the supreme divinity, was composed of six gods, namely, Jupiter, Neptune, Mercury, Apollo, Mars, and Vulcan; and six goddesses: Juno, Ceres, Vesta, Minerva, Diana, and Venus. To this assembly no other deities were admitted.

As soon as fiction descends from Heaven to Earth, divine beings become more numerous. Imagination discovers life in fountains, groves, and hills;—and according to her pleasure, ascribes to this life corporeal form. In this manner all nature becomes sacred: deity fills the whole, and the whole is deity, revealed only in various forms. The ancients not only deified the virtues, but distempers, storms, and passions, and worshipped them that they might be saved from all harm.

This practice of personifying natural and moral qualities, seems to have been coëval with Grecian poetry and religion. It was not, however, by any means peculiar to Greece; it will probably be found wherever poetry exists

THE COUNCIL OF JUPITER. 181

But it was only in ancient Greece and Italy, that these personifications were made objects of worship, and regarded as having a real and personal existence.

The Genii or Dæmons were not considered as equal to the gods, but as superior to mortals. The four natures, Gods, Genii, Heroes and Men, were first distinguished by Hesiod.

PART THIRD.

GENII AND INFERIOR DEITIES.

According to the ideas of the ancients, man was intimately connected with the Deity by means of the genii or tutelary beings. The highest divinity is multiplied, as it were, in those beings, who, like guardian angels, lead by the hand every individual mortal through life, from the hour of his birth to that of his death. In this sense it was, that man swore by his Jupiter, and woman by her Juno, speaking of their own genius, or tutelary deity.

On their birthdays, the ancients presented offerings of wine, incense, and garlands of flowers, to their respective genii, who were represented in the form of handsome youths, having their heads crowned with flowers. Thus man, following the dictates of his heart, venerated something higher and more divine than he could find in his own limited individuality, and brought to "this great unknown of himself" offerings as a god; thus compensating by veneration for the indistinct knowledge of his divine origin.

It was customary among the Romans to implore persons by their genius, as the orientals do by their souls; and in Latin writers it is not always easy to distinguish a man's genius from himself. The distinct worship of the

Genii continued down to the demise of paganism, for we find it noticed in the Theodosian code.

The worship of the Genius was a remarkable part of the religion of the Romans; they having derived it from the Tuscans, in whose system it formed a prominent feature. The word Genius is evidently a Latin translation of a Tuscan term, signifying *Generator*, and the Genius was therefore viewed as a deity who had the power of producing. In the Tuscan system he was the son of the gods, and the parent of men; according to the ancient Italian doctrine, all souls proceeded from Jupiter, and returned to him after death; therefore the Genius Jovialis was viewed as the great agent in giving life, and uniting the soul to the body.

When Ceres and Pallas bless the growth and animals of the fields, and thereby the house, so cares the Genius Jovialis for the continuance and bloom of the family itself. Through him is Jupiter an eternal, inexhaustible giver of life to the changing generation of man.

The Genii of the Romans are frequently confounded with the Manes, Lares and Penates; and they have indeed one great feature in common, viz., that of protecting mortals. There is, however, this essential difference; the genii are the powers that produce life, and accompany man through it as his second or spiritual self, and the other powers have no influence till life, the work of the genii, has commenced. Neither were they confined to man, but every living thing, animal as well as man, and also every place, had its genius, or protecting spirit.

Horace, in speaking of the Genius, calls him "changeable of countenance, white and black;" and in the well-known appearance of his evil genius to Brutus, the spirit was black, which would seem to intimate that a man had two Genii, a good and an evil one.

This does not appear to have been the Italian belief, though perhaps such a notion prevailed in Greece; for the philosopher Empedocles said, that two Moiræ receive us at our birth, and obtain authority over us.

The whole body of the Roman people also had its genius, who is often represented on the coins of Hadrian and Trajan. He was worshipped on sad, as well as on joyous occasions, as for instance at the beginning of the second year of the Hannibalian war.

When a local genius made himself visible, he appeared in the form of a serpent, that is, the symbol of renovation, or of new life. In works of art, the genii are usually represented as winged beings; and on Roman monuments, a genius generally appears as a youth dressed in a toga, with a patera or cornucopia in his hand, and having his head covered. The genius of a place is represented in the form of a serpent eating fruit placed before him.

The Greeks called their genii, dæmons, and appear to have believed in them from the earliest times, though they are not mentioned by Homer. Hesiod speaks of them as being thirty thousand in number, and says that they dwelt on earth. invisible to mortals, as the ministers of Zeus and the guardians of man and justice. He also considers them as the souls of righteous men who lived in the golden age. Upon this idea the Greek philosophers developed a complete theory of dæmons. Thus we read in Plato, that dæmons are assigned to men at the moment of their birth, accompany them through life, and after death, conduct their souls to Hades.* Pindar also speaks of the spirit that watches over the fate of man from the hour of his birth, which appears to be the same as the genius of the Romans—the protecting spirit, analogous to the guardian angels invoked by the church of Rome.

---

* Hades anciently signified the grave, or place of the dead in general. All therefore that die, must go to Hades.

Dæmons are further described as the ministers and companions of the gods, who bear the prayers of men to them, and the gifts of the gods to men, and accordingly float in immense numbers in the space between heaven and earth. Dæmons who were exclusively the ministers of the gods, seem to have constituted a distinct class. The Corybantes, Dactyls, and Cabeiri, are called the ministering dæmons of the great gods; Gigon, Tychon, and Ortharges, are the dæmons of Aphrodite; and Hadreus the dæmon of Demeter.

The Penates, or guardians of private families, who are also derived from the Etruscans, appear to have formed an especial class of deities among the Romans. The *dii penates* are those who are worshipped in the interior of the house. They were gods from whom blessings, cherishing, and prosperity were expected, as the name declares. There is no reason to suppose that the Penates were a class of gods distinctly divided from the others; but different gods and dæmons of different orders are honored in different houses. Therefore the great uncertainty and variety in the assertions of the ancients as to who the Penates were.

According to the Etruscans, they were divided into four classes: Penates of Jupiter, Penates of Neptune, those of the nether gods, and those of mortal men. They considered the dæmons who add to the possessions of families, as in part the souls of the dead, in part beings of the earth and lower world, of the water and the heavens; the fourth class comprised the Genii.

Among the various deities called Lares, are human souls, as among the Penates. Certain rites are described by which human souls are changed to gods called animals, because they arise from souls. These are Penates and way-gods. These rites are the same as those consecrated to the deities of the nether world, which were principally Etruscan; only the name, and perhaps certain usages, were borrowed from Greece, by which souls were redeemed and conjured out of the lower world, and thereby became gods. This is the doctrine of the genii. A genius is present at birth;—his power operates in the life of the mortal whom the gods favor, and also after death; and of the dead he becomes again the genius. Yet, these elevated and deified souls do not become gods of every sort, but first Penates. The old Latins called the soul of man, as soon as it had left the body, *Lemur;* and a Lemur, who retained an interest in posterity, and ruled the house with mild and peaceful disposition, *Lar Familiaris.* Those who, for a punishment, wandered about as powerless forms, empty bugbears to the good, and the torment of the bad, were *Larvæ.* But when the destiny of the man is uncertain, the term *Manes dii* is employed, and to the Manes was assigned a subterranean place of abode. There can be little doubt that Jupiter and Juno were worshipped as Penates. Vesta, also, is reckoned among them; for each hearth, being the symbol of domestic union, had its Vesta. The public Penates of the city of Rome had a chapel near the centre of the city, in a place called *Sub Velia;* the private had their place at the domestic hearth, which, as well as the table, was sacred to them. Every meal taken in the house resembled a sacrifice to the Penates.

After every absence from the hearth, the Penates were saluted like the living inhabitants of the house. Whoever went abroad, prayed to the Penates and Lares for a happy return; and when he came back, he hung up his armor and staff by the side of their images. No event, whether sad or joyful, occurred in the family, without offering prayers to the Lares and Penates

The Lares or domestic deities, were generally two in number, who had their abodes on the domestic hearth. They were represented as youths with hats on their heads, travelling staves in their hands, and dogs at their sides. Lamps, the symbol of vigilance, were consecrated to them; they were crowned with flowerets, and received offerings of food, which was prepared upon the hearth. Again, they are dressed in short habits, to show their readiness to serve, and hold a kind of cornucopia as a signal of hospitality and good housekeeping. Being witness of domestic happiness or misfortune, they hallowed the everyday occurrences of life by their presence, rendering every house, as it were, a sacred temple.

There are various classes of Lares, such as Lares *Urbani*, to preside over the cities; *Familiares*, over houses; *Rustici*, over the country; *Marini*, over the sea; *Viales*, over the roads, etc.

If we regard the nature of Lares and Penates, we shall readily perceive why the former have a higher rank assigned them in the hierarchy of the genii than the latter. The Penates were originally gods — the powers of nature personified—powers whose wonderful and mysterious action produces and upholds whatever is necessary to life, as well as to the common good and prosperity of families and individuals; in fine, whatever the human species cannot bestow upon itself.

The case is quite different with the Lares; they were originally human beings, who had lived upon earth, and who, becoming pure spirits after death, loved still to hover round the dwellings they had formerly inhabited, watching over their safety, and guarding them from evil. Having lived as mortals, they were familiar with the dangers that surround man, and knew what assistance was required by those whose situation in every respect was once their own. They were therefore supposed to avert danger from without, while the Penates, residing in the interior of the dwelling, pour forth benefits upon its inmates with bountiful hands.

The place in which the Lares were worshipped was called the Lararium—a sort of domestic chapel in the Atrium, where were also to be seen the images and busts of the family ancestors. In the sacrifices offered to them, the first-fruits of every year, with wine and incense, were brought to their altars; and their images were adorned with chaplets and garlands. The rich had often two Lararia, one large and one small; and also "Masters of the Lares" and "Decurios of the Lares;" namely, slaves specially charged with the care of these domestic chapels and images of their divinities. The common altar, on which sacrifices were offered to the Lares, was the domestic hearth; and in all family repasts, the first thing done was to cast a portion of the viands into the fire that burned on the hearth in honor of the Lares.

Certain public festivals were also celebrated in honor of the Lares, called Lararia and Compitalia. The period for their celebration fell in the month of December, a little after the Saturnalia. On this occasion the Lares were worshipped as propitious deities; therefore these festivities were gay and joyful. The Compitalia, dedicated to the *Lares Compitales,* were celebrated in the open air : the day of their celebration was not fixed. They were introduced at Rome by Servius Tullius, who left to the Senate the care of determining the period when they should be held.

In early times, children were immolated to the goddess Mania, who, according to some, was the mother of the Lares, in order to propitiate her favor for the protection of the family. This barbarous rite was subsequently abolished, and little balls of wool were hung up at the gates of dwellings, instead of human offerings. After the expulsion of the Tarquins, Junius Brutus introduced a new form of sacrifice, by virtue of which, heads of garlics and poppies were offered up in place of human heads, in accordance with the oracle of Apollo. During these festivals, every family brought a cake for an offering ; slaves enjoyed a perfect equality with their masters, as on the Saturnalia ; and slaves, instead of freemen, assisted the priests in the sacrifices offered on this occasion to the tutelary genii of the ways.

In case of death in a family, a sacrifice of sheep was offered to the family Lares. In the form of marriage, called *coëmtio,* the bride always threw a piece of money upon the hearth to the Lares of her family, and deposited another in the neighboring cross-road, in order to obtain admission, as it were, into the dwelling of her husband. Young persons, after their fifteenth year, consecrated to the Lares the *bulla* * which they had worn from infancy.

---

* The *bulla* was made of metal, and so called from its resemblance in form to a bubble floating upon the water. It was suspended round the neck of a child as a token of paternal affection, and a sign of high birth; as it was given to infants, it sometimes served to recognize a lost child. Probably it contained amulets.

Instead of the *bulla* of gold, the children of inferior rank wore one made of leather.

Soldiers, when their time of service was ended, dedicated to these powerful genii the arms with which they had fought the battles of their country. Captives and slaves, restored to freedom, consecrated to the Lares the fetters from which they had just been freed. Before undertaking a journey, or after a successful return, homage was paid to these deities, when their protection was implored, or thanks were rendered for their guardian care. The new master of a house crowned the Lares, in order to render them propitious; a custom which was most universal, and perpetuated to the latest times.

As regards the forms under which the Lares were represented, it may be observed that it differed slightly from that of the Penates. Thus, on the coins of the Cæsian family, they are represented as two young men, seated, their heads covered with helmets, and holding spears in their hands, while a dog watches at their feet. Sometimes the heads of the Lares are represented as covered with the skin of a dog, and sometimes it forms their mantle. At other times, we find the Lares resembling naked children, with the bulla hanging from the neck, and always accompanied by the attribute of the dog.

NYMPHÆ OR NYMPHS.

The imagination of the ancients, fond of connecting something divine with objects that are strong and lasting, and that outlive the generations of men, as the firmly-rooted mountain, the overflowing spring, and the solid oak, attributed to hills and fountains, to forests, and even to single trees, immortal souls; for in this light may those beings be considered, who, under the name of Nymphs, were thought to animate them.

The Oread roams on the mountains, pursuing with her sisters, in the retinue of Diana, the track of the deer; and, like the unyielding deity whom she follows, closes her heart to every tender affection.

At the lonely hour of noon, the Naiad sat with her water pitcher at her spring, sending forth from it the warbling brooks. Although less cruel than their mountain-sisters, the caresses of the Naiades proved dangerous. They embraced handsome Hylas, the favorite of Hercules, when he was sent for water, and drew him down into the fountain.

The sacred gloom of the forest was the abode of the Dryades, while the Hamadryad lived within her own single tree, with which she was born, and with which she died. Whoever therefore spared a tree laid the Nymph who dwelt in it under an obligation for life.

In this manner inanimate nature itself became to man an object of sympathetic benevolence.

The Auræ, or Sylphs, Nymphs of the air, a species of sportive, happy beings, and well-wishers to mankind, were winged and represented as flying.

SILENOS.

According to the Homerid, Hermes and the Silens mingle in love with the Nymphs in pleasing caverns, and Pindar calls Silenos the Naiad's husband. Socrates, on account of his wisdom, his baldness, and his flat nose, compared himself to the Silens born of the divine Naiades. Others said that Silenos was a son of Earth, and sprung from the blood-drops of Uranos; Marsyas is also called a Silen.

Like the sea-gods, Silenos was noted for wisdom; and it would therefore appear that a Silen was simply a river-god; and the name probably comes from the Greek verb, signifying *to roll*, expressive of the motion of the streams. The connection between Silenos, Bacchos, and the Naiades, thus becomes easy of explanation, all being deities relating to moisture.

Silenos was represented as old, bald, and flat-nosed, riding on a broad-backed ass, usually intoxicated, and carrying his can (*cantharus*), or tottering along, supported by his staff of fennel (*ferula*).

PRIAPOS.

Priapos, the emblem of fecundity, and fabled to have been the son of Bacchos and Aphrodite, was introduced late into the Grecian mythology. He was a rural deity, worshipped by the people of Lampsacus, a city on the Hellespont famous for its vineyards.

Priapos was not—as is supposed from the employment usually assigned him by the Romans after they adopted his worship—merely the god of gardens, but of fruitfulness in general.

Like the other rural gods, Priapos is of a ruddy complexion. His cloak is filled with all kinds of fruit; he has a scythe in his hand, and usually a horn of plenty. Sometimes his statue was placed in gardens, crowned with a wreath of herbs, and bearing a crooked knife in his hand.

SATYRS.

The forest, with its shades and deep recesses, is the scene also of those wanton beings, called Satyrs, whose human shape is disfigured by the horns and feet of a goat. They are, as it were, the middle link, which in nature's great chain connects the brute creation with the human world.

In these beings the slender feet of a goat is in a burlesque manner joined to a human form; and a similar contrast exhibits youthful wantonness and careless levity, blended with the higher spirit that dwells within them. Although mortal, they are superior to the cares and sorrows of mortal life.

Belief in the existence of these beings, as well as others of the same kind, must necessarily have been perpetuated from the idea that no one was permitted to behold a nymph or a satyr unpunished. Thus, instead of endeavoring to ascertain the truth or falsehood of their existence, every one shunned the sight of them, avoiding such places as they were reported to have chosen for their haunts. It was the inspired poet alone, who, amid lonely rocks, beheld in the train of Bacchos, nymphs and satyrs, listening to the instruction of the god, and goat-footed satyrs with erect and pointed ears. In the Greek mythology they were inseparably connected with the worship of Bacchos, and represent the luxuriant, vital powers of nature.

In the Satyrs, art has attempted to represent human form bordering as nearly as possible on brutal shape. A Satyr, exhibited upon an antique gem, as he is contending with a he-goat, and pushing him, is scarcely distinguished from that animal, except by his body and arms; the goat form being extended even to the face, which, although human, betrays the nature of the brute.

These comic Nymphs, Genii, and Cupids produce an agreeable contrast in the train of Bacchos; and it would seem as if they were a necessary part of those groups, and of the divine formations in general; fiction being as it were completed by those beings, half divine and half brute.

FAUNS.

The Fauns differ from the Satyrs; at least, according to the technical language of modern times. They are represented entirely in human form, but with erect and pointed ears, and the tail of a goat. Yet without these external marks, a Faun is easily recognized by his rough, ignoble features, which indicate the character attributed to him. Still there are some ancient monuments, which exhibit Fauns of admirable beauty, in whose features that half-brutish, sensual temper is but slightly indicated.

The peasants sacrificed lambs and kids to the Fauns with great solemnity.

SYLVANUS.

Sylvanus was a deity who presided over the woods and the fruits they produced, and was worshipped by the nations of Latium. He was represented like Pan, except that he bears a branch of cypress in his hand, which intimates night in the forest, and alludes also to the joyless and melancholy nature of his abode, which rendered him an object of terror to peasants and shepherds.

THEMIS.

Zeus, when Lord of all, united with Themis, which signifies possibility or aptitude arising from the necessary connection of things, or the laws of their existence. In action, Themis is the source of law, and her predictions of truth.

Themis, as goddess of justice, still maintains her place among the modern deities. In this character, presiding over the distribution of justice, she is represented as a noble and majestic woman, having her eyes covered with a fillet, holding a balance in one hand, and a sword in the other. She is said to have succeeded her mother Earth in the possession of the Delphic oracle, and to have voluntarily resigned it to her sister Phœbe, who gave it as a natal gift to Phœbos-Apollo.

By some mythologists, Themis is considered merely as an epithet of earth; and others consider her as the oldest purely allegorical personification of a virtue.

The ancient poets also mention her daughter Astræa,

who descended from Heaven to be the tutelary deity of mortals, distributing justice, settling differences, teaching the principles of integrity, and inculcating an abhorrence of injustice and crime. Pitying the unfortunate race of Prometheus, she dwelt with them for a long time; but when she found that, notwithstanding her endeavors, justice was overthrown by the misdeeds of men, and all reverence for what is holy banished from their lives, she left them in disgust and fled back to Heaven.

HORÆ.

Having become the wife of Zeus, Themis produced the three amiable guides and guardians of life, the Horæ, whose names are Eunomia (*order*), Dike (*punishment*), Irene (*peace*). Their office was to promote unanimity by the exercise of equity and justice. They likewise stand around the throne of Zeus, and their regular occupation is to open and shut the gates of Heaven, and yoke the steeds to the chariot of the Sun.

Under the name of the Horæ, the ancient fictions comprise, in the first place, the Genii of justice, children of Zeus and Themis; and then the Seasons; which, by a just partition of their benefits, as it were, preserve in continual succession the equipoise of nature.

The dancing Horæ, following each other in measured steps, are an emblem of fleeting time; and, as friends and companions of the Graces, often mingle with them in a common choir.

Winkleman's monuments contain a representation of the three Horæ, taken from an antique marble. One of them, crowned with palm leaves, and standing before an altar, bearing fruit in her hands, signifies Autumn; another, before whose feet a flower has sprung up, is an emblem of Spring; and near the third, on a pile of stones like an altar, a little fire appears, intimating Winter. Under the serene and mild sky of Greece, Summer and Autumn vary but little in temperature as well as products, therefore, one emblem is sufficient for both; the Athenians usually represented but two seasons, Thallo and Carpo, blossom and fruit, the whole year being divided by them into spring and autumn.

By poets and artists the seasons are all personified. They are frequently seen together on relievi, medals, and gems. On a medal of Commodus, they appear moving over a celestial globe, which lies by the goddess Tellus. The artists have also followed the poets in representing the four ages of life by depicting Ver (*spring*), as infantile and tender; Æstas (*summer*), as young and sprightly; Autumnus (*autumn*), mature and manly; and Hyems (*winter*), as old and decrepid.

Again Ver is a youth decorated with a coronet of flowers, or a basket of flowers in his hand; Æstas is crowned with corn or holds a sickle in his hand; Autumnus is usually distinguished by his crown of different fruits; and Hyems by his crown of reeds, the birds in his hand, or the beast at his feet; and also by his warm clothing.

EROS OR CUPID.

Eros or Cupid is unnoticed by Homer. In the Theogony he is one of the first beings, and produced without parents. In the Orphic poems he was the son of Kronos. Sappho made him the offspring of Heaven and Earth, while Simonides assigned him Aphrodite and Ares for parents. In Olen's hymn to Eileithyia, that goddess was termed the mother of Love; and Alcæus said, that well-sandalled Iris bore Love to gold-locked Zephyros.

Thespiæ in Bœotia was the place in which Eros was most worshipped. The Thespians celebrated games in his honor on Mount Helicon. The oldest image of the god in their city was of plain stone; but Praxiteles afterwards made for them one of Pentelican marble of rare beauty. Eros also had altars at Athens and elsewhere.

The God of Love was usually represented as a plump-cheeked, rosy boy, with light hair floating on his shoulders. He is always winged and armed with bow and arrows.

Under the appellation of Eros and Anteros, Love, and Love requited, ancient art represents two Cupids contending for the possession of a palm branch, to signify zeal in mutual love.

The divine person of Eros is multiplied by the ancients. Those little Cupids or Genii of Love, who every where appear in ancient fictions, are, as it were, sparks of this being. Poetry is inexhaustible in beautiful emblematic representations of the all-conquering god. Thus we find him as breaking the thunderbolts of Zeus; or as arrayed in the lion skin of Heracles, and armed with his club; or as stepping on the helmet of Ares, whose shield and spear are lying at his feet; or, finally, as riding on a lion, taming the beast by the strains of his lyre;—a beautiful emblem of the combined power of love and music.

CHARITES OR GRACES.

In the Graces are multiplied the eminently dazzling charms of the powerful Goddess of Love. The three sisters descended from Heaven, for the benefit of mortal men —instilling into their bosoms the lovely feeling of gratitude and mutual benevolence, and gracing their persons with the precious gift of pleasing.

The Graces were children of Zeus and Eurynome, the beautiful daughter of Oceanos; and their names were Aglaïa (*Splendor*), Thalia (*Pleasure*), and Euphrosyne (*Joy*). Temples and altars were every where erected to their honor; every age and every profession solicited their favor; arts and sciences paid homage to them; their altars were never without fragrant incense; and at every joyful repast, their names were mentioned with veneration.

Associated in friendly union with Love and the Muses, they had often a temple in common with the former, and still oftener with the latter. In Olympos they surrounded the throne of Jupiter. In heaven, as well as on earth, their dominion was acknowledged, and their influence, without which beauty itself is but a dead picture, was respected and honored. In the dancing attitudes of the three graceful sisters, are expressed the charms of personal dignity, of elegant movement, and of attitude and countenance by which beauty gains the soul of man; and walking hand in hand as loving sisters, they indicate also every tender emotion of a heart overflowing with affection, friendship, and benevolence.

The happy influence which the religious veneration of these lovely and significant beings exercised on the ideas and feelings of the ancients, is to be recognized in the whole life of the Greeks, as well as their works of art and science. The favor of the Graces was no where to be dispensed with; and in order to intimate that, to make even the most extravagant formations of fancy agreeable, grace must be concealed, hollow statues of Satyrs were formed, within which were found little figures of the Graces.

CAMENÆ OR MUSES.

Mnemosyne, the personification of memory as the source and repository of every art and science, belongs to the ancient deities; for she is the daughter of Heaven and Earth; and as mankind are indebted to memory for their progress in science, Mnemosyne is said to be the parent of the Muses, who divided among themselves that treasure of wisdom which their venerable mother alone possessed.

The Muses, as well as the Horæ and Graces, all of them daughters of Zeus, originally presided over the stars and the seasons; but the later Greeks took away these functions, giving them only such as were of a poetic character. An ancient bard thus sings the praises of the nine sisters: "They pour on the lips of man, whom they favor, the dew of soft persuasion; they bestow on him wisdom, that he may be a judge and umpire among his people, and give him renown among nations; and the poet who wanders on the mountain tops and in the lowly dales, is inspired by them with divine strains, which dispel sorrow and grief from the breast of every mortal."

Their appropriate employments are music, song, and dance; but playful fiction has given to each of the sisters a particular vocation. Calliope was the muse of eloquence and heroic poetry (to her the ancients gave precedence); Clio, of history; Erato, of amorous poetry; Euterpe, of music; Melpomene, of tragedy; Polyhymnia, of eloquence and imitation; Terpsichore, of dancing; Thalia, of comic and lyric poetry; and Urania, of astronomy. On a sarcophagus, in the Capitoline Gallery at Rome, there is a relievo in which the nine muses are represented; by the help of this, together with Ausonius' description of them (Idyl. 20), an attempt has been made to distinguish one muse from another. Herodotus has annexed their names to the nine books of his history; and from their arrangement, as well as from the relievos, it would appear that their order is quite arbitrary. In the relievo above mentioned, they are placed and distinguished in the following manner: Clio is first, and distinguished by the roll in her hand, or sometimes with the longer, bolder pipe. Her office was to celebrate the actions of departed heroes; though Statius makes her descend to lower functions, from the old notion that every thing penned in hexameters was an epic poem. (*See Engraving on opposite page.*)

Thalia was the Muse of comedy and pastorals, and is

distinguished by the comic mask in her hand, and her pastoral crook.

Terpsichore has nothing to distinguish her; Ausonius gives her the cithara (or lyre), and sometimes she is represented in a dancing attitude. On the medals of the Pomponian family, three Muses have stringed instruments in their hands, and are supposed to represent Terpsichore, Erato, and Polyhymnia.

Euterpe presided over music and performed on two pipes at once, as in the remarks before Terence's plays. By these pipes she is distinguished, though sometimes she holds the fistula (or pipe), and is so described by Ausonius.

Erato, who presided over amorous poetry, is represented at times as pensive, and again full of gaiety; both which characters, though directly opposite, suit with the ever-varying moods of lovers, and are appropriate to their patroness. Ovid invokes Erato in his Art of Love, and likewise in his Fasti for April, which among the Romans was considered as peculiarly the lover's mouth. But Virgil, in his Æneid, appears with less propriety to invoke her before a field of battle; unless, indeed, it was that a woman was the occasion of the war. Calliope is called by Ovid the chief of the Muses, and by Horace, Regina, as skilful on all instruments. The tablets in the hand mark her distinguishing character, which was to note down the worthy actions of men.

Polyhymnia is designated by a stringed instrument, perhaps what the Romans call *barbiton*, for which we have no name.

Urania presided over astronomy, and is distinguished by the celestial globe and the radius. In statues, the globe is sometimes placed in her hand, and sometimes on a column before her. Melpomene, the Muse of tragedy, was supposed to preside over melancholy subjects of all kinds. She is distinguished by the mask on her head.

In the Homeric poems, the Muses are the goddesses of song and poetry, and live on Olympos. There they sing the festive songs at the repasts of the immortals. At the funeral of Patroclus they sing lamentations.

The Muses were sometimes represented as dancing in chorus, to intimate the near and indissoluble connection that exists between the liberal arts and sciences; but more generally appeared differently attired, and with symbols of their respective characters.

Their worship was universally established, particularly in the enlightened parts of Greece, Thessaly, and Italy. Sacrifices were not offered to them, but no poet ever commenced his task without addressing a solemn invocation to the Muses who preside over verse.

The sacred retreats of these divine sisters, from whose lips flowed the stream of song and sweet eloquence, were the celebrated mountains Parnassus, Pindus, and Helicon.

HEBE.

Hebe, the goddess of youth, was daughter of Zeus and Hera. She was employed by her mother to prepare her chariot, and harness her peacocks, whenever requisite, and was cup-bearer to all the gods.

Fable says, that Zeus dismissed her from this office, declaring her to be unworthy of it, because, on one occasion, when handing nectar to the gods, she, by a fall, violated that gracefulness which must accompany every motion and gesture of the attendants at the table of Olympos.

She was superseded by Ganymedes (*Joy-promoter*), a son of Tros, and a great-grandson of Dardanos, the founder of Troy. The poets say, "he was the handsomest of mortal men;" and on account of his beauty, the gods took him from the earth, that in Olympos he might reach the nectar cup to Jove; henceforth partaking of the constant society of the immortals. In the shape of his eagle, the Thunderer carried away his favorite from the top of Mount Ida, softly bearing him in his crooked talons from earth upward to the sky. In this charming fiction, consoling Fancy veiled the loss of the youth, who, in the prime of life and beauty, could scarcely be thought mortal; and therefore his vanishing from the earth was explained as a removal to the seat of the celestials.

The fictions respecting the favorites of the gods, gain a peculiar charm by a kind of dim and melancholy twilight in which they are veiled. Whenever youth and beauty became the prey of death, some deity was said to have removed her favorite from the earth. In this manner, mourning was mingled with joy; and lamentations for the departed were mitigated. These fictions, therefore, are most frequently represented upon ancient marble coffins.

When Heracles was translated to the skies, and raised to the rank of a god, Hebe was given to him in marriage—a beautiful fiction, by which the venerated sun-god was united to immortal youth.

Hebe, the personification of youth, had the power of restoring gods and men to youth, and, at the instance of her husband, performed that kind office to his friend Iolaos. She was worshipped at Sicyon under the name of Dia, and at Rome under the name of Juventas. Hebe is represented as a young virgin, crowned with flowers, and arrayed in a variegated garment. Sometimes she holds the nectar cup; at others, the eagle stands by her side, which she is in the act of caressing.

PROTEUS.

Proteus, a sea-deity, was considered by some as a son of Oceanos and Tethys; by others, as a son of Poseidon and Phœnice.

Homer introduces him in the fourth book of the Odyssey, styling him a Sea-elder, and gives him the power of foretelling the future. He also calls him Egyptian, or servant of Neptune, and says that his office was to keep the seals, or sea-calves, belonging to the Ruler of the waves.

Proteus could assume any form at pleasure, changing himself into fire or water, plant or animal, which rendered him difficult of access; and sometimes, when consulted, evaded an answer by a sudden metamorphosis. To those only who held him fast with vigorous arms, did he appear in his real character, and by his spirit of divination reveal to them the truth.

ASCLEPIOS OR ÆSCULAPIUS.

The first beginning of medical science was likewise consid:red by the ancients as something divine, and its possessor and practiser as worthy of veneration. He who first applied medical art was looked upon, even after his death, as a beneficent human being, to whom the sick would not address their prayers in vain.

Æsculapius was the son of Apollo and Coronis, the daughter of a Thessalian king. By his father he was committed to the care of the wise Centaur, Cheiron, who taught him Botany, together with the secret efficacy of plants. By means of this information, Æsculapius became the benefactor of mankind, applying the various remedies that he had learned to the diseases which afflict mankind.

And so successful was he in the practice of the art, that

fiction speaks of him as having awakened the dead. Pluto, the ever-destroying power, considering this an encroachment on his rights, complained before the throne of Jupiter, of the awaker from the dead as a daring criminal. Jupiter then punished the second great benefactor of mankind, as he had done the first (Prometheus), by hurling lightnings upon his innocent head. He who had assuaged the pains of men, and healed their diseases, thus became himself a victim of his beneficent art.

After his death, groves, temples, and altars were consecrated to him; but Epidaurus, in Greece, was the principal seat of honor. His sons, Machaon and Podalcirios, were heroes and leaders in the Trojan war, and, at the same time, renowned for their skill in medical art.

The snake, as an emblem of recovery and health, was sacred to Asclepios, probably because of its renewing itself, as it were, by casting its skin. Hence the god of medicine always carries a staff, around which is twined a snake. The figure of a little boy is sometimes found with that of Asclepios, wearing a bonnet on his head, and entirely muffled in a cloak. His name is Telesphoros; and his infant form, together with his usual covering, seems to allude, in a certain manner, to his convalescence, as well as the mysterious art of his master.

Of his four daughters, Hygeia, Ægle, Panacea, and Iaso, Hygeia was the most celebrated. To her, divine honors were paid; and her occupation, like that of her father, was the preservation of health. This benefit she distributes among mortals as a mild gift, whenever she descends from the higher regions to earth. She is represented with a snake eating out of a flat cup which she holds in her hand.

The temples of Asclepios were regarded as sanctuaries which none of the profane could approach without repeated purifications; and the statue of Hygeia at Ægrium, in Achaia, could only be viewed by the priests. The temple at Tithorea was surrounded by a hedge in the vicinity of which no edifice could be erected. This hedge was forty stadia from the building itself.

The worship rendered to Asclepios had for its object the diversion of the sick, by the ceremonies of which they were the witnesses.

JANUS.

The worship of Janus must be ascribed to the Etruscans, by whom he was regarded as the inspector of Heaven, and therefore of all transactions. An image of the god with four faces came from Valerii to Rome, which is supposed to have reference to the four regions of Heaven.

In Italy he was usually represented with two faces, one before and one behind, and hence called Bifrons and Biceps. Sometimes he is represented with four faces, and then called Quadrifrons. There was an ancient statue of this deity in the Forum, said to be as old as the time of Numa, of which the fingers were so formed that those of one hand represented three hundred (CCC), those of the other fifty-five (LV), the number of the days of the ancient lunar year. All this is explicable on the supposition of Janus being the sun, the author of the year, with its seasons, months, and days.

Janus was invoked at the commencement of most actions; even in the worship of the other gods the votary began by offering wine and incense to Janus. The first month in the year was named from him; and under the title of Matutinus he was regarded as the opener of the day. Hence he had charge of the gates of Heaven, and hence, too, all gates, *Januæ*, were called after him, and supposed to be under his care. Hence, perhaps, it was, that he was represented with a staff and key, and that he was named the Opener (*Patulcius*), and the Shutter (*Clusius*).

The Janus Geminus, or Janus Quirinus, was the celebrated gate (not temple) which stood on the way leading from the Palatine Quirinal, and which was to be open in time of war, and shut in time of peace. To understand this much mistaken subject (for nothing is more common than to speak of opening or shutting the *temple* of Janus), we must go back to the early days of Rome.

The temples of Janus Quadrifrons were built with four equal sides, each side containing a door and three windows. The doors were emblematic of the four seasons, and the windows of the three months belonging to each.

Comus, the god of gay humor and merry jests, presided at banquets, and in general at all social feasts.

Hymen, the god of marriage, presided at all nuptial feasts.

Plutus, the god of riches, was represented by the ancients as blind, and as bestowing his favors indiscriminately upon the good and the bad.

Libertas (Liberty) was a goddess of Rome. She is represented in the figure of a woman, holding in one hand a rod, and in the other a cap. This cap was a badge of liberty used on all occasions.

Vertumnus presided over the growth of Spring, the crops of Summer, and the fruits of Autumn.

Terminus was worshipped at Rome as the guardian of landmarks.

Pales, the goddess of shepherds, presided over cattle and pastures.

Flora, the goddess of flowers, is fabled to have married Zephyros.

Pomona, the wife of Vertumnus. presided over fruit trees.

Feronia was the guardian deity of woods and groves.

Victory attended the conquests of all heroes.

Fortuna, the goddess of fortune, was supposed to distribute riches and poverty, blessings and misfortunes, pleasures and pains.

Fortitudo (Fortitude), a deification of courage and bravery, was one of the moral deities of the Romans.

Veritas (Truth) is said to be the parent of Justice and Virtue.

Virtus (Virtue), daughter of Truth, is represented as clothed in white, as an emblem of purity.

Honos (Honor) was worshipped as a virtue at Rome.

Pax (Peace) wears a crown of laurel, and holds in her hand the branch of an olive tree.

Fidelitas (Fidelity) presided over the virtues of men, and the conduct of human life.

Felicitas (Felicity) was a symbolical, moral deity of the Greeks and Romans. She was the goddess of happiness and prosperity.

Amicitia (Friendship) was represented by the Greeks in a clasped garment, her head bare, her dress open near the heart, holding in her left hand an elm around which a vine is clinging, filled with clusters of grapes.

At Rome she was represented as a young maiden with a white robe, her bosom partially covered, her head adorned with myrtle and pomegranate flowers intermixed. On the border of her tunic was written "Death and Life;" on her front, "Summer and Winter." Her side was open, and her heart visible, bearing these words, "Far and near."*

---

* For a full account of these deities see large edition.

PART FOURTH.

DEMI-GODS AND HEROES.

In the assembly of the gods, Jupiter is represented as ruling supreme. He frowns, and Olympus trembles; he smiles, and the sky brightens. But heaven is not his only theatre of action; enveloping his deity in illusive forms, he descends to earth to propagate his power in a race of heroes.

From his seat on high, he descends to Danaë in the form of a golden shower, and the valiant Perseus springs forth; who, with powerful arm, subdues monsters.

In the form of Amphitryon he appears to Alcmena, and makes her the mother of Hercules.

With the majestic neck of a swan, he clings to Leda for protection, and she becomes the mother of the magnanimous Pollux, and the god-like Helena, the most beautiful woman that earth ever produced.

In the strength of a mettled bull, he invites the virgin Europa to mount his back, and carries her through the floods of the sea to the shores of Crete, where she brings forth Minos, the wise and powerful law-giver of nations.

In these fictions all nature is deified; even animals are considered as sacred beings. Thus nothing mean or abject lies in the idea of representing the supreme divinity in any form that is offered by all-comprising nature. As the wind stirs up the quiet sea, so the jealousy of Juno brings life into these fictions of imagination; and this jealousy is not destitute of sublimity, for, being endowed with divine power, it checks even the boasted omnipotence of the Thunderer.

That an opposing, jealous, yet eminent power strives to check the highest authority, is likewise entirely appropriate to the genius of these fables; according to which, the beautiful and strong, in developing itself, must struggle against opposition and difficulties, and sustain many trials and dangers before its value is acknowledged and approved.

The demi-gods were also called Semones, as being descended from a mortal and an immortal. The deified mortals, or peculiar gods of any country, were called Indigetes.

In the poems of Homer, the heroes are described merely as warriors who had distinguished themselves by extraordinary strength, courage, and prudence; these qualities being essential to those who were charged either with the government of the people, or the conduct of the wars. The poets, posterior to Homer, placed the heroes in an intermediate rank between gods and men; therefore they were called demi-gods, and temples were erected, and sacrifices offered to them. Their time is called the *Heroic*, and in the period to which the achievements of the heroes are attributed, much fable is mingled with true history.

The heroic times of the ancients is the period when they passed from the savage to the civilized state. That of the Greeks is the most celebrated; perhaps from its history having been handed down to us by the most distinguished poets. Those times commenced with the establishment of the kingdom of Sicyon (an ancient city of Greece), about 2164 B. C., and were closed after the siege of Troy, 1245; but the greatest events are embraced in the six last centuries of that period.

PERSEUS.

The history of Perseus belongs to the earliest period of the heroic age, and is therefore the most involved in clouds and fable.

To trace the earthly descent of this hero, it is necessary to go back to old Inachos, whose daughter, Io, gave Zeus a son in Egypt, named Epaphos. Libya, the regal daughter of Epaphos, became the mother of Belos and Agenor, the sons of Neptune. Belos was the father of Danäos and Ægyptos.

Danäos came from Ægyptos over to Greece, to assert and maintain his claims to the kingdom of Argos, against Gelanor, who at that time actually reigned over the country. The claims of the former rested upon his descent from Inachos; those of the latter, on the right of possession. The people were called upon to decide to whom the royal crown belonged; while they were yet wavering, a wolf rushed into a herd of cows and destroyed the bull that defended them. This unexpected accident was considered as a sign from the gods, that the stranger was destined to reign, instead of the native. Accordingly, Danäos ascended the throne; and to him the Argives are said to be indebted for the knowledge of digging wells and the building of ships.

Danäos, according to the legend, had fifty daughters, and Ægyptos as many sons. The latter came over to Greece, each of them intending to marry a daughter of Danäos. But Danäos had received warning from an oracle, that one of his sons-in-law would deprive him of his royal authority; and, anxious to retain his throne, he commanded each of his daughters to kill her husband on the first night of their marriage. This cruel order was obeyed by all of them except Hypermnestra, who, notwithstanding the danger that threatened her own life in consequence, suffered Lynceus, her beloved husband, to fly. But he afterwards returned; for Danäos became reconciled to his daughter, and Perseus and Hercules, the god-like heroes, are descendants of Lynceus and Hypermnestra. Endless labor was the punishment inflicted on the Danaïdes for this crime. They were condemned to pour water incessantly into a vessel full of holes, and to see every moment that their labor is vain.

Atlas, a son of Lynceus, reigned over Argos after the death of his father, and left two sons, Prœtos and Acrisios, who at different times contested with each other for the royal authority.

Acrisios in his turn feared destruction from his descendants. It had been predicted to him that he should be killed by one of his grandsons. He therefore shut up his only daughter, Danaë, in a brazen tower, that he might thwart the prediction of the oracle. But his precaution was rendered ineffectual by Jupiter, who, descending in a golden shower through an opening in the roof of the building, made her the mother of Perseus.

When Perseus was born, his grandfather committed both mother and child to the sea, in a crazy bark. The benevolent goddess of the deep, tenderly taking up the divine boy, together with his mother, in the lap of the waters, brought the bark to a haven on the shores of the small island of Seriphos, in the Ægean sea. Here they were found by Dictys, a fisherman, and carried by him to Polydectes, king of the island, who kindly received both mother and child, and superintended the education of young Perseus, intrusting him to the care of the priests of Minerva's temple.

His rising genius and manly courage, however, soon displeased Polydectes; and the monarch, who wished to get Danaë into his power, feared the resentment of her son. Yet Polydectes resolved to remove every obstacle, and in-

vited his friends to a sumptuous entertainment, requiring all who came to present him with a beautiful horse. Perseus was included, knowing that it was not in his power to furnish the requisite gift. But Perseus, who wished not to appear inferior to the other guests in magnificence, told the king, that as he could not bring him a horse, he would bring the head of Medusa, the only one of the Gorgons who was subject to mortality. This offer was particularly agreeable to Polydectes, as it would remove Perseus from Scriphos; and as his undertaking seemed impossible, the attempt might perhaps end in his ruin.

The innocence of Perseus was protected by the gods. Pluto lent him a helmet which had the power of rendering the wearer invisible; Minerva gave him her buckler, which was as resplendent as glass; and from Mercury he received wings and the talaria, with a short dagger made of diamonds, and called *harpe*. With these arms Perseus commenced his expedition, and traversed the air, conducted by the goddess Minerva.

He first went to the Grææ, the sisters of the Gorgons, and with the aid of Pluto's helmet, which made him invisible, stole from them the eye and tooth which they shared in common, and refused to return them until he was informed of the residence of their sisters. When he had received every necessary information, he flew to the habitation of the Gorgons, and found the monsters asleep. He knew that, by fixing his eyes upon them, he should be instantly changed to stone, he therefore looked continually upon his shield, which reflected all objects as clearly as the best mirror. He approached them, his courage supported by the goddess Minerva, and with one blow struck off the head of Medusa. The noise awoke the two immortal sisters, but Pluto's helmet rendered Perseus invisible, and the attempts of the Gorgons to revenge their sister's death proved fruitless. The conqueror made his way through the air, and from the blood which dropped from the head of Medusa sprang those innumerable serpents which have ever since infested the sandy deserts of Libya.

Minerva was the chief instigator to this bloody deed; having resolved on the destruction of Medusa, because, in company with Neptune, the monster had profaned her sanctuary. But when Perseus had brought down the deadly stroke, Stheino and Euryale sighed and groaned so loud at the view of their slain sister, and the hissing of the snakes upon their heads echoed so mournfully to their groaning, that Minerva, moved at the terrible concert, invented a flute with which she endeavored to revive these mournful sounds, by imitating their different strains. Thus, even in the midst of sanguinary and terrible destruction, the goddess of Art shines forth.

Chrysaor also, with his golden sword, sprang from these drops of blood, as well as the horse Pegasos, which immediately flew through the air, and stopped on mount Helicon, where he became the favorite of the Muses. Meantime, Perseus had continued his journey across the deserts of Libya; but the approach of night obliged him to alight in the territories of Atlas, king of Mauritania. He went to the monarch's palace, where he hoped to meet with a kind reception, by announcing himself as the son of Jupiter. But in this he was disappointed; for Atlas recollected that, according to the prediction of an ancient oracle, his gardens were to be robbed of their fruit by one of the sons of Jupiter; he therefore not only refused Perseus the hospitality he demanded, but even assailed his person with violence. Perseus, finding himself inferior to his powerful enemy, showed him the head of Medusa, and Atlas was instantly changed into a large mountain, which bore the same name, in the deserts of Africa.

On the morrow Perseus continued his flight, and passing the territories of Libya, he fixed his eyes upon the Ethiopian coast, where he beheld a maiden fastened with chains to a rock, and a monster rising out of the sea ready to devour her; while her parents stood on the shore wringing their hands in despair. Perseus rushed down upon the monster at the very moment it was seizing its prey, struck the deadly blow, and delivered the fair maiden. It was Andromeda, who, to atone for a crime of which she was guiltless, was to have become the victim of divine anger. Cassiopeia, mother of Andromeda, and wife of Cepheus, had dared to compare the beauty of her daughter with that of the powerful daughters of Nereus, and in consequence, the whole country was laid waste with plagues, which, according to the oracle of Jupiter Ammon, were not to cease until Andromeda, swallowed up by a sea-monster, should, by her death, expiate the crime of her mother.

The parents of Andromeda having been witnesses of their daughter's rescue, readily complied with the wish of her deliverer, and gave her to Perseus in marriage. Phineus, however, brother of Cepheus, to whom Andromeda had been betrothed, accompanied by an armed body, appeared at the wedding feast, and furiously assailed the bridegroom, who would have been overpowered but for the head of Medusa. Warning his friends of the dangerous power of the Gorgon's head, they turned away their eyes; but on showing it to his adversaries, they in a moment became petrified statues, each in the posture and attitude in which he then stood.

After having accomplished these exploits, Perseus conducted his bride to Seriphos, where he again saw his mother and Polydectes. But alas! he was here compelled to turn the petrifying head against his foster-father and benefactor. Polydectes, fearing him and his mighty arm, made an attempt upon his life; but was punished for his cowardly suspicion by being transformed into a rock. Dyctis had protected his mother during his absence; and Perseus, sensible of his merits and humanity, placed him upon the throne of Seriphos.

He afterwards restored to Mercury his talaria, harpe, and wings; to Pluto his helmet; and to Minerva her shield; but as he was more particularly indebted to the Goddess of Wisdom for her assistance and protection, he placed the Gorgon's head on her Ægis.

When Perseus heard that his grandfather, Acrisios, had been deprived of his throne by his brother Prœtos, far from seeking revenge for the cruelty with which he and his mother had formerly been treated by Acrisios, he magnanimously hastened to Argolis with the design of replacing his grandfather in possession of his kingdom. He vanquished and killed Prœtos, and after having restored to Acrisios the royal crown, he was recognized by him with joy and gratitude as his beloved grandson, his friend and benefactor. But Fate, who trifles with the hopes of mortals, had not recalled her former threat, and a tragic end was lurking beneath the seducing appearance. Perseus, knowing how much Acrisios was delighted with his skill in every bodily exercise, was one day resolved to give him a splendid proof of his dexterity; but alas! the fatal quoit, as if directed by an evil dæmon, missing its aim, struck the head of Acrisios, and he fell lifeless to the ground.

In consequence of this unfortunate accident, Perseus passed his future days in melancholy sadness, calling himself a parricide notwithstanding his innocence of the fatal event. His residence at Argos became insupportable to him, and therefore he induced the son of Prœtos to exchange territories. But finding nothing at Tyrius, the capital of his new dominion, to obliterate from his memory the event which distracted him, he built the new city of Mycenæ.

One of the children of Perseus and Andromeda was Alcæus, the father of Amphitryon, who was married to Alcmena, Electryon's daughter, and the mother of Heracles. Another son of Perseus, whose name was Sthenelos, was the father of Eurystheus, who ruled over Mycenæ, and whom Heracles was compelled to serve.

Perseus himself, as well as the chief persons connected with his history, Andromeda, Cassiopeia, and others, were, according to fiction, transposed among the constellations of the sky, where their names are immortalized. In this sense, the heroes of old were really raised to heaven, and a monument most durable and shining was erected to their names.

The ancients represented the Gorgons as winged, and with a broad, flat face, and a long tongue protruding from an enormous mouth, which opened from ear to ear. Later artists banish this hideous mask from their compositions, and represent Medusa as the unhappy beauty who attracted the love of Neptune, giving her a melancholy air, expressive of her regret at finding serpents mingled with her beautiful locks. But few serpents are represented, and so placed as to destroy all deformity; sometimes brought under the chin, and again forming a necklace. The wings, gracefully placed upon the head, add to the beauty of the composition.

BELLEROPHONTES OR BELLEROPHON.

Bellerophon was a son of Glaucos; and his adventures form a pleasing episode in the Iliad, where they are related to Diomedes by Bellerophon's grandson.

The same Prœtus by whom Acrisios was deprived of his kingdom, and who was at last vanquished and slain by Perseus, urged on by a false suspicion, gave to Bellerophontes the first occasion for his heroic feats. He was a grandson of Sisyphos, the founder of Corinth, who was a descendant of Deucalion, and the son of Æolus, from whom the Æolic race of heroes spread through many royal families of Greece.

Having committed a murder, Bellerophon was forced to flee from Corinth, and he came to Prœtus, who at that time was reigning in Argos, with whom he found an asylum. The gods had endowed the hero with manly vigor and beauty; and Antæa, the wife of Prœtus, a daughter of Iobates, king of Lycia, conceived a tender affection for the handsome youth, which was soon changed to hatred because it found no return on the part of Bellerophon. She basely accused him of an attempt on her honor, and enjoined her husband to avenge both her and himself. But the rites of hospitality were too sacred to allow of Prœtus killing Bellerophon; he therefore sent him to Iobates, his father-in-law, with a letter, in which he was desired to avenge the crime of which the bearer was accused, by putting him to death. Iobates, however, did not read the letter until he had hospitably received Bellerophon, after which, he also abhorred the thought of violating the sacred rites of hospitality. He therefore trusted to chance, to effect his ruin, bidding him embark in the most dangerous enterprises, in which his destruction seemed inevitable.

Of the monsters which descended from Phorcys and fair Ceto, one, the terrible Gorgo, was vanquished by Perseus; but another, not less formidable, was assigned to Bellerophon as a trial of his valor. It was the fire vomiting Chimæra, with the head of a lion, the body of a goat, and the tail of a dragon. To this bold adven ture the gods lent their assistance, granting Bellerophon the winged horse Pegasos. The hero bestrode him and then in the air commenced the fight. The monster defended herself to the utmost, sending from her mouth whole masses of fire, and coiling her dragon tail in formidable windings. But all this availed her not. After a persevering and obstinate struggle, the monster lay stretched on the ground weltering in her blood.

Not enough that Bellerophontes had vanquished Chimæra, the scourge of the land; he must now conquer the human enemies of Iobates, the courageous Solymians, and the manlike Amazons. As he was returning victorious, the king laid an ambush for him composed of the bravest men of Lycia, of whom not one returned home, as Bellerophontes slew them all. The king, now perceiving him to be of divine origin, gave him his daughter in marriage and shared his kingdom with him.

But the happiness of this hero was of short duration; for when, elated by his victories, he attempted by means of Pegasos to ascend to Heaven, Zeus, incensed at his boldness, sent an insect to sting the steed, which made Pegasos bound so furiously in the air as to throw his rider to the earth, where he wandered in solitude and melancholy until death relieved him of his grief.

HERACLES OR HERCULES.

The first Greek tragedian (Æschylus) introduces Prometheus when chained to a rock, complaining of his sufferings to the equally unfortunate Io, and predicting the birth of his deliverer, Heracles.

Io, transformed into a cow, was by Juno's jealousy driven in frantic fury over the whole earth. She wandered to the solitary corner where Prometheus was suffering, who revealed her future fate as well as his own, telling her that the thirteenth of her descendants would be his deliverer. The thirteen members of the family in uninterrupted descent are, Io, Epaphos, Libya, Belos, Danaös, Lynceus, Atlas, Acrisios, Danaë, Perseus, Alcæus, Alcmena, Heracles.

The sons of Perseus, were Electryon, Sthenelos, Alcæus, and Mestor, of whom Electryon succeeded his father in the government of Mycenæ. The children of Alcæus were, Anaxo and Amphitryon. Electryon married Anaxo, and from this marriage sprung Alcmena, the mother of Heracles. Amphitryon lived at Electryon's court, and had confident hopes of becoming his uncle's successor in the government, by his marriage with Alcmena; in which he was disappointed.

Taphios, a grandson of Mestor, had founded a colony on the island of Taphos, whose inhabitants called themselves Taphians, or, from their living at a great distance from their native country, Teleboans. After the death of Taphios, Pterelaos, his son and successor, claimed a part of the inheritance of Mycenæ, on account of his descent from Mestor, a son of Perseus, and sent his children thither to enforce his claims. Upon Electryon's denying the justice of them, and refusing to restore any thing of Perseus' inheritance, the sons of Pterelaos, with their people, laid waste the country, and drove away the royal herds. The sons of Electryon immediately collecting a body of men, fought a battle with the invaders, in which the leaders on both sides were killed, with the exception of one son of Electryon, Lycimnius, and one of Pterelaos, Eueres.

Upon this, Electryon resolved on going in person against the Teleboans, to avenge the death of his children; in the mean time transferring his government to his daughter Alcmena and his nephew Amphitryon, with the promise that they should be united in marriage as soon as he should return victorious. He returned conqueror, bringing back the herds of which he had been deprived by his enemies

Amphitryon, now quite secure of his happiness, went joyfully forth to meet him; but as one of the recovered cows strayed from the herd, he, with the intention of turning her back, threw a club at her, which unfortunately hit Electryon, who fell lifeless to the ground.

This occurrence blighted his hopes of one day becoming king of Mycenæ, for though the act was unintentional, it brought upon him the hatred of the people, and Sthenelos, the brother of the slain Electryon, seized upon the royal crown of Mycenæ, without resistance, and Amphitryon was compelled to flee to Thebes, whither Alcmena followed him. Creon, who was at that time king of Thebes, took them under his protection. Alcmena, however, refused to become Amphitryon's wife, until he had avenged the death of her brothers. Amphitryon accordingly entered into an alliance with Cephalos, Eleus, and several other neighboring princes, for the purpose of waging a new war against the inhabitants of the Taphian islands. Pterelaos was vanquished, and Amphitryon divided the conquered islands among his allies; the one of which, called in ancient times Cephalene, and in ours Cephalonia, received its name from the above-mentioned Cephalos.

Meanwhile, however, Alcmena's charms having attracted the Thunderer, he assumed the form of Amphitryon returning as victor from his expedition and came down from Olympos to see her; and was afterwards obliged to reveal his divinity to Amphitryon, in order to appease his anger against Alcmena.

On the day in which Heracles was to be born, Jupiter boastingly spoke in the assembly of the gods, "I give you to understand, all ye gods and goddesses, that to-day a hero will be born, of a race of men who derive their origin from me, who is destined to reign over all his neighbors." Brooding artifices, the cunning Juno replied, "I shall, nevertheless, very much doubt the accomplishment of thy words, unless thou swear with the inviolable oath of the gods, that he, who to-day shall be born of the race of men that derive their origin from thee, will indeed reign over all his neighbors." Scarcely had Jupiter uttered the fatal oath, ere Juno left Olympos, and hastening to Argos, forwarded the birth of Eurystheus, and retarded that of Heracles; then, returning to Olympos, she thus triumphantly accosted Jupiter, " The hero who will rule over the Argives is already born ; he is descended from the race of men that sprang forth from thee; for he is Eurystheus, a son of Sthenelos, whose father Perseus was thine offspring ; the promised kingdom, therefore, is fallen to the lot of no unworthy one." (Il. xix. 101.)

The luckless father of the gods, not able to recall his oath, nor to avenge himself against the wily Juno, burst out in unspeakable wrath, and seizing the bright hand of Ate, the evil breeding power, who was his own daughter, and until now a member of the divine assembly, he hurled her from heaven to earth, swearing with a great oath, that she should never return to Olympos. Since that time, Ate hovers over the heads of mortal men, every where sowing dissensions, broils, and ruin.

Alcmena became the mother of two sons; Hercules, whose father was Jupiter, and Iphicles, the son of her husband Amphitryon. Which of these was the son of the Thunderer soon became evident. While the two children were cradled in a hollow buckler (a part of the booty which Amphitryon had taken in the war against Pterelaos), Juno sent two serpents to destroy Hercules; but the divine babe stifled them with his infant hands. Jupiter then recognized his son ; and finding Juno sleeping, laid Hercules by her side, who by this means obtained the divine milk without her consent. When Juno awoke, she flung far away from her the bold suckling, sprinkling upon the vault of the sky the milk that fell from her breast, the

10*

226   GRECIAN AND ROMAN MYTHOLOGY.

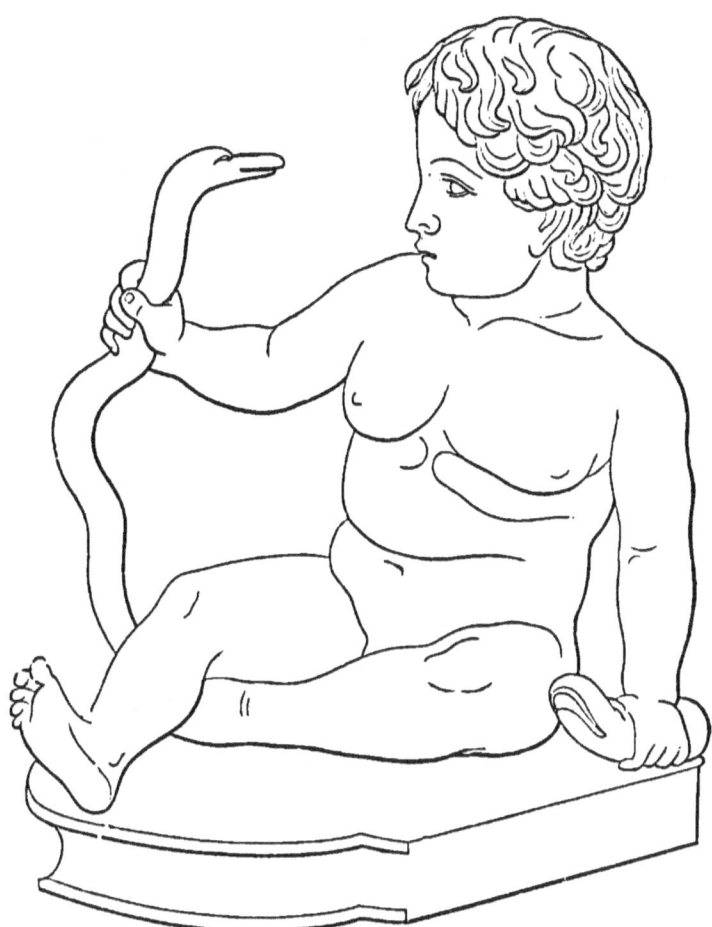

marks of which formed the galaxy or milky way, on which the gods walk. Fiction here becomes Colossean, and the atmosphere through which the stars shine, appears therein as Juno's chief archetype.

At the command of Jupiter. Mercury committed Hercules to his tutors, who were to instruct him in warlike occupations. as well as in peaceful arts. Several of them were themselves sons of deities;—Linus, the son of Apollo, taught him to play on the lyre, and Eumolpos to sing;

Castor taught him how to fight; Eurytos how to shoot with a bow and arrows; Autolicus to drive a chariot; and like the rest of his illustrious contemporaries, he became the pupil of the wise Centaur, Cheiron, and under him, perfected his accomplishments, and made himself the most valiant of the age.

When in pursuit of these occupations, Hercules one day betook himself to a lonely spot, to muse undisturbed on his future life and fate; and seating himself on a crossway he sank into deep reflection. On this occasion two females appeared to him, the one of whom was Luxury and the other Virtue. Each endeavored to win the youth to her interest. Luxury, by promising him all the enjoyment of a cheerful, careless life, if he would follow her; Virtue, by announcing to him troublesome and laborious days, but afterwards glory and immortality, if he would choose her for his guide in the path of life. "Thee will I follow; to thee devote my life," exclaimed the youth, with glowing heart, grasping at the same time the hand of Virtue; and followed her with firm step, resolved to endure patiently every trial that awaited him, to bear every burden that should fall to his lot, and to shun no labor that should be appointed him, however difficult the task might be.

Two of the most terrible children of Phorcys and Ceto were vanquished by Perseus and Bellerophon, but the greatest feats of valor, as well as merit, are reserved for Hercules, who is to conquer monsters, to subdue tyrants, and to set bounds to the injustice of the Thunderer himself, by delivering Prometheus from his torments, who was still suffering for the benefits which he had conferred upon mankind. The fate of Hercules was woven in the commencement of his life's thread by the inexorable Parcæ. Born to be a ruler, he was forced by the power of the Fates to obey, and to achieve his most glorious actions at the command of one, who was in every respect his inferior, and who dreaded the strength with which he was endowed.

He was not permitted to live long in quiet at the house of his foster-father, Amphitryon; for jealous Juno had infused into the heart of the latter dread, and suspicion against the young hero. Heracles was therefore sent by him to the court of Eurystheus, at Mycenæ, where from time to time he was charged with the most difficult labors, and the most dangerous undertakings, which put his courage and firmness to the severest test. On his journey to Mycenæ, he inquired of the oracle at Delphi concerning his future fate; and received for answer, that twelve labors awaited him at the court of Eurystheus, after the performance of which, immortality should be his reward. For these undertakings the favors of the gods had completely armed him. From Minerva, he received a coat of arms and a helmet; from Mercury a sword; from Neptune a horse; from Jupiter a shield; from Apollo a bow and arrows; and from Vulcan, a golden cuirass and a brazen buskin.

Eurystheus, seeing so powerful a man completely subjected to him, and apprehensive of such an enemy, commanded him to achieve the most difficult and arduous enterprises ever known; generally called,

THE TWELVE LABORS OF HERCULES.

1st. *The Nemæan Lion.*—A monstrous lion, near the forest of Nemæa, wasted the surrounding country and threatened destruction to the herds. His first labor was to destroy this beast of prey, which he did by throwing his sinewy arms around his neck and strangling him. In memory of this deed of valor, he ever afterwards wore the lion skin, which, with the knotty branch of the wild olive tree, was the external mark of his strength and courage.

2d. *The Lernæan Hydra.*—The morasses of Lerna, near Argos, was the abode of the Hydra with many heads. Hercules attacked the monster with his sickle-shaped sword, but no sooner severed one head from the trunk than a new one grew out. At last, he commanded his companion, Iolaus, the son of Iphicles, to burn the root of the head with a hot iron before a new one could spring up. This was no sooner accomplished, than Juno sent a crab to gnaw at the heels of Hercules while he was struggling with the monster. The hero soon dispatched his new enemy, and after a long fight, drove the last head of the Hydra into the ground, and covered it with an immense stone. As a reward for his labor, he dipped his arrows into the blood of the Hydra, which, by this fatal poison, became doubly dreadful.

3d. *The Erymanthian Boar.*—From the Erymanthian mountains, a monstrous boar descended, laying waste the fields of Arcadia. This afforded Eurystheus a wished for occasion to send Hercules on a new and dangerous expedition. To the conqueror of the Nemæan Lion and the many-headed Hydra, however, it was no difficult task to catch the boar alive and carry him to Eurystheus, who, terrified at the sight of the monster, concealed himself in a brazen butt.

4th. *The Stag of Diana.*—In order to put to the proof the swiftness and agility of Hercules, he was in his fourth labor ordered to bring alive and unhurt into the presence of Eurystheus, the stag of Diana, famous for its swiftness, its golden horns, and brazen feet.

Hercules, accepting the task, pursued the tracks of this nimble animal during a whole year, and at last caught him in a thicket, and carried him on his shoulders to the gates of Mycenæ. This celebrated stag frequented the neighborhood of Oenoë, and as Hercules was returning victorious, he met Diana, who snatched the stag from him with a severe reprimand for molesting an animal sacred to her. He pleaded necessity, and by representing the commands of Eurystheus, he appeased the goddess, and obtained the stag.

5th. *The Stymphalides.*—A kind of ghastly birds inhabited the Stymphalian lake, to which the imagination of the poets ascribes the most frightful aspect.. They were represented as furnished with claws and bills of brass, enabling them to pierce any armor, and according to several fictions, were armed with darts, which they flung at their aggressors.

These monsters, which Eurystheus commanded Hercules to destroy, had taken up their abode in the deep recesses of an inaccessible morass. And here the divine hero would have been at a loss, notwithstanding his strength and courage, but for the aid of Minerva, who wished him success, and gave him a rattle of brass, the noise of which frightened the birds from their haunts, driving them into the air, where Hercules easily dispatched them with his arrows.

6th. *Augias' Stables.*—Augias, a king in Elis, and called a child of the sun, from the immense number of flocks and herds which he possessed, was one of the wealthiest princes of his time. In those ages, a man's wealth was estimated in proportion to the abundance of his cattle; and the occupations required by possessions of this kind were not degrading; neither was it considered disgraceful to clean a stable.

According to the tale of antiquity, Augias had three thousand oxen in his stables, which had not been cleansed for thirty years, so that at last it seemed an impossibility to clear them of the prodigious accumulation. But Hercules, at the command of Eurystheus, undertook the enormous task, which was to be accomplished in the space of a few days. Augias, who doubted the possibility of the performance, promised Hercules, as a reward, the tenth part of his herds.

By turning the course of the river Alpheus through the stables, Hercules completed the task in one day. After the work was done, Augias withheld the promised reward, on the pretext that Hercules had made use of artifice; and the son of Alcmena, enraged at this faithlessness, made war upon him, and having conquered and killed him, proclaimed his son Phyleus his successor upon the throne.

Out of the treasures which he gained in this war, he built a temple in honor of Olympian Jupiter, and renewed the Olympic games.

7th. *The Cretan Bull.*—Neptune, being angry at the inhabitants of Crete, because they were deficient in their veneration for him, sent into the island a furious bull, which exhaled fire from his nostrils, and as no one would venture to approach him, laid waste the country.

Scarcely had Eurystheus heard of this, ere he imposed on Hercules the new task of catching the beast alive. Hercules, whose bodily strength measured itself as it were with the whole animal world, subdued the bull sent by Neptune, and carried him on his shoulders to Mycenæ.

8th. *The Horses of Diomedes.*—Diomedes, a king of Thrace, and son of Mars, had in his possession four fire-vomiting horses, which were fed by him with human flesh. All strangers who fell into the hands of this barbarian, were thrown to his horses to be torn and devoured.

The report of this cruelty having spread every where, Eurystheus commanded Hercules to bring to him the fire-vomiting steeds. The hero obeyed, overpowered Diomedes, and by throwing him to the carnivorous beasts, made him suffer the just punishment of his cruelty.

9th. *The Girdle of the Queen of the Amazons.*—The precious girdle worn by the queen of the Amazons, and which Hercules was to win, was a present from the god of war, and defended as it was by fortitude and bravery, it could only be obtained by invincible courage.

In this expedition, Hercules was accompanied by Theseus, and at the river Thermodon the fight commenced, in which the Amazons with their allies were vanquished, and the queen herself taken prisoner. Hercules, after having on his way accomplished several other bold feats, returned to Mycenæ, and presented the girdle to Eurystheus.

10th. *The Triple-bodied Geryon.*—Geryon, the savage monarch of three islands, situated in the dusky west of the ancient world, has already been mentioned in the pedigree of the monsters.

He was in possession of what, in times of antiquity, was considered the greatest treasure; and the fame of Geryon's oxen had spread so far, as to induce Eurystheus to impose upon Hercules the commission of leading them away from their pastures, and bringing them as a warlike treasure from the remotest bounds of the earth to Mycenæ.

Hercules made his way over mountains and rocks, performing on this expedition many other great exploits. After having overcome the two-headed dog, which guarded the herds, as well as Eurytion the herdsman, he took possession of Geryon's oxen. The triple-bodied monster then rushed upon him, but was killed by Hercules with his club.

11th. *The Golden Apples of the Hesperides.*—The greatest treasure which imagination transferred to the widest distance, and which was thought to be altogether unattainable, was the golden apples in the gardens of the Hesperides. These gardens were watched by a monstrous dragon, and to bring the golden fruit to Eurystheus, was one of the tasks which Hercules was to accomplish in obedience to the command of another.

The hero, ignorant of the situation of these celebrated gardens, applied to the nymphs in the neighborhood of the Po for information; and was told that Nereus, if properly managed, would direct him in the pursuit. Hercules seized Nereus as he was sleeping, and the sea-god, unable to escape from his grasp, answered all the questions that he proposed.

After reaching the gardens, Hercules gave the dragon a potion which threw him into a deep sleep; he then succeeded in killing him, gathered the apples, and returned in triumph to Eurystheus. They were afterwards carried back to the gardens by Minerva, as they could be preserved in no other place.

12th. *Cerberus, the Watch-dog of Orcus.*—Hercules had now given eleven proofs of the strength and agility of his body, as well as the greatness of his soul; the last only remained. He had not done enough in conquering the monsters of the higher world—Eurystheus also commanded him to descend into the world of shades, and drag to the light of day the triple-headed dog Cerberus, that watched the gates of Pluto.

Before Hercules went on his way to the lower world, he was initiated in the Eleusinian mysteries, to be as it were prepared for any event, whether life or death: he then boldly entered the cavern at the Promontory of Tænarus, which led to the abode of the shades. He compelled Charon to row him across the Styx, and when reaching the opposite shore, he first beheld the three-headed dog Cerberus, and then, chained to a rock, two well-known heroes, Theseus and Pirithoös, who had ventured to descend into Orcus, with the intention of delivering Proserpine, the Queen of the dead, from Pluto's dominions. They were overpowered, fastened to an enchanted rock, and doomed never again to see the light of the sun.

Hercules fought with Pluto himself; seized upon the triple-headed watch-dog of his dominions, loosened Theseus' bonds, and hastened out of the land of terrors. He

had also endeavored to free Pirithoös from his fetters, but in vain, for Pluto defended his prey with his whole power.

Hercules brought Cerberus in triumph to the upper world. The terrified Eurystheus could not bear the sight of the monster, and Hercules, after having kept him tamed between his knees, delivered him from the pain of beholding the light of day, and the black monster slunk back to the lower world to resume his watch at its gates.

These are the proofs which Hercules gave of his strength, his perseverance, invincible courage, and patient submission to the decrees of Fate, in performing the most difficult tasks at the command of an inferior. But besides these labors imposed upon him by Eurystheus, he voluntarily achieved other deeds of valor, not less glorious, equally celebrated, and perhaps of higher merit.

He rescued Hesione, who was chained to a rock to be devoured by a sea-monster; he killed the giant Antæos, who forced all strangers to wrestle with him who came within his reach; he slew Busiris, a cruel king of Egypt, who sacrificed all foreigners to Jupiter; he destroyed Cacus, a famous robber, who was represented as a three-headed monster, vomiting flames; he delivered Alceste from Orcus; he slew the vulture that gnawed at the liver of Prometheus; and erected the pillars at the straits between Europe and Africa.

Hercules' first marriage was with Megara, the daughter of Creön, prince of Thebes, who was given to him by her father out of gratitude for having freed the city from a burdensome tribute, which had been exacted by the Orchomenians. After Megara had presented him with four sons, he is said to have been driven distracted by Juno, and in a fit of frenzy to have slain both mother and children. In their memory obsequies were annually celebrated at Thebes.

In order to expiate this horrible deed, although it was not perpetrated with design, Heracles the more readily submitted to the labors imposed upon him by Eurystheus; but when he had nearly completed his tasks, he was enchained by a new love, and married again, notwithstanding the tragical end of his first nuptials.

Upon one of his expeditions he came to king Œneus, at Calydon, in Ætolia, where he saw the beautiful Deianeira, the royal daughter, who was the affianced bride of the river-god, Acheloös. Hercules engaged in battle with him, and Deianeira was the prize of his victory. The hero then proceeded on his way, accompanied by his wife. When they arrived at the river Euënus, on the banks of which Nessos, the Centaur, had his dwelling, Heracles committed to him the charge of carrying Deianeira on his back through the river. The Centaur complied the more willingly with the request of one in whose mouth a request amounted to a command, because he harbored the secret intention of depriving Heracles of his wife. Accordingly, when he reached the other bank of the river with his fair burden, he galloped off; but hearing Deianeira's cries for assistance, Heracles bent his bow, and sent through the faithless Centaur one of those arrows which had been dipped in the poisonous blood of the Lernæan Hydra. Nessos, brooding revenge at the very moment of his death, handed to Deianeira a flask filled with his blood, beseeching her to keep it as a precious gift, by means of which she could secure to herself the attachment of her husband, as well as banish every other love from his breast, by rubbing the blood on the garment which he wore next his body.

Before his marriage with Deianeira, Heracles had seen Iole, the daughter of king Eurytos, who reigned over Œchalia, in Eubœa, and was conquered by her charms. He sued for her hand from her father, but met with a refusal, at which he was angry, and left the house of his host meditating revenge. And soon after, when Iphitos, the son of Eurytos, came to Heracles in quest of his strayed horses, which the hero himself kept concealed, Heracles conducted the son of his host to the rocky walls of Tyrins, and suddenly pitched him from the steep height.

By this deed he stained his glory, and was, by the command of the gods, compelled to atone for it in a humiliating manner. He must suffer himself to be sold as a slave to the voluptuous queen Omphale, in Lydia, at whose command he was obliged to do female work.

Plastic art represents Omphale wearing the skin of the Nemæan lion round her shoulders, and holding the club in her hand, while Heracles is seen in a female dress, sitting at the distaff and spinning. The hero, who had already completed his heroic course, must nevertheless become sensible of the lot of mortals, before he could take his seat in the assembly of the celestials, sinking down from his greatness in proportion to the height of his former elevation.

The fixed period of his servitude in Lydia having expired, Heracles made war upon Eurytos, because of his having refused him his daughter; and carrying the city Œchalia by assault, he destroyed it, slew the king himself, and sent his daughter Iole as a slave to Deianeira, by whom she was received with kindness.

Understanding, however, that this very captive was her rival, she thought it was time to make use of the gift of Nessos. Accordingly, she took the long-preserved blood of the Centaur, and having rubbed with it a splendid tunic, she sent it to her husband by her servant Lichas, with the request not to wear the garment until he should have occasion to show himself finely dressed to the immortals at a sacred festival.

Heracles had long since received the oracle, that his death was not to be apprehended from a living being, but from a dead one. The fulfilment of this prediction was now drawing nigh.

After his victory over Eurytos, Heracles erected an altar to Jupiter upon the promontory of Cenæum, in Eubœa, and was about to kill the victims, when Lichas appeared, bringing with him Deianeira's present. The hero was the more rejoiced at the gift, because it arrived at so seasonable a time. Instantly arraying himself in the costly attire, he presented a hecatomb to the immortals, and made the flames blaze from the altars to the sky. Suddenly his newly-received tunic adhered to his body as if glued to it, and convulsions seized all his limbs. It was the poison of the Hydra, mingled with the blood of Nessos, which penetrated his body, and was now consuming the very marrow of his bones.

Suffering unspeakable pain, he called the unfortunate Lichas, who had brought him the garment, and hurled him against a rock with such force that his skull and bones were crushed to pieces. In the midst of his tortures the hero was carried to the city of Trachinia, in Thessaly. The unhappy Deianeira no sooner heard of the dreadful effect of her present than she put an end to her life.

Hyllos, the son of Heracles and Deianeira, assisting his father in his torments, at his command carried him to Mount Œta, where Heracles resolved to put an end to his sufferings by a voluntary death. On Mount Œta a pile of wood was erected and kindled; it was the funeral pile of Heracles. After having recommended to his son Hyllos his much-loved Iöle, and given to Philoctetes, the son of Pœas, and his faithful companion, his bow and arrows as an inheritance, the hero ascended his fatal death-bed.

There, surrounded by the blazing flames, his face became resplendent. Heracles had finished the sufferings of humanity, and atoned for her foibles; his mortal covering, subject to pains and distress, fell off; his shade went down to Orcus, but he himself rose to Olympos, and was received into the assembly of the immortals. Juno was reconciled, and Hebe, the goddess of eternal youth, became, according to the decree of Fate, the spouse of the new deity.

Heracles, according to the theory of Dupuis and others, is the Sun, and his twelve labors are a figurative representation of the annual course of that luminary through the signs of the zodiac. He is the powerful planet which animates and imparts fecundity to the universe; whose divinity has been honored in every quarter of the globe, by temples and altars, and consecrated in the religious theories of all nations.

To illustrate the fable of his labors (altering the order in which they are usually given), let us suppose the sun to commence his annual course at the summer solstice, which was indeed considered as the opening of the year, by different ancient nations.

In the first month the sun passes into the sign *Leo* The first labor of Hercules was the slaying of the Nemæan *lion*. In the second month the sun enters Hydra. The second labor of Hercules was the killing of the Hydra, or dragon of many heads. The constellation Hydra is peculiar for its length. Its head rises with Cancer; its body extends under the sign Leo, and only ends at the later degrees of the sign Virgo. Hence the fable of the continual re-appearance of the heads of the monster whom Hercules slew. In the third month the sun enters the sign Libra, when the constellation of Centaur rises, represented as bearing a wine-skin full of liquor, and a thyrsus adorned with vine-leaves and grapes. Bayer represents him with a thyrsus in one hand, and a flask of wine in the other; and the Alphonsine tables, with a goblet in his hand. At this same period, what, by some, is termed the constellation of the Boar rises. In his third labor, Hercules, after being hospitably entertained by a Centaur, encountered and slew the other Centaurs, who fought for a cask of wine. He slew also the Erymanthian Bear. In the fourth month the sun enters Scorpio, when Cassiopeia rises, who was represented, anciently, by a stag In his fourth labor, Hercules caught the famous stag with golden horns and brazen feet, and breathing fire from its nostrils; aptly representing a constellation studded with blazing stars, and which unites itself with the solstitial fires of the sun. In the fifth month, the sun enters Sagittarius (the archer), when also appear the constellations of the vulture, swan, and eagle. In his fifth labor, Hercules destroyed, with arrows, the three birds near the lake Stymphalus. In the sixth month, the sun enters Capricornus, said to be a grandson of the luminary. At this period, the stream which flows from Aquarius sets. Its source is between the hands of Aristæus, son of the river Peneus. In his sixth labor, Hercules cleansed, by means of the river Peneus, the stables of Augias, son of Phœbus. In the seventh month, the sun enters the sign Aquarius; the constellation of the Lyre, or Vulture, sets, which is by the side of the constellation Prometheus; and the celestial bull, the bull of Pasiphaë, or of Marathon, or of Europa, passes the meridian. In his seventh labor, Hercules brought alive, into the Peloponnesus, a wild bull which laid waste the island of Crete. He also slew the vulture which preyed upon the liver of Prometheus. It should be observed that the constellation of the Vulture *sets*, and that the Vulture was *killed;* that the constellation of the bull *crosses the meridian* merely, and that Hercules brought his bull to Greece *alive*. In the eighth month, the sun enters Pisces, and the celestial horse Pegasus, or Arion, rises. Hercules, in his eighth labor, overcame and carried off the horses of Diomedes. In the ninth month the sun enters the sign Aries (sacred to Mars), the same with the ram of the golden fleece; the celestial ship Argo rises; Cassiopeia and Andromeda set; Andromeda is remarkable for its many beautiful stars, one of which is called her girdle. In his ninth labor, Hercules embarked on board the Argo in quest of the golden fleece; contended with female warriors, and took from their queen, Hippolyta, the daughter of Mars, a famous girdle. In the tenth month, the sun enters Taurus; the constellation Orion, fabled to have pursued the Pleiades, daughters of Atlas; the conductor of the oxen of Icarus, and the river Eridanus, also; the

Pleiades rise, and the she-goat, fabled to have been the spouse of Faunus. The tenth labor of Hercules was restoring from pirates, employed by Busiris, the seven Pleiades to their father; slaying Busiris, the same as Orion; bearing away the oxen of Geryon, and vanquishing Cacus. In the eleventh month, the sun passes into the sign of Gemini; Procyon sets; the Dog-star rises, and the swan. In his eleventh labor, Hercules conquered the Dog Cerberus, and triumphed over Cycnus (Swan), at the time when the dog-star's influence is felt upon the fields.

In the twelfth month the sun enters the sign *Cancer*, the last of the twelve, commencing with Leo. The constellations of the river and the Centaur set, that of Hercules Ingeniculus also descends towards the western regions, or those of *Hesperia*, followed by the dragon of the pole, the guardian of the golden apples of the Hesperides, whose head he crushes with his foot. In his twelfth labor, Hercules travelled to Hesperia in quest of the golden fruit, guarded by the dragon. After his, he offers up a sacrifice, and clothes himself in a robe dipped in the blood of the *Centaur*, whom he had slain in crossing a river. The robe takes fire, and the hero perishes amid the flames, but only to resume his youth in the heavens, and become a partaker of immortality.

The Centaur thus terminates the mortal career of Hercules; and in like manner the new annual period commences with the passage of the sun into Leo, marked by a group of stars in the morning that glitter like the flames that issued from the vestment of Nessos.

Heracles, with Omphale, is the solar god descended into the Omphalos, or navel of the world, amid the signs of the southern hemisphere; and it was the festival of this powerful star, in some degree enervated at the period of the winter solstice, which the Lydian people celebrated by the change of vestments made between the weaker and stronger sex.

DIONYSOS OR BACCHUS.

Dionysos and Heracles, although born of mortal mothers, are associated in the assembly of the immortal gods. Yet, Dionysos is by far the higher, the more divine person. From the beginning, the plenitude of his being is revealed; and from his very birth, he is ranked among the celestials, while Heracles, by bold deeds and invincible valor, must prepare himself the path to immortality. For this reason, too, the latter, during his life-time, was ranked only among the God-like heroes; while Dionysos was always entitled to the society of the gods.

The archetype of Dionysos (the reproductive force of nature, of which wine is the symbol) was the inward swelling fulness of nature, typified in the foaming cup, from which she bestows animating enjoyment on the initiated. The worship of Dionysos, therefore, like that of Demeter, was mysterious; for both deities are the emblems of the whole of nature, which no mortal eye penetrates.

The fiction of the birth of Dionysos contains a deep meaning. The jealous Hera, appearing to his mother in the character of an old woman, instigated the daughter of Cadmos to express the extravagant wish of enjoying Zeus in his divine character. Semele accordingly, first desired the Thunderer to swear compliance to the request she was about to make to him, and when he had taken the oath, she demanded that he should appear to her in his true, divine person. Zeus, not daring to break the terrible oath by Styx, was compelled to approach her by thunder and lightning. The wretched Semele, killed by the thunder, and consumed by the lightning, fell a sacrifice to her rash request. Zeus snatched from her his son Dionysos, yet unborn, and placed him in his thigh, where he remained till the regular time of his birth. Mortality is destroyed ere immortality rises. Man, during his life-time on earth, not being able to bear the glory of divinity, is annihilated by its terrible majesty.

At the birth of the child, Zeus gave him the name of Dionysos, and sent him by Hermes to Ino, sister to Semele with directions to rear him; but Hera, whose revenge was not yet satiated, caused Athamas, the husband of Ino, to go mad. Zeus, to save Dionysos from the machinations of Hera, changed him into a kid, under which form Hermes conveyed him to the nymphs of Nysa, who were to take charge of his education, and by whom he was reared with the greatest tenderness.

In his boyhood, Dionysos, as if yet half reeling in sweet slumber, does not comprehend the fulness of his being, and appears apprehensive of injuries inflicted by men, until his formidable power suddenly reveals itself through miraculous events. Lycurgus, king of the Edones, a people of Thrace, surprised the nurses of Dionysos on Mount Nysa, and wounded several of them. The terrified Dionysos threw himself into the sea, when Thetis took him up in her arms; but he avenged himself by driving Lycurgus mad, when he killed his own son, Dryas, with a blow of an axe, mistaking him for a vine-branch. His subjects afterwards bound him, and left him on Mount Pangæon, where he was destroyed by wild horses, for such was the will of Dionysos.

When Dionysos grew up, he discovered the culture of the vine, and the mode of extracting its precious liquor; but Hera struck him with madness, and in this state he roamed through a great part of Asia. In Phrygia he was met by Rhea, who cured him, and taught him her religious rites, which he resolved to introduce into Greece. In his course he met with various adventures.

At one time a body of pirates, who took him for the son of a king, in the hope of obtaining a large ransom, carried him off and placed him on board their ship. No sooner, however, had they left the shore, than the cords with which the smiling boy was fastened fell off, and a fragrant stream of wine ran through the ship; then suddenly a vine rose to the top-sail, which expanded its branches, loaded with heavy grapes: the mast became entwined with dark ivy, and all the oars were covered with vine leaves. On the deck of the vessel a terrible lion made its appearance, casting around him fierce, threatening glances; terror seized the offenders, who leaped from the ship into the raging sea, where suddenly appearing as swimming dolphins, they bore witness to the power of the all-conquering deity.

When Dionysos reached Thebes, the women readily received the new rites, and ran wildly through the woods of Cithæron. Pentheus, the ruler of Thebes, set himself against them; but Dionysos caused him to be torn to pieces by his mother and aunts. The daughters of Minyas, Leucippe, Aristippe, and Alcathoë, also despised his rites, and continued plying their looms, while the other women ran through the mountains. Dionysos appeared to them as a maiden and remonstrated, but in vain; he then assumed the form of various wild beasts; serpents filled their baskets; vines and ivy twined round their looms, while wine and milk distilled from the roof; still their obstinacy was unsubdued. He finally drove them mad, when they tore to pieces the son of Leucippe, and then went roaming through the mountains, till Hermes touched them with his wand, and changed them into a bat, an owl, and a crow.

Dionysos next proceeded to Attica, where he taught Icarios the culture of the vine. Icarios having made wine, gave it to some shepherds, who, thinking themselves poisoned, killed him; recovering themselves, they buried him. His daughter, Erigone, being shown the spot by his faithful dog Mæra, hung herself through grief.

At Argos the rites of Dionysos were received by the women as at Thebes, and opposed by Perseus, the son of Zeus and Danaë; Zeus, however, reduced h s two sons to amity, and Dionysos thence passed over to Naxos, where he met with Ariadne. Afterwards he descended to Erebos, whence he brought his mother, whom he named Thyone, and ascended with her to the abode of the gods.

The expedition of Bacchos to India, is a beautiful and sublime fiction. With an army of both men and women, who advanced with joyful tumult, he extended his beneficent conquests as far as the Ganges, teaching the conquered nations the cultivation of the vine, together with a higher enjoyment of life, and giving them laws. In the divine person of Bacchos, men revered the more cheerful delights of life, as a particular, sublime being, who, under the form of an eternally flourishing youth, subdues lions and tigers that draw his chariot, and who, in divine ecstasy, accompanied by the sound of flutes and timbrels, proceeds in triumph, from east to west, through all countries

The victorious expedition, undertaken for the benefit of the nations of earth, was accomplished by Bacchos in three years; for which reason the festivals afterwards instituted in remembrance of it, were always celebrated after the same interval of time. Then, the joyful tumult which accompanied the march of the god through the earth was repeated, and celebrated anew from every hill and mountain. The priestesses of the god of wine, roaming with dishevelled hair upon the mountains, filled the air with the noise proceeding from the beating of timbrels, playing upon flutes, &c., and the wild, continual cry, of Euöi! Bacche! The threatening thyrses in their hands, from which the colored ribbons waved, while the pine-apple on its top concealed the wounding point, is an emblem of the expedition to India; on occasion of which, the clamor of war and din of battle were hidden under song and the sound of musical instruments.

Mythologists differ in opinion as to the origin of Bacchos. Creutzer and others consider his worship as evidently of eastern origin, and that he is identified with the Osiris of the Egyptians and the Schiva of India. The fable of his birth, and his strange translation to the thigh of the monarch of Olympos, bear the impress of oriental imagery. An ivy branch is made to spring forth from a column to cover him with its leaves when he is taken from his mother, and the Ivy was in Egypt the plant of Osiris. In like manner, the coffin of the Egyptian deity is shaded by the plant *erica*, which springs from the ground and envelopes it. Bacchos and Osiris both float upon the waters in a chest, or ark, and both have for one of their symbols the head of a bull.

The Lingam and equilateral triangle, symbols of Bacchos, were also symbols of Schiva. The two systems of worship have the same obscenities and the same emblems. Schiva is represented, in the Hindoo Mythology, as assuming the form of a lion during the great battle of the gods. He seizes the monster that attacks him with his teeth and fangs, while Dourga pierces him with his lance. In the Grecian Mythology, the same exploit is attributed to Bacchos, under the same form, against the giant Rhœtos.

The Grecian festivals, in honor of Dionysos, called Dionysia, were observed at Athens with more splendor and superstition than in any other part of Greece. The years were numbered by their celebration, the archon assisted at their solemnity, and the priests who officiated were honored with the most dignified seats at the public games. They were at first celebrated with great simplicity, and the time was consecrated to mirth. It was then usual to bring a vessel full of wine, adorned with a vine branch, after which followed a goat, a basket of figs, and other emblems. In imitation of the poetical fictions of Dionysos, his worshippers were clothed in fawn skins, fine linen, and mitres, and crowned themselves with garlands of ivy, vine, and fir, and carried thyrses, drums, pipes and flutes. Some, in the uncouth manner of their dress, and their fantastic motions, imitated Pan, Silenos, and the Satyrs; and some rode on asses, while others drove the goats to slaughter for the sacrifice, and in this manner both sexes joined in the solemnity, and ran about the hills and country, nodding their heads, dancing in ridiculous postures, and filling the air with hideous shrieks and shouts, crying Bacche! Io! Io! Euöi! Iacche! etc., beating on drums and sounding various instruments.

With such solemnities were the Greek festivals of Bacchos celebrated. In one of these a procession was formed, bearing the various emblems of his worship; and among them a select number of noble virgins carried baskets of gold, filled with all kinds of fruit; serpents were some times put in the baskets, and by their wreathing and crawling out amused and astonished the beholders. This was the most mysterious part of the solemnity.

These festivals, in honor of the god of wine, contributed much to the corruption of morals among all classes of people. They were introduced into Etruria, and from thence to Rome, where both sexes promiscuously joined in the celebration during the darkness of the night; but their vicious excesses called for the interference of the senate, who passed a decree, banishing the Bacchanalia for ever from Rome.

The women who bore a chief part in these festivals were called *Mænades*, *Bacchæ*, *Thyiades*, and *Euades*.

As the god of wine, Bacchos is generally represented

crowned with vine and ivy leaves, with a thyrse in his hand. His figure is that of an effeminate young man.

The golden horns upon the head of Bacchos, which by the plastic art of the Greeks were either entirely hidden, or partly concealed, are a token of the high antiquity of this god; such horns having been in the remotest times connected with the ideas of inward, divine power.

Among animals, the spotted panther is sacred to Bacchos; fierceness, nay, even cruelty is tamed by him, and cringes at his feet; and he is said to have been clothed in the skin of this animal on his expedition to India. The ever-verdant ivy, and the snake, which, casting its skin, renews itself, are pleasing emblems of perpetual youth; in which the divine form of Bacchos resembles that of Apollo, only with this difference—the former is represented as more delicate and feminine. His beauty is compared to that of Apollo, and both are represented with fine hair flowing loosely on the shoulders.

The thyrse was one of the most common and ancient attributes of Bacchos and his joyous crew. It consisted of a lance, the iron point of which was concealed in a pine cone, in memory of the stratagem of his followers in concealing their pikes. It was used at all the festivals held in his honor, and often twined with wreaths of ivy or bay.

MINOS, RHADAMANTHYS, AND SARPEDON.

Zeus, says the legend, becoming enamored of the beauty of Europa, the daughter of Phœnix or Agenor, changed himself into a beautiful white bull, and "breathing saffron from his mouth," he approached her as she was gathering flowers with her companions in a mead near the shore. Europa, delighted with the tameness and beauty of the animal, caressed him, crowned him with flowers, and at length ventured to mount his back. The disguised god immediately made off with his lovely burden, ran along the waves of the sea, and made no stop till he arrived at Crete, not far from Gortyna. Here he resumed his own form, and beneath a plane-tree embraced the trembling maiden. By him she had three sons, Minos, Rhadamanthys, and Sarpedon.

These three brothers fell into discord for the sake of a beautiful youth named Miletos, the son of Apollo, or of Zeus. The youth testifying the most esteem for Sarpedon, Minos chased them out of Crete. Miletos went to Caria, where he built a town which he named from himself. Sarpedon went to Lycia, where he aided Cilix against the people of that country, and obtained the sovereignty of a part of it. Zeus is said to have bestowed on him a life of triple duration.

Rhadamanthys ruled with justice and equity over the islands. Having accidentally committed homicide, he retired to Bœotia, where he married Alcmena, the mother of Heracles. According to Homer, Rhadamanthys was placed on the Elysian Plain, among the heroes to whom Zeus allotted that blissful abode. Pindar seems to make him a sovereign or judge in the island of the Blest. Later poets place him with Minos and Æacos in the under-world, where their office is to judge the dead.

Minos is chiefly remarkable for belonging to a period when history and mythology interlace; and as uniting in his own person the chief characteristics of both. He is a son of Zeus, and yet the first possessor of a navy; a judge in Hades, and at the same time a king in Crete.

It is worthy of remark, that Crete, so famous at this age, both for its naval power and for being the birth-place of the Olympian gods, should never afterwards have attained any thing like the celebrity which its position seemed to promise. Its office seems to have been that of leading the way in naval supremacy. Too isolated for power of a durable nature, it was lost in the confederate or opposing glories of

Athens and Sparta; but while they were yet in their infancy, the insular form of Crete (together perhaps with some Asiatic refinement) gave it that concentrated energy, which in an early age is irresistible.

According to fiction, Minos, in a grotto on Mount Ida, had occasional secret converse with his father Zeus, the purport of which he announced to the listening people as the fundamental part of legislation. In consequence of this wise government and justice, fiction transferred to him, together with his brother and counsellor, Rhadamanthys, as the most righteous of mortals, the judicature over the dead in the lower world; associating with them Æacos, the father of Peleus, and sometimes Triptolemos too, the benefactor of mankind.

Minos, the legislator, was at the same time a warlike and valiant prince, who, sweeping the pirates from the Mediterranean sea, rendered sailing and commerce safe. But the hero, who in many respects was the benefactor of mankind, was obliged to endure misfortunes which shaded his glorious victories in gloom.

The wife of Minos was Pasiphaë, a daughter of the Sun and Perseis, and sister of Ætes. By her he had several children, the most celebrated of whom were Androgeos, Glaucos, Deucalion, Ariadne, and Phædra.

After the death of Asterion, the Cretans hesitated whether to give Minos the royal dignity; to prove his claim to it, he asserted that he could obtain whatever he chose to pray for. Then, sacrificing to Poseidon, he besought him to send him a bull from the bottom of the sea (a bull with the ancients being an emblem of power), promising to sacrifice whatever should appear. Poseidon sent the bull, and Minos received the kingdom. According to Homer, he ruled nine years at Cnossos, and was the intimate friend of Zeus. He was victorious in war, and extended his dominion over the isles of the Ægean.

The bull which Poseidon had sent out of the sea, being of a large size and brilliant white hue, appeared to Minos too beautiful an animal to be slain; he therefore put him in his herd and substituted an ordinary one in its place. This act offended Poseidon, and he caused the bull to run wild, and at the same time inspired Pasiphaë with a strange passion for him, and she became the parent of the monster, half man and half bull, which, under the name of the Minotaur, often makes its appearance in ancient fictions.

Dædalos, the most skilful artist and architect of that time, had fled to Crete, on account of a crime committed in his native city of Athens; and Minos, in compliance with an oracle, charged him with making that subterranean building, with many walks and innumerable winding passages, which is known by the name of the Cretan Labyrinth. In the middle of this Labyrinth was the abode of the Minotaur, visible only to those unfortunate victims who were thrown to the monster to be devoured, or those who had dared to enter the Labyrinth, but were unable to extricate themselves, and thus came within the reach of its terrible inmate.

In the mean while, Androgeos, a son of Minos, accompanied by many of his friends, had undertaken a voyage to Athens to participate in the celebration of the Athenian games. Having there excited the jealousy and suspicion of Ægeus, the childless king of Athens, because he had taken the prize in every combat, and gained the applause of the whole people, the promising son of Minos was basely assassinated. No sooner was his father informed of this new misfortune that had befallen him, than he went over to Athens with his whole force to avenge the murder.

He first besieged Nisa, where Nisos, brother of Ægeus, was king. Nisos, with his city, was betrayed by his own daughter, Scylla, who having an admiration for Minos, in disregard both of filial love and duty, went to her father while he was sleeping, and cut from his head a golden lock, by means of which he had been invincible. She handed this lock, the strength of her father, to Minos; but instead of gaining favor with the Cretan ruler, as she had expected, she was punished by him according to her deserts: he employed the gift to his advantage but treated the giver with scorn and contempt.

After the attack on Nisa, which city was afterwards called Megara, Minos immediately moved with his army towards Athens, which oppressed by drought and famine, was already groaning under the wrath of the gods and its distressing fate. In addition to the miseries which they suffered, it was declared by an oracle, that the immortals would not cease to send misfortunes on the city, until it should have given to Minos ample satisfaction for the murder of his son. Upon this, the Athenians sent ambassadors to the ruler of Crete, who appeared before him with humble demeanor, and supplicated peace. Minos granted peace on this hard condition;—that Athens should send annually seven of her handsomest youths, and as many of her most beautiful maidens to Crete, in order, as victims of their native land, to expiate the murder of Androgeos, by becoming the prey of the Minotaur.

When Theseus had at last killed this monster and fled with Ariadne, the daughter of the Cretan monarch, Minos, unable to avenge himself in any other manner, shut up the Athenian Dædalos, together with his son, Icaros, in the Labyrinth, the work of his own hands. The art of Dædalos, however, supplied him with the means of flying with his son out of prison, and of reaching Sicily, where he met with a friendly reception by Cocalos, king of the island.

Minos demanded that Dædalos should be delivered up to him; and having been invited by Cocalos to a personal interview, went to Sicily, where he was received by the king in a friendly manner; but in the end was secretly suffocated when bathing. Thus Minos, the wise Legislator, the valiant warrior, the benefactor of mankind, found his death in a foreign country, while pursuing the artist who was protected by the immortals. He was succeeded in his kingdom by his son Deucalion, whose son, Idomeneus led the troops of Crete to the war of Troy.

THESEUS.

Theseus, king of Athens, and son of Ægeus by Æthra, the daughter of Pittheus, monarch of Trœzen, was one of the most famous heroes of antiquity. Ægeus, who was privately married to Æthra, before leaving Trœzen, concealed his sword and sandals under a stone, and told Æthra, that if she should have a son, not to send him to Athens until he had become strong enough to raise it. She obeyed the injunction, and Theseus was educated by Connidas under the supervision of his grandfather, the wise Pittheus; and as often as the Athenians celebrated a festival in honor of Theseus, the name of Connidas was mentioned with veneration.

When Theseus was grown to the proper age, his mother led him to the stone on which he was to try his strength. Lifting it, he took from beneath his father's sword and sandals, with which he entered upon his journey to Athens.

Imitating the example of Heracles, whom the glowing soul of the young hero had embraced as his model, he chose the more dangerous way by land, where he must encounter robbers, who made the roads unsafe, and who treated all strangers who fell into their hands in the most cruel manner. As Theseus, armed with his father's good sword, was passing on his way from Trœzen, through the country of Epidauros, he first met with Periphates, a son of Hephæstos. This ferocious savage was famous for his cruelty, and trusting to his gigantic strength, laid wait for travellers with no other weapon than a club, which, how ever, was the terror of all the surrounding country. Theseus, assaulted by him, stretched him to the ground by the aid of his good sword, and ever after carried the club of his foe in remembrance of his victory.

Upon the Isthmus of Corinth he fought a still more cruel murderer, Sinis (*Evil-doer*), who was also called the *Pine-bender*. His strength was so great that he was able to take pine trees by the top, and bend them to the ground. Placing himself by the road-side, he obliged all passengers to take hold of a pine with him and bend it; he would then let go, and the tree flying up, the unhappy stranger was dashed to the ground and killed. Theseus, on being challenged, though he never before attempted such a feat, held down the tree with ease; he then conquered the monster, and obliged him to undergo the punishment that his cruelty and crimes deserved, by putting him to death in the same manner in which he had been accustomed to destroy his fellow-creatures.

Theseus likewise delivered the countries through which he passed from the monsters by which they were infested; killing, among others, the Cromyonian Swine, which, wasting the fields, and threatening destruction every where to the inhabitants, was both a plague and a terror to the land.

As he approached the borders of Megara, he came to the narrow path overhanging the sea, where the robber Sciron (from whom the pass derived its name) had fixed his abode. When any stranger came to him, it was the custom of Sciron, instead of giving water to wash the feet of his guest, to insist upon the guest's washing his feet. This ceremony was performed on the pass; and Sciron, taking advantage of the opportunity it gave him, tumbled every one into the sea, where was a huge tortoise always ready to devour the bodies of those who were thrown down. Theseus conquered Sciron, and threw him down to the tortoise.

In Eleusis, Theseus fought with the robber Cercyon, whom he vanquished and killed; and upon arriving a short distance further, at Hermione, he found the formidable Damastes, who, from the particular kind of cruelty with which he abused foreigners, was called Procrustes (*the Stretcher*). For this tyrant is said to have had two iron bedsteads, of different lengths, in which he placed all strangers who arrived within his reach; and in such a manner as to lay the short ones upon the long bedstead, and those who were of a larger stature, upon the short one. He then by force stretched the former to the extremity of the bedstead, and cut off the limbs of the latter to fit their couch of torture. Theseus, after having subdued him in a combat, subjected him to the same pain that he had inflicted upon others, and then delivered the earth from the monster.

It seems as if fiction here aimed at representing the violation of the rites of hospitality in its most heinous light; for what can be imagined more cruel and barbarous than to change the very place of repose into a rack! It was under the sacredness of hospitality, that men could first commune with each other, and contribute to their mutual civilization. To rid the earth of such as violated these sacred rites, and thereby hinder the progress of improvement among mankind, was a task worthy of the heroes, whose proper reward is, having their names immortalized as the benefactors of the world.

When Theseus arrived at Athens, he was recognized and acknowledged by Ægeus as his son and successor on the royal throne; upon which, the sons of Pallas, the brother of Ægeus, who had already flattered themselves with the hope of succeeding their childless uncle in the government of Athens, excited a revolt, which, however, was immediately quelled by Theseus.

It was then the third year that the Athenians had been obliged to send the sad tribute of fourteen of its handsomest children to the island of Crete, as an atonement for the murder of Androgeos, son of Minos; and as long as the Minotaur was alive, the Athenians dared not hope to be released from the tribute. When, therefore, the youths and maidens had drawn their lot of death, and as the destined victims for the present year were departing, in spite of the entreaties of his father to the contrary, Theseus voluntarily offered himself as one of their number, in the hope of conquering the monster.

Before his departure, he made a vow to Apollo that, if he should be successful in this undertaking, he would send annually to his temple on the island of Delos, a ship laden with offerings and presents; and, upon inquiring of the oracle what the event should be, he received for answer, that if he chose Love for his guide, it would be successful.

The ship departed as usual, under black sails, which Theseus promised his father to exchange for white in case he should return victorious. The vessel, wafted by favorable winds, soon arrived at Crete, where, when the victims were presented to Minos, the eyes of Ariadne, his royal daughter, rested upon Theseus, whose beauty and noble stature made an impression on her heart. Theseus chose Love for his guide, receiving from Ariadne the clew that made him secure of a passage out of the Labyrinth. Holding Ariadne's thread in his hand, he confidently descended into the mazes of the subterranean building, where, as soon as he had found the Minotaur, he began a desperate fight with the monster, and killed him, aided by the advice which he had received from Ariadne.

The death of the monster freed the Athenians from the horrible tribute which they had twice paid with their own children; and their sons and daughters, already destined to die a cruel death, owed their preservation to Theseus. The expression of their gratitude became a favorite subject of plastic art, in ancient as well as in modern times.

A picture, found in Herculaneum, shows the hero surrounded by tender boys, who were saved from death by his exertions, and who, in gratitude, are embracing his knees and kissing his hands.

Ariadne fled with her beloved Theseus to the island of Naxos, where, however, Theseus was forced by the will of the gods to desert her, because Bacchos, the deity of the island, was captivated by her charms. The god found her sleeping at night in the open air, and when she awoke, he, in token of his divinity, cast the golden crown which he wore upon his head towards the sky, where it immediately appeared as a splendid constellation, and bore witness to the marriage of Bacchos and Ariadne.

Before returning to Athens, Theseus sailed to the island of Delos, in order to pay his vow to Apollo. At the same time, he there consecrated to Aphrodite, in gratitude for the assistance he had received from her, a statue made by Dædalos; and to preserve the memory of his victory over the Minotaur, he instituted a dance, which imitated the windings of the Labyrinth.

The sacred vow which Theseus had made to the god of Delos, was, long after his death, fulfilled with the greatest care by the Athenians. In the very same ship in which the hero had returned from Crete, ambassadors, crowned with olive wreaths, were sent every year to Delos; and to make the vessel, as it were, everlasting, the injuries of time were carefully repaired, so that at last, although considered the same, she was an entirely different ship from that which had borne the hero. Neither was any criminal put to death while this ship was on its passage to and from Delos—a circumstance which long afterwards spared for a short time the life of Socrates. It was a law worthy of the sublime sentiments of the Athenians during their better times, that while celebrating the delivery of their children from destruction, no one should become the victim of a violent death.

From Delos, Theseus steered directly to Athens, to announce there the happy issue of his enterprise, which was yet to terminate in a tragical event. For when Ægeus, standing on a high rock near the sea-shore, and looking anxiously over the waters for the returning ship, descried at last a black sail, which the pilot had forgotten to exchange for a white one, in despair he threw himself into the sea, which after him is called the Ægean.

Theseus was received with loud applause by the Athenians, as their protector and deliverer from the most distressing tribute; and, succeeding his father on the royal throne, he availed himself of the affection of his people, and introduced a wise course of government, as well as an improved code of laws. Indeed he may be called the creator of the Athenian state, because he united the people (who, until his day, had lived scattered) in small districts, and brought them into one compact body in the city, which he divided into certain sections; he also settled the borders of the Athenian territory, by treaties with the neighboring tribes. Having succeeded in modelling the people according to his views, he instituted the religious service of *Peitho*, the goddess of persuasion.

After having accomplished his task as a royal magistrate and legislator, Theseus gave an example of magnanimity which rendered him worthy the admiration of all successive ages. Voluntarily divesting himself of the greater part of his authority, in compliance with the voice of an oracle, he endeavored to prepare Athens for becoming a republic. In honor of Poseidon, whom Fame called his father, he renewed the Athenian games; and as all Greece assembled at their celebration, he in this way promoted the intercourse and general improvement among his people.

Theseus' civic cares did not prevent him from engaging

in warlike occupations. He accompanied Heracles in his expedition against the Amazons, who then dwelt on the banks of the Thermodon; and as a reward for his distinguished services in the conflict, Heracles, after the victory, bestowed on him the hand of the vanquished queen. When the Amazons in revenge afterwards invaded the Attic territory, they again met with a signal defeat by the Athenian prince.

An amiable feature in the history of this hero, is the inseparable friendship which united him with Pirithoös, a Thessalian prince, who ruled over the Lapithæ. Their friendship, nevertheless, originated in arms. The renown of Theseus having spread widely over Greece, Pirithoös became desirous not only of beholding him, but of witnessing his exploits; he accordingly made an irruption in the plain of Marathon, and carried off the herds of the king of Athens.

On receiving the information, Theseus went to repel the plunderers. The moment Pirithoös beheld him, he was seized with secret admiration, and stretching out his hand in token of peace, exclaimed, "Be judge thyself! what satisfaction dost thou require?" "Thy friendship," replied the Athenian, and they thereupon swore eternal fidelity.

There was now no danger too great for Theseus and Pirithoös to brave; none that could separate the heroes. They were present at the Calydonian hunt, and both took part in the famous conflict between the Centaurs and Lapithæ. The cause of the contest was as follows—Pirithoös having obtained the hand of Hippodamia, daughter of Adrastos, king of Argos, the chiefs of his nation, the Lapithæ, were all invited to the wedding, as well as the Centaurs who dwelt in the neighborhood of Pelion. Theseus, Hercules, and Nestor were likewise present. Heated by wine, the Centaurs began to quarrel during the repast, and threatened to carry away Hippodamia; and would have made good their threat but for Heracles and Theseus, who valiantly assisted Pirithoös, and punished the haughty pride of the Centaurs, not only on that occasion, but afterwards also in a regular battle. This is the famous battle between the Centaurs and Lapithæ, so often a subject of poetry with the ancients, as well as of art.

Like faithful comrades, Theseus and Pirithoös aided each other in every project, and the death of Hippodamia having subsequently left Pirithoös free to form a new attachment, the two friends, equally ambitious in love, resolved each to possess a daughter of the king of the gods. Theseus fixed his thoughts on Helena, the daughter of Zeus and Leda, then a child of nine years old. The friends succeeded in their plan of carrying her off, and placing her under the care of his mother, Æthra, at Aphidnæ. Theseus then prepared to assist his friend in a bolder and more perilous attempt; for Pirithoös resolved to venture on the daring deed, of carrying away from the palace of the monarch of the under-world his queen, Proserpina, to take vengeance as it were on Pluto, for having deprived him of his wife, Hippodamia. There is a deep sense hidden in this latter fiction. The undertaking was one which inevitably involved the most imminent danger, and Theseus, faithful to his friend even unto death, descended with him

"To the seat of desolation, void of light."

They descended together to the region of shadow; but Pluto, knowing their design, seized them, and placed them upon an enchanted rock, at the gate of his realm. Here they sat, unable to move, till Heracles, passing by in his descent for Cerberos, freed Theseus; but when he would have done the same for Pirithoös, the earth quaked, and he left him. Pirithoös, therefore, remained everlastingly on the rock, as a punishment for his audacious attempt, and thus death separated the most faithful of friends.

This loss was the forerunner of many misfortunes which afterwards befel Theseus, embittering the rest of his days. It was the common lot of heroes to end their lives in a tragical manner, and from this Theseus was not exempt.

When he returned to Athens, he found the fickle and ungrateful people excited against him by his enemies, and while struggling against a public enemy, a domestic foe arose in the bosom of his family. After Antiope's death, Theseus married Phædra, a daughter of Minos, and sister of Ariadne. Conceiving a hatred against Hippolytos, Antiope's son, she preferred a false charge against him, in consequence of which he lost his life. When Phædra heard of the fate which had befallen her innocent victim, in bitter repentance she put an end to her own life; and Theseus, learning too late the innocence of his son, was well nigh driven to despair.

The invasion of Attica by Castor and Pollux, for the recovery of their sister, Helena, and an insurrection of the Pallantidæ, brought on Theseus the usual fate of all great Athenians—exile. Oppressed by misfortunes, as well as the ingratitude of his people, he banished himself from Athens, uttering before he went on board the ship that was to take him to a foreign country, the bitterest curses against the Athenians. The place where this occurred was afterwards called the place of imprecations.

He retired to the isle of Scyros, where he hoped to spend the rest of his days in quiet, but the treacherous Lycomedes, who was king of the island, feared the enemies of Theseus, and violated the sacred rites of hospitality. Under the pretext of showing his guest the island, he conducted him to the summit of a steep rock, and hurled him down unawares.

Long after his death, the Athenians built temples and altars in honor of Theseus, and revering him as a demigod, brought offerings to his altars, and instituted festivals to his memory. They also obtained his bones from the island of Scyros, and interred them beneath the soil of Attica.

CASTOR AND POLYDEUKES OR POLLUX.

Œbalus, a king of Lacedæmon, sprung from a scion of the old stem of Inachos, was the father of Tyndareos, who succeeded him in the government. Tyndareos married Leda, a daughter of Thestias, king of Ætolia.

The beauty of Leda attracted the eyes of Zeus; and, descending from his Olympian seat under the disguise of a swan, he took refuge in her lap, while Aphrodite was pursuing him in the shape of an eagle. According to the common legend, Leda produced two eggs: from the one came Pollux and Helena, children of Zeus; and from the other, Castor and Clytemnestra, children of Tyndareos. The former were immortal, the latter mortal.

Notwithstanding their different descent, Castor and Pollux were inseparable, loving one another as dear brothers and friends. Both were valiant and glowed with heroic fire, and both were skilled in every bodily exercise; with this difference only, that Castor was pre-eminent in the art of riding and managing horses, and Pollux in wrestling.

They were contemporaries of the most renowned heroes, and accompanied the Argonauts in their expedition to Colchis. On their way thither Pollux slew Amycus, a son of Poseidon, in single combat. It was also in this voyage that, in the midst of a dreadful storm, two flames were seen hovering over the heads of Castor and Pollux, whereupon the storm abated. In remembrance of this, when ever fires appeared to seamen in boisterous weather, they were called Castor and Pollux, and considered as a sure sign of health and safety. Nay, the Dioscuri (or twin sons of Zeus, under which name Castor and Pollux are generally designated) were revered above all other deities as benign beings, ever present to those who were in danger, and ready to aid them—and were addressed in every emergency, on land as well as at sea, by the prayers of such as stood in need of assistance.

After their return from the expedition to Colchis, they were informed that, during their absence, Theseus had ravished their sister, Helena, and delivered her to the care and custody of his mother, Æthra, in Aphidnæ. Castor and Pollux conquered the city, delivered their sister, and took with them the mother of Theseus as prisoner; they, however, committed no violence in the besieged city, or in the whole territory of Attica. This forbearing benignity, which attends the heroic deeds of the Dioscuri, is probably the chief reason why mortal men afterwards looked up to them with truth and confidence, as to friendly-assisting genii.

The fidelity, likewise, with which these inseparable brothers assisted each other in dangers, rendered them an object of love and veneration to mankind; and their fraternal friendship is indeed one of the most beautiful circumstances which fiction has interwoven into the records of the splendid heroic age.

When Castor and Pollux sued for the daughters of Leucippus, Phœbe and Ilaïra, each of them was obliged to win his bride by a combat with a rival—Castor with Lynceus, and Pollux with Idas, the sons of Aphareus. Castor, being mortal, was conquered and slain by Lynceus. Although Pollux avenged his brother's death on Lynceus, and fought with Idas also, until the latter was struck by a thunderbolt from Jupiter, yet he could not awaken his beloved brother from death. He then implored Jupiter either to deprive him also of life, or allow his brother to share his immortality. Jupiter gave him his choice, and Pollux descended one day to his brother, in the abode of the shades, in order to enjoy life with him on the next, under the light of the sky.

Human love and veneration often dedicated temples and altars to the Dioscuri. Imagination frequently presented them to mortals, when in imminent dangers; they then appeared in the form of two youths on white horses, arrayed in shining armor, and bearing little flames or stars upon their heads. And thus they were commonly represented in works of art, either riding side by side, or standing near together, their spears bent, the stars sparkling on their heads, and each holding a horse by the bridle. The egg-shaped caps allude to the manner of their birth.

JASON.

Jason was a shoot of the heroic stem of Æolus, but not the son of a god; and Juno, while she persecuted the sons of Jupiter, took him under her especial protection.

Æolus, Deucalion's grandson, who reigned in Thessaly, was the father of Salmoneus, Sisyphos, Athamas, and Cretheus. Salmoneus was killed by Jupiter's lightnings; Sisyphos atoned in the lower world, for the tyrannical exercise of his power while on earth; and Athamas died in a state of madness.

Tyro, a daughter of Salmoneus, became the mother of Pelias and Neleus, sons of Neptune. Afterwards marrying her father's brother, Cretheus, she gave him a son called Æson, who succeeded his father on the throne, and was the parent of Jason, the god-like hero, whose mother's name was Alcimede.

Æson was dethroned by his brother Pelias, but was not obliged to fly from the city of Iolcos, which was the seat of the Thessalian kings. Of young Jason, however, Pelias was anxious to rid himself; considering him as a member of the legitimate royal family who might become dangerous to him. The parents of the child, Æson and Alcimede, perceiving the intention of the tyrant, spread the rumor that Jason was sick, and soon after, that he had died. At the same time, he was taken by his mother to Mount Pelion, where the wise Centaur, Cheiron, well versed in every science, devoted himself to the education of the young hero, sheltering him in his lonely grotto.

When Jason had attained his growth, and manful courage began to awaken in his breast, following the advice of an oracle, he threw the skin of a panther over his shoulders, armed himself with a couple of darts, and went to the court of Pelias, at Iolcos.

Pelias had received an oracle, guarding him against a person who would one day appear before him with only one sandal, having the other foot bare. When Jason, on his way to Iolcos, was going to pass the river Anauras, Juno appeared to him in the shape of an old woman, and entreated him to carry her over the river. Jason readily complied with the request, but on going with his burden through the water, he lost one of his sandals in the mud, and thus presented himself before the palace of Pelias. On perceiving him, Pelias recollected, with consternation, the sentence of the oracle.

When the stranger was required to tell who he was, Jason demanded, before all the people, the royal crown which the usurper had received from the head of his father, Æson. "The revenues of the kingdom," added he, "thou mayest keep and enjoy, but of the supreme authority thou must divest thyself."

Pelias, being enabled, by this proposal, to penetrate the soul of the young hero, did not doubt that for the present he might avert the storm which was pending over his head.

and remove the lion, by offering as a bait, the enticing charm of an extraordinary as well as a glorious enterprise. He therefore feigned a willingness to restore the crown to its rightful possessor, or his family, provided the manes of Phrixos, another descendant of Æolus, who had found an untimely death in Colchis, were propitiated, and that golden fleece recovered which he had deposited there.

This Phrixos, who died in Colchis, was a son of Athamas, and a grandson of Æolus. Athamas, king of Bœotia, had, by his first wife, Nephele, two children, Phrixos and Helle; but after Nephele's death, Athamas married Ino, a daughter of Cadmos, who persecuted these two children, and even resolved to deprive them of life. The shade of Nephele then appeared to her children, apprising them of the danger they were in of becoming the victims of Ino's hatred, unless they would seek safety in distant flight; and, for this purpose, a ram with a golden fleece stood ready, which, at the command of the gods, would bear them on his back over the land and through the sea.

Phrixos and Helle mounted the ram, which carried them towards the east to the distant country of Colchis, where Æetes reigned, whose father was the sun. But they were not both destined to reach that country; for, on their journey, Helle fell from the back of the animal into the sea, between Sigeon and the Chersonese, and was drowned. This sea was named from her Hellespontos (*Helle's Sea*), and still retains its name. Her brother Phrixos arrived safely in Colchis, where he sacrificed to Zeus Phyxios the ram which had borne him thither, and, as a holy token, suspended the skin, or golden fleece, in a grove sacred to Ares. He then married the daughter of Æetes, but soon died in a foreign land.

The report of the golden fleece which had spread over the earth, had for a long time excited the desire of every one who wished to obtain something particularly excellent

It was in the distant east, what the golden apples of the Hesperides were in the west—a treasure worthy of the greatest toils, pains, and perils. The image of the ram, and its richly covered skin generally implies, with the ancients, the idea of wealth; and this probably gave rise to the fiction of the golden fleece, involving the ideas of riches and treasures, as well as the means of gaining them.

The miraculous which was intermingled with the tales of the golden fleece, and the adventures that were connected with an expedition to a far distant land, were most alluring calls on the heroes of yore, for a trial of courage, as well as of fortune. No sooner did the words of Pelias touch the ear of Jason, than his ardor was excited to perform the glorious deed; and, pledging his word to bring the treasure, or never to return, he invited the most renowned heroes of Greece to embark with him in the bold adventure.

For making the voyage to Colchis, a ship was built of pines cut from Mount Pelion, which, although larger than any other previously constructed, moved lightly and easily, and was therefore called the Argo (*swift-sailing*). From her name, those who embarked in her were called Argonauts.

The mast of the Argo was taken from the forest of Dodona, where the oaks were endowed with the power of making predictions; therefore, the ship was regarded as an animated being, in concord with Fate, to which a man might commit himself with confidence. Among the number of heroes who accompanied Jason, the following names are most conspicuous: Heracles, the son of Zeus; Castor and Pollux, the Dioscuri; Calais and Zetes, sons of Boreas; Peleus, the father of Achilleus; Admetos, the husband of Alceste; Neleus, the father of Nestor; Meleagros, the Calydonian; Orpheus, the divine bard of Thrace; Telamon, the father of Ajax; Menœtius, the father of Patroclos;

Lynceus, the son of Aphareus; Theseus, the Athenian, and his friend Pirithoös, the Lapithæan.

The fathers of the most renowned heroes who shone in the Trojan war, were still in youthful vigor at the time of the voyage to Colchis. A race of heroes, they advance with their united force to recover a precious treasure; afterwards, a second race unites to avenge the robbery of beauty by the destruction of Troy.

When the heroes were all assembled, fifty in number, the auguries being favorable, Jason, standing at the poop, poured a libation from a golden cup, and called on Zeus, the Winds, the Sea, the Days, the Nights, and the Fate presiding over their return. Thunder then rolled in the clouds, lightnings flashed through the sky; Orpheus struck his lyre in concert with his voice, and the joyful heroes, each grasping an oar, kept time to his harmony. The gods looked down from the sky, the nymphs of Pelion gazed in wonder at this first of ships, and Cheiron, leaving his mountain cave, cheered them, and prayed for their happy return. The piercing eye of Lynceus penetrated the most distant regions, and the experienced pilot, Tiphys, managed the helm with skilful hands. For a time all things went on successfully; when suddenly a dreadful storm befel the adventurers, and forced them to seek refuge in the harbor of Lemnos.

It is a remarkable circumstance, that while the heroes were struggling against the raging elements, several of them made a vow to consecrate themselves, by becoming initiated in the Samothracian mysteries; just as Heracles, when about to engage in the most dangerous enterprise, was first initiated into those of Eleusis.

At Lemnos, a greater danger threatened the Argonauts than that caused by the storm which drove them thither; for the charms of the Lemnian women kept the heroes in bonds, protracting, for some time, the progress of their voyage to Colchis.

Not long before the arrival of the Argonauts at Lemnos, the female inhabitants had murdered all the males of the island, except king Thoas, who was secreted by his daughter Hypsipyle. The anger of Venus, whom the Lemnian women had not sufficiently honored, was the occasion of this atrocious deed. For the goddess infused into the men of Lemnos, who were at that time warring against the Thracians, an invincible dislike to their wives, and, at the same time, a preference for the female slaves who had become their prisoners in the Thracian war. Such an insult the women of Lemnos could not bear; they conspired, rose in one night upon their sleeping husbands, fathers, and brothers, and murdered them all. Those who conducted the war in Thrace were saved by their absence.

When the Argonauts were landing at Lemnos, they were at first opposed by the women, who mistook them for the Lemnians returning from Thrace to avenge the death of their fellow-citizens. But as soon as they perceived their error, they received the strangers with hospitality, who remained on the island two years.

From Lemnos the heroes sailed to Samothrace, where they were inspired with new courage by their initiation into the mysteries. On landing near Troas, they were abandoned by Heracles, who with Telamon went into the country in search of Hylas. In the city of Cyzicus, on the descent of Mount Dindymus, where the Argonauts next landed, they were hospitably received by the king, who bore the same name as his city, and who dismissed them with presents. But the night after their departure, when the ship was forced back into the harbor by a storm, king Cyzicus mistook the heroes for enemies and attacked them in a hostile manner. In this fight, Jason had the misfortune to kill his kind and friendly host. To atone for this deed, although unintentional, he brought offerings on Mount Dindymus to the mother of the gods, and built a temple there to her honor. The Argonauts then proceeded on their course, and steering always towards the east, arrived in Bebrycia, where the royal crown was worn by Amycus, who challenged every stranger to fight him with clubs, and who was at last vanquished and slain in a combat with Pollux.

On their further course, the bold navigators were driven near the coast of Thrace by a storm, and compelled to enter the harbor of Salmydessus, where the prophesying Phineus reigned, whom the immortals had punished with blindness. To complete his misery, he was perpetually vexed by the daughters of Thaumas, the direful Harpies. Phineus had delivered up his two sons, the children of his first wife, a daughter of Boreas, to the hatred of their stepmother, Idaea, and at her calumnious instigation, had even deprived them of sight;—a crime which he was obliged to expiate by his own blindness, while the Harpies, those ghastly birds of prey, with maiden faces, seized upon his food, or ruined and defiled whatever he was about to partake. Phineus was deprived of the external light, but with his mental vision anticipated the future, and gave to the Argonauts prudent advice concerning their further voyage; and also furnished them with a guide to lead them through the Cyanean rocks, or Symplegades, the dangerous passage of which now awaited the bold navigators. Grateful for these services, the winged sons of Boreas, Calaïs and Zetes, by their swords affrighted the Harpies from Phineus' table, pursuing them as far as the Strophades, where, at the command of the gods, they stopped their pursuit, and returned to their companions. From this return, those islands derived their name.

The Cyaneæ, or Symplegades, through which the Argonauts were obliged to sail, were two immense rocks, im mediately opposite each other, at the entrance into the Black Sea; and which seemed, according to the different directions in which they were approached, to open and then again to close. This phenomenon gave rise to the ancient fiction, that the rocks really opened and closed like a pair of scissors, crushing every thing that happened to pass between them as they were moving together. Quite natural, therefore, is the subsequent fiction, after the Argonauts had successfully ventured on the passage, and the optical illusion was thus discovered, that Neptune had made the rocks immovable.

After having safely passed the Symplegades, the heroes next landed in the territory of Lycus, who, being by birth a Greek, gladly received the strangers from his native land. Here the pilot Tiphys died, and his place was succeeded by Ancæus; and the sacred Argo, after having long sustained the beating of the briny flood, and experienced many a storm, was at last happily conducted into the longed-for harbor of Colchis. It was here, however, that the greatest danger awaited Jason, the leader of the expedition; a danger which could hardly be avoided without divine assistance. King Æetes received the strangers, not in a hostile or even unfriendly manner; but he prescribed to Jason, who demanded the restitution of the golden fleece, such conditions as he thought could not be complied with; for to the dangers which he had planned, the most undaunted hero must necessarily succumb.

In order to gain the golden fleece, Jason was, in the first place, to put two fire-exhaling bulls, sacred to Hephæstos, to an adamantine ploughshare, and to break up with them four acres of land, sacred to Ares, and which had never before been ploughed. Then he was to sow the dragon-teeth of Cadmos, which yet remained in the possession of Æetes, in the newly-ploughed furrows, and the armed warriors who would immediately arise from the dreadful seed, he must kill to the last man. This done, he was at last to fight with, and conquer the dragon that guarded the golden fleece.

Medeia, a daughter of Æetes, skilled in charms and witchcraft, had scarcely beheld Jason, when, through the influence and disposal of the gods, a tender affection for the hero was raised in her bosom, which soon kindled to a flame of the most violent passion.

Jason went to the temple of Hecate to supplicate the mighty goddess, where he was met by Medeia She disclosed her love to him, at the same time promising her assistance in the dangers which threatened him, and her powerful help in accomplishing his glorious undertaking, provided he would swear fidelity to her. Jason complied, and Medeia, reciprocating the oath, rendered the hero invincible by means of her magical incantations. She gave him a stone which he was to cast among the warriors, that would spring up from the dragon-teeth, and also herbs, and a potion for lulling to sleep the dragon that guarded the golden fleece.

On the following day, Jason, surrounded by his companions, appeared on the field of Ares in the presence of the king and a multitude of people ; the fire-breathing bulls were about to be set free, and the hearts of the assembled multitude were chilled with awe and expectation ; a deadly silence reigned, and all eyes were anxiously turned upon the hero, who alone quietly expected his fire-vomiting foes. Fierce and snorting, the bulls rushed upon him ; but tho powerful charm with which Medeia had armed him, suddenly made them tame and obedient ; without resistance they bent their necks under the yoke, suffering Jason to put them to the plough, and quietly made the furrows into which he sowed the dragon-teeth. No sooner were they scattered, than a harvest of armed warriors sprang from the ground, all of them turning their swords against Jason.

The hero then following the directions received by Medeia, flung the enchanted pebble, which she had given him for that purpose, into the midst of the thronged crowd of his enemies; this stone had the power of troubling their senses as well as hardening their hearts, causing them to rise furiously against one another, until the ground from which they had just sprung, was covered with their slain bodies.

Before the king and people could recover from the amazement into which this spectacle had thrown them, Jason was already hastening towards the grim guardian of the fleece, to lull him to sleep. He succeeded, and afterwards killed the monster, and triumphantly held in his hand the golden fleece. The conqueror then returned with his companions to the ship; and Medeia, leaving in nightly silence the house of her father, followed her lover, and went on board the Argo, which immediately set sail.

Æetes, soon roused by the discovered flight of his daughter, went himself with his ships in pursuit of the swift-sailing Argo. Near the mouth of the Danube, Medeia descried the sails of her father, and to save herself as well as her lover from the impending danger, she adopted a measure both cruel and desperate. She had taken her little brother Absyrtus, as a kind of hostage, and in the present emergency, seeing no other means of safety, she killed, and cut him in pieces, planting his head and hands upon a high rock, and scattering the rest of his members upon the shore, with the view of retarding her father's pursuit, or of inducing him to desist from it altogether. In order to mark this horrible deed in all times to come, several small islands in that region were afterwards called Absyrtides.

Medeia's expectation was realized. Her father, first retarded by collecting together the remains of his unfortunate son, afterwards desisted entirely from pursuit, and the Argonauts quietly proceeded on their voyage. Having received advice from Phineus not to return to their native land by the same course which they had pursued in coming to Colchis, they sailed up the Danube; "and when they could ascend the river no farther, the strong heroes," says the fiction, " took up their lightly-built vessel on their shoulders, carrying her for the space of four miles over hills and dales, as far as the Adriatic gulf." But here, when they were about to embark again, the following oracle was heard to issue from the mast of the Argo: " You are not destined to reach your home until Jason and Medeia are absolved from the murder of Absyrtus, after having atoned for their crime by a penalty imposed on them."

With a view to this atonement, the Argonauts entered the port of Ææa, the abode of Circe, a daughter of the sun, and sister of Æetes. She, however, refused to absolve Jason and Medeia, by presenting the usual offerings to the offended immortals, and by imposing a penalty on the criminals; but announced to them, that they could not blot out their guilt until they had reached the promontory of Malea.

Thence the bold navigators steered towards the dangerous straits of Scylla and Charybdis, which they passed under the guidance of Hera. By the persuasion of Orpheus, they escaped the danger which threatened them from the Sirens, and happily reached the island of the Phæacians, where, however, they met with an unexpected enemy. After the funeral obsequies of Absyrtus had been properly celebrated, the Colchian fleet, which had desisted from its pursuit at the mouth of the Danube, took another way to intercept the fugitives; and here, at the island of the Phæacians, it was stationed to watch for them. The anger of the Colchians against Medeia, as well as the Argonauts, having in the mean time somewhat abated, they demanded no other restitution than the person of Medeia, provided she had not yet been married to Jason. She had not yet been made the wife of Jason, but the king of the Phæacians immediately procured a private celebration of the matrimonial rites, announcing to the Colchians, on the following day, that his guests, Jason and Medeia, were lawfully married; whereupon the former, satisfied with the answer, spread their sails to the wind and steered for Colchis.

The Argonauts, after having taken leave of their friendly host, the king of the Phæacians, endeavored to reach the promontory of Malea, when suddenly a storm cast them on the Libyan Syrtes, where the vessel would have been lost but for the appearance of a Triton, who, for the reward of a precious tripod which Jason carried with him in the ship, promised the heroes to show them the only course by which they could escape. After having received the tripod, at the sight of which he was highly delighted, the Triton kept his word, and conducted the Argo in safety out of the surrounding Syrtes. Moreover, he presented Euphemos, one of the Argonauts, with a clod of earth, as a pledge that his descendants should reign in Libya. This pledge was afterwards redeemed.

Argo at last reached the longed-for promontory of Malea, where Jason and Medeia, after having brought rich offerings to the immortal gods, obtained absolution of their crime committed against Absyrtus. They were now, according to the oracle which they had received from the oak of Dodona, as well as the promise of Circe, permitted to expect soon to reach their native port. And, indeed, without meeting any farther accidents, the Argonauts soon after entered the harbor of Iolcos. The good ship Argo was devoted by Jason to Poseidon, on the isthmus of Corinth, from whence fiction afterwards transported her to the vaults of the sky, where she shines as a glittering constellation.

The golden fleece was now gained; but the purpose for

which alone Jason had exposed himself, as well as his friends, to every imaginable danger, was frustrated; his father, Æson, having in the mean while become a decrepid, childish old man, unable to reign, or to enjoy the glorious feats of his son.

The first request, therefore, which Jason made to Medeia, was, to use her magic powers to renew, if possible, the mental as well as physical abilities of his father. Medeia, complying with her husband's request, infused a new juice of life, prepared of secret herbs, into the veins of the old man, so as to make him sensible of the return of his gay youth and the renewed strength of life. The daughters of Pelias deprived their father of life in imitating the work of Medeia, so that Æson now reigned undisturbed, sole king of Iolcos.

Jason, with Medeia, then went to Corinth, formerly called Ephyra, where Æetes had reigned before going to the fertile Colchis. Medeia took possession of the government for her husband, and they lived there quietly during ten years. Behind this calm of peaceful life, however, a dreadful storm was lurking, which threatened Jason with a tragical fate, as was the case also with Heracles, Perseus and Bellerophontes.

Weary of Medeia, whom he always seems to have secretly despised, he was about to marry Creon's royal daughter, unmindful of the revenge of despised jealousy or disregarded faith. Medeia feigned patience and mildness, enduring with apparent resignation what she could not prevent; she even sent to the bride a costly wedding garment. But scarcely had the latter made use of the dangerous present, than she suddenly felt a consuming fire raging through her body, which produced an agonizing death. Medeia, giving full scope to revenge, rained fire upon Creon's palace, which consumed the king himself, murdered her two children, and then hastened through the air in her chariot drawn by two dragons, leaving Jason to grief and despair, which embittered the remainder of his days.

MELEAGROS OR MELEAGER.

Œneus, who reigned in Calydon, was the father of renowned children; of Deianeira, the wife of Heracles; of Meleagros and Tydeus, whose valorous son, Diomedes, engaged with the gods themselves in dangerous combat during the siege of Troy. Œneus had the misfortune to draw the wrath of Artemis upon himself as well as his country, by having forgotten her divine personage, while he brought thank-offerings to all the other deities, for the thriving growth of the fruits of the field.

To punish him and his subjects for this offence, the goddess of the forest sent a monstrous boar into the Calydonian land, which wasted the fields, and threatened death and ruin to the inhabitants of the surrounding country. Œneus, anxious to subdue this monster, desired the assistance of the strongest, both in his own territories and those beyond them. Thus the chase of Diana's Boar again united the flower of the Greek heroes.

To hunt the Calydonian Boar, some of those heroes again assembled who had shared the dangers of the voyage to Colchis. The most renowned of the Argonauts who assisted Meleagros in this hunt, were Jason, Castor and Pollux, Idas and Lynceus, Peleus, Telamon, Admetos, Pirithoös, and Theseus. To this noble troop, the brothers of Althæa, the wife of Œneus, and daughter of Thestius, who reigned in Pleuron, and Atalanta, the daughter of Schœneus, associated themselves. Atalanta, like Diana, had devoted herself to a state of virginity, and, like her, was a lover of the chase.

Atalanta first wounded the boar with her arrow; Meleager then cut off the head of the monster, and presented it to her as the deserved price of victory. The brothers of Althæa were offended by this preference given to a woman, and disputing the prize, took it from Atalanta. Diana setting no bounds to her wrath, kindled the spark of anger between Meleager and the sons of Thestius into a flame, that burst out in a bloody fight, and gave to the Calydonian chase a tragical termination.

Meleager, in the fray, killed the two brothers of his mother, who, beholding the bodies of the slain, swore to avenge their death, even on her own son. An easy, too easy means of vengeance was in her power; for on the birthday of Meleager, the Fates had placed a piece of wood on the hearth near the fire, with the hint that Althæa's newborn son should live as long as that piece of wood remained unconsumed. Althæa had preserved the fatal billet as a precious treasure, until the moment when she was provoked to anger by the death of her brothers. Then, seizing it in her passion, she threw it into the blazing fire. As it was gradually consuming to ashes, Meleager felt his body withering away, and the marrow of his bones drying up, until he died in convulsive agony. Scarcely had Althæa heard the cruel result of what she had done, than repenting the deed, she put a period to her own life.

CADMOS.

Poseidon, says the legend, was by Libya the father of two sons, Belos and Agenor; the former reigned in Egypt, and the latter, having gone to Europe, married Telephassa, by whom he had three sons, Cadmos, Phœnix, and Cilix, and one daughter, Europa. Zeus, becoming enamored of Europa, carried her away to Crete; and Agenor, grieved for the loss of his only daughter, ordered his sons to go in search of her, and not to return until they had found her. They went, accompanied by their mother, and by Thasos, a son of Poseidon. Their long search was to no purpose, for they could obtain no intelligence of their sister; and fearing the indignation of their father if they returned without her, they resolved to settle themselves in various countries. Phœnix therefore established himself in Phœnicia, and Cilix in Cilicia; Cadmos and his mother went to Thrace, where Thasos founded a town, calling it after himself.

After the death of his mother, Cadmos went to Delphi for the purpose of consulting the oracle about Europa. The answer was, to cease from troubling himself about her, but to follow a cow as his guide, and to build a city where she should lie down. On leaving the temple, he went through Phocis, and meeting a cow belonging to the herds of Pelagon, he followed her through Bœotia till she came to where Thebes now stands, where she laid herself down. Wishing to sacrifice her to Athena, Cadmos sent his companions to the fount of Ares for water; but the serpent that guarded the fount killed a greater part of them. Cadmos then fought the serpent and destroyed it; by the direction of Athena he sowed its teeth, and immediately a crop of armed men sprang up, who slew each other, either quarrelling or through ignorance; for it is said that when Cadmos saw them rising, he flung stones at them; and thinking it was done by some one of their number, they fell upon and slew each other. Five only survived; and they joined with Cadmos to build the city of Thebes.

For killing the sacred serpent, Cadmos was obliged to spend a year in servitude to Ares. At the expiration of that period, Athena herself prepared a palace for him, and Zeus gave him Harmonia, the daughter of Ares and Aphrodite. All the gods assembled in Cadmeia, the palace of Cadmos, to celebrate the marriage. The bridegroom presented his bride with a magnificent robe, and a collar, the work of Hephæstos, and said to be the gift of the divine artist himself.

Cadmos endeavored to civilize the people whom he had

gathered around him, and to whom he is said first to have communicated letters, brought by him from Phœnicia. The date given for the settlement of this colony is B. C. 1550.

The offspring of Cadmos and Harmonia, who is sometimes called Harmione, were Ino, Agaüe, Autonoë, Semele, and a son named Polydoros. All these children were persecuted by an inimical fate, or the hatred of Hera, which rested upon their father's house. Semele, the mother of Bacchos, was consumed by Zeus' lightnings. Agaüe married Echion, one of those five warriors who had arisen from the dragon teeth. She became the mother of Pentheus, who opposed the worship of Bacchos, and was torn in pieces by his own mother, and the other votaries of the god. Ino was persecuted by the wrath of Hera, because she had taken care of young Bacchos. She was married to Athamas, who, seized by a sudden fury, dashed their first son, Zearchus, against a rock, and then pursued the hapless mother, who fled with her younger son, Melicertes, to the very verge of a rock on the shore. Ino, with her son in her arms, flung herself down, and both were henceforth numbered among the deities of the sea; Ino under the name of Leucothea, and Melicertes under that of Palæmon. Both were worshipped as benign beings, who assist seafaring people in the dangers of their element. Autonoë, the fourth daughter of Cadmos, married Aristæos, son of Apollo and king of Arcadia. He was said first to have taught man how to manage bees and raise honey, as well as to use the milk of animals. Autonoë became the mother of Actæon, who was punished for the crime of beholding Diana when bathing.

After the various misfortunes which befel their children, Thebes became odious to Cadmos and his wife, and they migrated to the country of the Enchelians; who, being harassed by the incursions of the Illyrians, were told by the oracle, that if they made Cadmos and Harmonia their leaders, they would be successful. They obeyed the god, and the prediction was verified. Cadmos became king of the Illyrians, and had a son named Illyrios.

Cadmos lived with Harmonia to his latest years; and in order to ascribe to them a kind of immortality, fiction suffers them at last to be transformed into serpents, and sent by Zeus to the Elysian Plain; or, as some say, they were conveyed thither in a chariot drawn by serpents.

When Cadmos left Thebes, he placed his son Polydoros upon the throne. Labdacos, the son of Polydoros, married Nicteis, the daughter of Nycteus, and became the father of Laïos. At the time of his father's death, Laïos was a minor, and therefore his uncle Lycos reigned in his place over Thebes.

Antiopë, another daughter of Nycteus, beloved by Zeus, and rejected by her father, fled to Epopeus, king of Sicyon, who married her. But Lycos, having given to the dying Nycteus a solemn promise to avenge him on his daughter, killed Epopeus, and carried Antiopë prisoner to Thebes, where he prepared for her the most cruel treatment, by committing her to his wife, Dirce.

Antiopë had borne Jupiter two sons, Amphion and Zethos, who were brought up secretly. As soon as she found means to escape, she hastened to her sons, bidding them avenge the injury of their mother. Amphion and Zethos immediately invaded Thebes, slew Lycos, expelled Laïos, and fastened Dirce, by whom their mother had been so cruelly treated, to the horns of a wild bull, thus devoting her to a painful death.

Amphion then built the walls of Thebes, with their seven gates; and the persuasive eloquence with which he prevailed on the rude inhabitants to assist him in this undertaking, has been veiled by fiction in the fable, that he moved the stones by the notes of his lyre, so that they vol untarily united, and formed themselves into walls and turrets.

After the death of Amphion and Zethos, the Thebans invited the expelled Laïos to take charge of the government, which belonged to him by hereditary right. He returned and married Jocasta, a Theban princess.

ŒDIPUS.

It had been predicted to Laïos that he should have a son who would be the murderer of his father. Therefore, when Jocasta became the mother of a son, Laïos ordered the child to be exposed in a wild desert. The servant who was intrusted with this commission, perforated the ankles of the child, in order to recognize it, if it should ever appear. In this condition it was found by Phorbas, the overseer of the herds of king Polybos, who reigned in Corinth. The latter, to whom Phorbas delivered the hapless infant, adopted it, and from its swollen feet, gave it the name of Œdipus.

The foster-parents of Œdipus kept his descent carefully concealed from him, so that until he approached to manhood, he believed them to be his real parents. But some doubts having been raised in his mind as to his birth, he resolved to inquire at the oracle of Apollo. The oracle, leaving the question of his descent untouched, confined itself to the warning never to return to his native country, because he would there slay his own father, and marry his own mother.

To escape a fate so horrible, Œdipus voluntarily banished himself from Corinth, which he supposed to be his native land, and took his way towards Thebes. Thus went the hapless youth directly to meet that doom of fate which he intended to avoid. For on his journey he encountered his father, Laïos, in a narrow pass, accompanied only by his herald, Polyphontes. Œdipus was ordered to give way; and upon his refusal, the herald killed one of his horses, which so exasperated him, that he slew the king and Polyphontes. He was unconscious of having killed his own father, but he thus made true a part of the oracle which he had received at Delphi.

Upon his arrival at Thebes, Œdipus found the Sphinx in its vicinity; a monster in the shape of a lion, with the head of a maiden, the progeny of Echidna, and sent by Juno to terrify the inhabitants of the city and surrounding country. The monster, lying on a steep rock, proposed this riddle to all who passed by: "What animal is it that goes in the morning upon four feet, at noon upon two, and in the evening upon three?" Every one who was unable to interpret this riddle, was hurled into the abyss by the Sphinx, and hundreds had already perished in this way ere Œdipus arrived. He came and explained the riddle. "Man," said he, "as a child, in the morning of life, creeps upon hands and feet; at the noon-tide of life, when strength dwells in his members, he goes upright on two feet; and in the evening, when old age has stolen upon him, he needs a staff for his support, and goes, as it were, upon three feet."

Œdipus had scarcely spoken the last words, when the Sphinx flung herself down from the rock; or, according to another fiction, she was killed by Œdipus.

Laïos was dead, and in order to get rid of the monster that desolated the country, the Thebans had promised his widow, together with the throne of Thebes, to the man who should be able to unriddle the enigma of the Sphinx. To Œdipus this apparent fortune, envied by many, was destined, and thus was the second part of the oracle fulfilled without mercy; for in taking Jocasta, the queen of Thebes, for his wife, he ignorantly married his mother, after having slain his father. His hard and unfriendly fate, having drawn a veil over all these horrors, granted him yet for a short time the enjoyment of life. Œdipus and Jocasta had two sons, Eteocles and Polyneices, and two daughters, Antigone and Ismene; their wretched father being as ignorant of his own fate, as of the future destiny of his children.

Yet the days of this happy ignorance drew to an end. A wasting pestilence spread itself over Thebes. Œdipus himself proposed to ask the oracle whether any man had drawn down the wrath of the gods by secret crimes, and whether the whole land was suffering for the misdeeds of an individual. His advice was followed, and the dreadful sentence fell upon himself. He determined not to cease investigating until he should succeed in bringing the truth to light, or in setting the calumny to rest; but with every inquiry, the horrible story developed itself with additional evidence.

When, at length, every doubt had vanished, and Œdipus, with dreadful certainty, had found himself guilty of the worst crimes, no longer able to bear the light of day, he blinded himself. Thus deprived of his eyes, he wandered until death in foreign lands, led by the hand of his daughter, Antigone. The unfortunate Jocasta strangled herself.

Eteocles and Polyneices succeeded their father in the government, with this arrangement: that each of them should enjoy, by turns, the supreme power, every other year. But neither could they escape that hostile destiny which hung over Thebes, and the house of Cadmos.

ETEOCLES AND POLYNEICES.

These two brothers became victims of their own discord, arising from envy, and the desire of despotic power Eteocles first entered upon the government; but when his year had expired, he refused to cede the royal authority to Polyneices for the succeeding year.

Upon this, Polyneices left Thebes, retiring to Adrastos, the ruler of Argos, who kindly received him, gave him his daughter in marriage, and promised to defend his claim to the Theban throne to the utmost of his ability. Tydeus also, the son of Œneus, and brother to Meleager, came at that time as a fugitive to Adrastos, and to him the king of Argos married his second daughter.

The first step taken by Adrastos, in order to secure for his son-in-law the portion of authority that was due to him in Thebes, was to send Tydeus to Eteocles, that he might prevail on the usurper to share with his brother the throne of their common father. But before he could reach Thebes, Tydeus was treacherously attacked by armed men, who, at the command of Eteocles, lay in wait for him; and he returned to Argos, after narrowly escaping with his life. Upon relating this treachery, Adrastos immediately prepared war against Eteocles.

THE THEBAN WAR.

Adrastos and his two sons-in-law, Tydeus and Polyneices, united in the expedition against Thebes, in which several other heroes were eager to share with them the danger and the glory. The valiant Capaneus of Messene joined them, and Hippomedon, a son of Adrastos' sister; also Parthenopæos, a handsome and brave youth from Arcadia, the son of Melanion and Atalanta.

Amphiaraös, the husband of Eriphyle, sister of Adrastos, could not, for a long time, be prevailed upon to take part in the enterprise, because, anticipating the future, his mind foreboded not only the misfortune that awaited the besiegers of Thebes, but also his own inevitable death. He therefore retired to a private place, where he concealed himself from Adrastos and Polyneices, until his wife, bribed by the latter with a costly necklace, discovered his hiding-place, and thus Amphiaraös was obliged to embark in the enterprise against his will.

The leaders in this expedition were seven in number:

Adrastos, Polyneices, Tydeus, Amphiaraös, Capaneus, Parthenopæos, and Hippomedon.

On their way to Thebes they met with an accident, which involved unfavorable auspices. Hypsipyle, whose name has already been mentioned in the history of the Argonauts, was compelled, after the departure of Jason and his companions from Lemnos, to leave her home, because she had spared the life of her father, Thoas. At the sea-shore, whither she had fled and where she was wandering, she fell into the hands of pirates, who sold her as a slave to Lycurgos, king of Nemea, and there she was employed as nurse to the king's infant son, Opheltes.

At that time the seven heroes, with their army, were passing through the dominions of Lycurgos, and found the royal daughter of Thoas with her little nursling in a wood. Hastening to point out a fountain to the Greeks, who were suffering from thirst, she left the little Opheltes alone on the turf; she returned again to the child, who, in the mean time, had been killed by a snake. The Greeks were confounded at this accident, but celebrated the funeral of the child in a splendid manner, and, under the name of Archemorus, instituted sacred games in his honor, which were afterwards periodically repeated at Nemea.

Having completed these funeral rites, the heroes proceeded on their way, and arrived under the walls of Thebes. Here the seven leaders distributed their army around the seven gates, so that one was to be blocked by each of the heroes with his troop, and thus take the city, if possible, by a regular siege.

To oppose each of the leaders in the army of Adrastos, Eteocles placed within the walls one whom he regarded as his equal: against Tydeus, Melanippus; against Capaneus, Polyphontes; against Hippomedon, Hyperbius; Actor against Parthenopæos; Lasthenes against Amphiaraös; and stationed himself against his brother, Polyneices

If the besiegers were animated by their just cause, by hatred against the usurper, Eteocles, and by confidence in their superior power, the besieged, on the other hand, were urged to the most desperate struggle by a still more powerful motive—the fear of hunger. They made a furious sally, and a battle ensued equally fatal to both parties. Hippomedon and Parthenopæos fell under the swords of the enemy; Capaneus, who had mounted the walls, was killed by a flash of lightning; Tydeus fell under the hand of Melanippus; Eteocles and Polyneices, the two unnatural brothers, killed each other in single combat; Amphiaraös was swallowed up by the earth; and Adrastos owed his life only to the swiftness of his good steed, Arion, whose sire was the ruler of the waves.

The sovereignty of Thebes now devolved on Creon, the brother of Jocasta. He ordered the corpse of Eteocles to be buried with the usual rites and due honors; but commanded, on pain of death, that the bodies of Polyneices and his fallen friends should remain unburied, a prey to the fowls of the air.

Antigone, the faithful daughter of Œdipus, prompted by her sisterly love, notwithstanding the interdict of Creon and the danger to which she exposed her life, stole out of the city in a moonlight night, and with her own hands covered the body of her brother with sand.

Her disobedience to the command of the tyrant was discovered, and she was condemned to die by being buried alive; but she prevented a public execution and a cruel death by strangling herself.

Hæmon, Creon's son, who had tenderly loved this victim of his father's cruelty, upon finding Antigone dead in her prison, plunged his sword in his breast; neither did Hæmon's mother survive the loss of her beloved son. Thus stood Creon, bereft of all who had been related to him by the sacred ties of nature, accusing his destiny.

In the mean time, Adrastos had solicited the assistance of Theseus, who conquered Thebes, and forced the inhabitants to surrender all the slain bodies that belonged to the army of Adrastos, in order to their interment with solemn funeral rites.

The misfortunes attending this war were insufficient to extinguish the enmity that subsisted among the sons of the fallen heroes. Ten years after, it burst forth in a new war, which, from its being carried on by the descendants of the former leaders, was called the war of the Epigones.

Creon was succeeded on the throne of Thebes by Laodamas, a son of Eteocles. Thersander, the son of Polyneices, assisted by the sons of those heroes who were slain in the former war, together with Ægialeus, the son of Adrastos, undertook a new expedition against Thebes, conquered Laodamas, and seized upon the royal authority, of which his father Polyneices had been unjustly deprived. Laodamas fled to Illyria, which had formerly been also the asylum of Cadmos. In the first Theban war, Adrastos was the only one of the leaders who escaped; in the second, his son, Ægialeus, was the only one who fell.

THE PELOPIDÆ.

Pelops, a son of that Tantalos, who, after having been raised by the gods even to their own assembly, was hurled down by them into the depths of Tartaros, came from Phrygia to Œnomaos, king of Pisa, by whom he was hospitably received. Struck by the charms of the beautiful Hippodameia, the king's daughter, Pelops requested her from her father as his wife. But it had been predicted to Œnomaos that his son-in-law would deprive him of life; and he therefore proposed to every suitor for his daughter to contend with him in the chariot race, putting to death all whom he overtook in the course. The race was from the banks of the Cladios in Elis to the altar of Poseidon, at the isthmus, and was run in the following manner: Œnomaos, placing his daughter in the chariot with the suitor, gave him the start; he then followed with a spear in his hand, with which, on overtaking the suitor, he ran him through. Thirteen had already lost their lives when Pelops appeared.

"In the dead of night," says Pindar, "Pelops went down to the margin of the sea, and invoked the god who rules it. Suddenly Poseidon stood at his feet; and he conjured him by the memory of his affection, to grant him the means of obtaining the lovely daughter of Œnomaos, declaring, that even if he should fail in the attempt, he regarded fame beyond inglorious old age. Poseidon, assenting to his prayer, gave him a golden chariot, and horses of winged speed."

Pelops then went to Pisa, and by alluring promises prevailed on Myrtiles, the charioteer of Œnomaos, to adjust the king's chariot in such a manner that it would break down in the middle of the course. The king was thrown out and lost his life, when Hippodameia became the bride of Pelops. To celebrate the wedding, Poseidon assembled the Nereïdes upon the strand of the sea, and raised a bridal chamber of the waves, which arched in bright curves over the marriage bed.

After his marriage with Hippodameia, Pelops, unwilling to fulfil his promise to Myrtilos for the aid he had given him, threw him unawares from a rock into the sea, which from him derived the name of Myrtœan. One misfortune after another followed this act of injustice and cruelty, although the power of Pelops increased to such a degree, that the whole Peninsula of Greece was called after him Peloponnesus.

Hippodameia had two sons, Atreus and Thyestes, who became jealous of their father's affection for their step-bro ther, Chrysippos, and put him to death. Pelops supposed Hippodameia to have instigated this murder, and upon being charged with it, she destroyed herself, and her two sons fled from the wrath of their father.

Atreus went to Eurystheus, king of Mycenæ, who received him kindly, and gave him his daughter Aëropé in marriage. After the death of Eurystheus, Atreus mounted the throne of Mycenæ.

Thyestes followed Atreus, and shared his brother's good fortune; but soon brought reproach and misfortune upon himself by his own misdeeds. During the absence of Atreus, Aëropé bore two sons to Thyestes. As soon as Atreus became apprised of it, he expelled them, as well as their father from his dominions. Thyestes, breathing revenge, contrived to get a son of Atreus into his power, and educated him as his own, at the same time instilling into his youthful heart a deadly hatred against his father, and finally sent him away to commit a murder at which the Sun veils his face.

But the youth was unsuccessful in his attempt, and upon the discovery of his design, he was put to death under the most cruel tortures; and Atreus learned too late that by his command his own son, instead of his brother's, had suffered a cruel death. Atreus, now brooding over a still deeper revenge, feigned a reconciliation with his brother, and by various marks of affection induced him to come to Mycenæ and bring his sons with him. He then had them secretly murdered and their flesh served up on the table at which their father sat. After Thyestes had eaten the food prepared for him, Atreus cast their heads and hands before his eyes. "On beholding the scene," says the fiction, " the Sun swiftly turned back his course."

Thyestes then fled to Sicyon, where he had a son by his daughter Pelopia, whose name was Ægisthos, who, on attaining the years of manhood, murdered Atreus. and expelled his sons Agamemnon and Menelãos from the kingdom, when Thyestes usurped the royal throne of Mycenæ.

The fugitive sons of Atreus found a friendly reception at the court of Tyndarëos, king of Lacedæmon, where each married a daughter of their host; Agamemnon, Clytemnestra, and Menelãos, the beautiful Helena, who afterwards brought wo throughout Greece and destruction on Troy. The two brothers avenged the death of their father, Atreus, and once more expelled Thyestes from Mycenæ. Agamemnon then took the reins of government in his father's dominions, while Menelãos succeeded Tyndarëos in the government of Sparta.

Menelãos and Helena had no children. Agamemnon and Clytemnestra had two daughters, Iphigeneia and Electra, and one son, Orestes.

When Agamemnon afterwards took the chief command of the army destined to call Troy to account for the offence which his brother Menelãos had suffered from Paris, forgiving Ægisthos, the murderer of his father, he became reconciled to him, and even intrusted him with the care of Clytemnestra and his house during his absence. Ægisthos, however, abused this confidence, misleading Clytemnestra to infidelity, and bringing ruin upon her husband. For when Agamemnon returned to Mycenæ after an absence of ten years, to enjoy the remainder of his days in quiet and domestic happiness, he was murdered by Ægisthos and Clytemnestra.

With regard to the children of Agamemnon, Iphigeneia was to have been sacrificed on entering upon the expedition against Troy; but was rescued by Diana, who carried her to Tauris, where she became a priestess in her temple. Orestes, whose life was threatened with great danger from the hands of Ægisthos, was secretly sent by his sister to Strophios, king of Phocis, and the husband of Agamemnon's sister. Electra remained at home, exposed to the abuse of an unnatural mother.

After the death of her husband, Clytemnestra, fearing neither gods nor men, married Ægisthos. and put the royal crown of Mycenæ on his execrable head. But Destiny had already decreed the punishment of that guilty couple, although it was to be executed only by the means of a new crime.

In Orestes, Agamemnon's son, rose an avenger both of his father's death and his mother's infamy. A false report, intentionally circulated. had announced him as dead ; and while Ægisthos and Clytemnestra rejoiced in the thought of being rid of him, Orestes was planning their destruction. As soon as Orestes felt his arm strong enough to meet a foe with his sword, he went to Mycenæ and slew the murderer of his father, not sparing his own mother who shared in the crime. But on account of this horrible deed, Orestes was punished by the Furies wherever he went ; that is to say, his conscience would not allow him any rest, and suffered him not to be reconciled to himself, until he went to Delphi and consulted the oracle of Apollo, which promised him alleviation of his torments if he would go to Tauris, and carry the statue of Diana from thence to Greece.

Orestes had been brought up with Pylades, the son of king Strophios, at Phocis, and both were so intimately and inseparably united by the tie of friendship, that their union became proverbial in antiquity, and is so even in our own times. This faithful friend, Pylades, who had never left Orestes during all his sufferings, was now his companion on the voyage to Tauris. It was there an old and barbarous custom to bring human offerings to Diana, the se vere goddess who was the tutelary deity of the country. and whose image Orestes was to carry away. Orestes and Pylades had no sooner landed, than they were made pris-

oners, and doomed to be for ever separated by the sacrifice
of one of them to Diana. In the trying hour, when the
sentence of the high priest was received, each of the friends
offered his life to save that of the other. A contest that
was pleasing in the sight of the gods, and worthy of heavenly assistance.

Orestes recognized his sister Iphigeneia, the priestess of
Diana, and made himself known to her; and she found
means not only to bring the statue of the goddess on board
her brother's ship, but also to rescue both the friends and
fly with them to Greece. The oracle of Apollo proved true.
The Furies ceased to torment Orestes, who henceforth
reigned quietly over Mycenæ, and the wrath of the gods
which had borne so long and so heavily upon the house of
Pelops, seemed now to abate.

ACHILLEUS OR ACHILLES.

Achilles was the son of Peleus (a descendant of Zeus)
and of Thetis, the goddess of the sea. At the festivity of
their marriage, the gods brought gifts, the Muses sang,
the Nereïdes danced, and Ganymedes poured forth nectar
for the guests.

When Achilles was born, Thetis plunged him in the
river Styx, which made him invulnerable in every part except the heel, by which she held him. And in this heel
he received a fatal wound. Achilleus, like the other heroes, was reared by the wise Centaur Cheiron. In the
Iliad he appears as one of the most prominent heroes.*

---

* For the story of the Iliad, see large edition.

PART FIFTH.
MYTHIC FICTIONS.

LETO AND THE FROGS.

While wandering from place to place with her children, Leto arrived in Lycia. The sun was shining fiercely, and the goddess was parched with thirst. Seeing a pool of water, she knelt down by it to drink, when some clowns who were there refused to allow her to slake her thirst. In vain the goddess entreated, representing that water was common to all, and appealing to their compassion for her babes. The brutes were insensible, and not only mocked at her distress, but jumped into and muddied the water. The goddess, though the most gentle of her race, was roused to indignation; and raising her hands to heaven, cried, "May you live for ever in that pool!" Her wish was instantly accomplished. and the churls were transformed into frogs.

PHAËTHON.

Phaëthon (*Gleaming*) was a son of Helios and the ocean-nymph Clymene. Venus intrusted him with the care of one of her temples. This distinguished favor of the goddess rendered him so vain and aspiring, that Epaphos, a son of Zeus, to check his pride, disputed his claims to a celestial origin. Phaëthon, to refute this bitter reproach, resolved to know his true origin; and, at the instigation of his mother, visited the palace of the Sun, to beg that Helios, if he really were his father, would give him some proof of his paternal tenderness, and convince the world of his legitimacy. Helios swore by the Styx, that he would grant him whatever he required. The ambitious youth instantly demanded permission to guide the solar chariot for one day, in order to prove himself the undoubted progeny of the Sun-god. Not daring to violate the oath by Styx, and finding entreaties and remonstrances unavailing to dissuade him from his perilous enterprise, Helios complied with his wish, and Phaëthon courageously and joyfully mounted the chariot of the Sun.

No sooner, however, did the celestial coursers discover that they were guided by a feebler hand than that of Helios, than they disregarded the efforts of the new charioteer, and leaving their usual course, now approached too near the heavens, and now again so close to earth, that the mountains began to blaze, and the rivers and fountains dried up. Earth, in her extremity, besought Jupiter for help. Enraged at the presumption of this new driver of the celestial horses, Jupiter struck him with one of his thunderbolts, by which he was precipitated into the river Eridanos. There his three sisters, the Heliades, or daughters of the sun, Lampetia, Phaëthusa, and Ægle, who tenderly loved their brother, lamented his loss so long, that at length the gods were touched with compassion for their grief, and changed them into poplar trees. Their tears, which still continued to flow, became amber as they dropped into the stream.

Cycnos, also, the chosen friend of the ill-fated Phaëthon, lamented his death on the banks of the Eridanos, till his form, dissolved in tears, was changed to that of a swan, which always remained on the water that swallowed his beloved friend.

PHILEMON AND BAUCIS.

In Phrygia, as a beautiful ancient tale relates, Jupiter laid aside his thunderbolts and Mercury his caduceus, and assuming the form of wayfarers, wandered in disguise among men, in order to try their characters and actions.

One evening, when as weary travellers they sought for hospitality, the doors of the rich were closed against them. At length they approached the abode of Philemon and Baucis, a pious couple, but poor, and already advanced in years, and in their humble cottage they were received with hospitality and kindness. The gods were served with a supper such as the cottage afforded, and the wine bowl being spontaneously replenished, the quality of the guests was revealed.

The guests after having declared themselves to be Jupiter and Mercury, told their host that they intended to destroy the neighboring town, and desired them to leave their dwelling and ascend the adjacent hill. The aged couple obeyed, and ere they had reached its summit they turned round and beheld the waste and destruction wherewith the gods had punished the hard-heartedness of the inhabitants of the country. The houses and palaces of the rich were ruined by a deluge, while the poor, hospitable cottage still raised its roof above the floods, and before the astonished eyes of its late inhabitants, was transformed into a magnificent temple.

On being desired by Jupiter to express their wishes, they prayed that they might be appointed to officiate in that temple, bringing offerings to Jove, the patron and rewarder of hospitality, and finally be united in death as in life. Their prayer was granted; and as they were one day standing before the temple, they were changed into trees, an oak and a lime. These trees overshadowed the temple, and in their memory were long afterwards called Philemon and Baucis.

In this and similar traditions of old, the dreadful as well as beneficent power of the deities was recognized. Altars were every where erected to Jupiter Hospitalis. Strangers arriving at any place where they were destitute of friends, were under his immediate protection, and guests were considered as sacred and inviolable persons; for in strangers and guests the celestials were revered, who often came down from Olympos in human form, in order to mingle among mankind.

ORPHEUS.

Thrace is fabled to have been the native place of Orpheus, son of Apollo and the muse Calliope ; that divine bard, who, by his song and the tones of his lyre, tamed the fierceness of forest beasts, moved rocks and trees, and, like a being sent from heaven, first taught mortals to listen to his harmonious notes, when he was chanting the praises of the celestials. The divine bard, not less renowned for his wisdom than for his skill in poesy and music, became also the founder of religious mysteries.

His wife, a nymph named Eurydice, died from the bite of a serpent. Orpheus, disconsolate at her loss, determined to descend to the lower world, and obtain permission for his beloved Eurydice to return to the regions of light. Armed only with his lyre, he entered the realms of Hades, and gained an easy admittance to the palace of Pluto. At the music of his "golden shell," to borrow the beautiful language of ancient poetry, the wheel of Ixion stopped, Tantales forgot the thirst that tormented him. the Vulture ceased to prey on the vitals of Tityos, and Pluto and Proserpina lent a favoring ear to his prayer.

Eurydice was allowed to return with Orpheus, on condition that he should not look back at her until she had reached the higher world, and again beheld the light of day. But when they had nearly attained the opening above, and were about to leave the gloomy abode of the shades, tender anxiety, and doubt whether his dear companion was really following him, induced Orpheus to look back. He beheld his wife close behind him, but for the last time. Falling back she again disappeared in the nightly darkness of Orcus, and all the sweet hope of Orpheus vanished like a dream. The joy of life was now for ever lost, and his lyre was silent.

From the Thracian mountains resounded the ferocious clamor of the Mænades, at a Bacchic festival, who, angry at the bard for the contempt shown to them by his sorrow for Eurydice, fell upon him and tore him to pieces. Thus Orpheus, the son of Apollo, the divine poet, musician, and philosopher, fell a victim to the frantic fury of the devotees of Bacchos.

CUPID AND PSYCHE.

One of the most charming fictions transmitted to us from antiquity, is that of Cupid and Psyche. It involves the most sublime ideas of life, death, and immortality, as far as we may look for such ideas among the religious heathens of ancient times. The name of Psyche signifies both a butterfly and the human soul. Therefore, when represented with the wings of a butterfly attached to her shoulders, Psyche is, as it were, the emblem of a tender spiritual being, who, freed from the coarser covering of her chrysalis, is too sublimated for this lower world, and rises to a higher existence, where, united with Love, in sacred and mutual marriage, she participates in that bliss which the immortals themselves enjoy. This fiction forms the veil, which in a most agreeable manner conceals the terrors of the lower world.

Psyche, the most lovely of mortals, was the daughter of a powerful monarch, and the youngest of three sisters. So transcendent was her beauty, that no mortal man dared sue for her hand; and her father's subjects, neglecting the worship of Venus, raised altars to Psyche. Her parents exulted in this general homage paid to their daughter, and her sisters, somewhat jealous of her superior beauty, pleased themselves with the thought that while they were married, she would never have a husband. Both parents and sisters, however, soon found themselves disappointed in the anticipations in which they had indulged. The former consulted an oracle as to her future fate, and were commanded to array their daughter in festive attire, and then conduct her as if to her burial to the summit of a mountain, and there to abandon her till her destined husband should come for her.

Venus, resolving to revenge herself upon the innocent Psyche, sent Cupid to inspire her with a passion for the ugliest of mortals. But Cupid no sooner saw Psyche, than he laid aside his bow and arrows, and resolved to make her his wife. For this purpose he went to Zephyros, the god of the west-wind, and Somnus, the god of sleep, to ask their assistance. No sooner did Psyche find herself alone, than a profound sleep stole over her senses, and then she was tenderly raised by Zephyr, who carried her to the abode prepared for her by Love. She found herself transported to an unknown region, but the most charming she had ever seen. A magnificent palace, surrounded by beautiful groves and beds of flowers, was at her disposal; she was mistress of many invisible attendants, by whom her commands were instantly obeyed. But he who had bestowed upon her this delightful abode, she was not permitted to behold. He visited her only at night, telling her with a sweetly-sounding voice, that he was the husband allotted to her by the immortals, at the same time warning and entreating her never to inquire who he was, for then she would for ever lose his love, and become miserable.

But in the midst of a heavenly happiness, Psyche longed to see her parents once more, or at least her sisters, that she might dissipate the grief of her family on account of her fate. Her husband, seeing that all the entreaties and remonstrances with which he endeavored to banish this wish from her heart were vain, at last consented that she should receive a visit from her sisters. Zephyr was accordingly ordered to convey them to Psyche's abode. No sooner had they arrived and beheld the happiness which was allotted to their sister, than envy filled their hearts, destroying every better feeling; and after having heard the particular circumstances under which Psyche enjoyed her matrimonial happiness, they infused into her mind the suspicion that her husband must be a hideous monster, because he dreaded to be seen. Their malevolence even went so far as to persuade their sister, by every possible art, to transgress the positive commands of her husband, and, by the use of a dagger, to rid herself of the monster when buried in sleep.

The sisters were carried away by Zephyr, and poor Psyche, whose mind was agitated by contending passions, resolved at last to follow the malevolent counsel which they had given her. When Night had expanded her wings over her blessed abode, and her husband was buried in repose, she took the lamp, and a dagger which she had concealed, and stepped, with fainting knees and a trembling hand, to the couch of the unknown. But instead of the monster whom she had expected to see, she beheld the most beautiful of the immortals, Cupid, God of Love! She attempted gently to withdraw the lamp, but her hand trembled, and a drop of hot oil fell on the god's shoulder. Cupid started up from his sleep, and beholding his wife, with a lamp and dagger, cast a look on the wretched Psyche, in which rage, scorn, and pity were intermingled. He then mounted on his wings, never more to return.

When Psyche felt that she had lost the love and esteem of her adored husband, despair took possession of her mind, and she attempted to put a period to her existence. She threw herself into the neighboring stream, but the river-god feared Love, and gently carried her to the opposite bank. Here she met with Pan, who endeavored to console her by the prediction that she was destined at a future period to be once more happy.

Psyche's sisters, who had anticipated the consequences of their fatal counsel, and who now wished to succeed their unfortunate sister, placed themselves one after the other on the summit of the mountain, from which Psyche had been carried away, hoping that Zephyros would convey them to the wished-for residence; but being hurled into the abyss by sudden blasts of wind, they atoned by their deaths for the envy and treachery which they had displayed towards their innocent sister.

Poor Psyche overran the whole earth in search of her lost husband. But finding all her endeavors vain, she at last took the resolution of applying to Venus, and imploring mercy from her. Venus, incensed with the fair suppliant, because she had charmed Cupid, and because of her celestial beauty, received her with reproaches, imposing upon her the severest tasks, the performance of which seemed impossible. Psyche, however, assisted by beneficent beings, whom Cupid, who still loved her, sent to her aid, surmounted all difficulties; yet for a long time she was obliged to suffer the consequences of her imprudence, until she was again thought worthy of her forfeited happiness. At last, she was ordered by Venus to descend into Orcus itself, and to fetch from Proserpina a box containing the highest charms of beauty. Psyche obeyed the command of the cruel goddess, and set out on the dreadful enterprise, despairing of success; but the voice of her invisible protector and guide taught her every necessary precaution, and warned her of every danger.

Provided with a cake to tame the fury of Cerberos, and a sum of money to gain the good-will of Charon, she ventured down to the gloomy regions, and arrived safely at the palace of Proserpina. The desired box was delivered to her, but with a strict injunction not to open it. Psyche, who had surmounted so many difficulties, and sustained with heroic fortitude so many trials, suffered herself to be overpowered by this last. Scarcely had she left the dominions of Pluto, when curiosity and vanity induced her to open the box. She was instantly involved in a black and noxious vapor, which threw her into a deep sleep, from which she would never have risen, had not Cupid, her invisible protector, hastened to her assistance. He restored her to life, collected the vapor again into the box, and conducted his beloved Psyche safely to the throne of Jove, there proclaiming her as his lawful wife, and supplicating for her admission among the immortals. Jupiter complied with his request, endowed her with immortality, and Venus became reconciled to her beauteous daughter-in-law. The Hours shed roses through the sky, the Graces sprinkled the halls of Heaven with fragrant odors, Apollo played on his lyre, the Arcadian god on his reeds, the Muses sang in chorus, while Venus danced with grace and elegance, to celebrate the nuptials of her son. Thus the celestials celebrated the second, the heavenly marriage of Cupid and Psyche.

TRITON.

According to Hesiod, Triton was a son of Poseidon and Amphitrite, who " keeping to the bottom of the sea, dwelt with his mother and royal father in a golden house." Later poets made him his father's trumpeter. He was also multiplied, and we read of Tritons in the plural num ber. Like the Nereides, the Tritons were degraded to the fish-form.

OTOS AND EPHIALTES.

The Aloeids, Otos and Ephialtes, were also sons of Poseidon. In their ninth year, they were nine cubits in width, and nine fathoms in height. At this early age they undertook to make war upon Zeus; and, in order to reach the heavens, they strove to place Mount Ossa upon Olympos, and Pelion upon Ossa; but (to use the graphic language of Homer) "they were destroyed by Apollo before the down had bloomed beneath their temples, and had thickly covered their chins with a well-flowering beard." According to the animated narrative of the same bard, they would have accomplished their object had they made the attempt, not in childhood, but after having "reached the measure of youth."

CENTAURS.

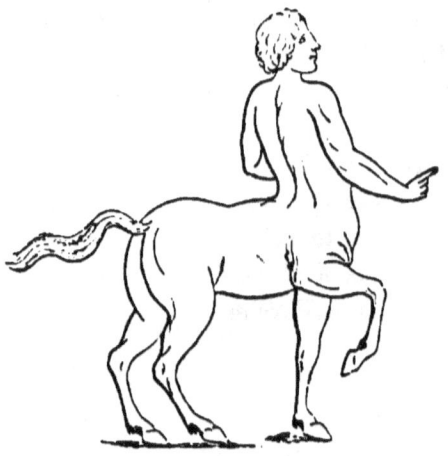

The Centaurs were a tribe of Thessaly, fabled to have been half men and half horse, and are always mentioned in connection with the Lapiths. The former are twice spoken of in the Iliad, under the name of *Wildmen*, and once in the Odyssey. They appear to have been a rude, mountain tribe, dwelling on and about Mount Pelion.

ATALANTA.

Iasos, or Iasion, a descendant of Arcas, was married to Clymene, a daughter of Minyas. He was anxious for a male offspring, and therefore, disappointed at her birth, he exposed the babe in the mountains, where she was suckled by a bear, and at last found by some hunters, who named her Atalanta, and reared her. She followed the chase, and was alike distinguished for beauty and courage. The Centaurs, Rhœcos and Hylæos, approaching her with evil intentions, perished by her arrows. She distinguished herself in the Calydonian hunt, and at the funeral games of Pelias, she won the prize in wrestling.

Atalanta was afterwards recognized by her parents. Her father wished her to marry, to which she consented, on condition that her suitors should run a race with her, promising, if she should be vanquished, to become the wife of the victor; but the vanquished suitor should be shot by one of her own darts. As she was almost invincible in running, many of her suitors perished in the contest.

Hippomenes, venturing to enter upon this dangerous race, implored the assistance of Aphrodite, who presented him with three golden apples, which, one after another, he let slip from his hands during the course. Atalanta, whose eyes were dazzled by the glitter and beauty of this golden fruit, repeatedly stopped to take it up from the ground, and thus Hippomenes gained time to reach the goal before her.

Atalanta became the wife of Hippomenes; but unmindful of the benefit which he owed to Aphrodite, both were obliged to atone for his offence against the goddess. Upon her impulse, they profaned a sanctuary of Cybele, who, with formidable power, transformed them into two lions, that under one yoke drew her chariot.

ARACHNE.

A Mæonian maid, named Arachne, proud of her skill in weaving and embroidery, in which arts the goddess of wisdom had instructed her, ventured to deny her obligation, and challenged her patroness to a trial of skill. The goddess changed her into a spider.

TANTALOS.

Tantalos, the favorite of the gods, was admitted to their table, where he feasted on nectar and ambrosia, which made him immortal.

He once so far forgot himself as to offend Jupiter with some intemperate language, and was immediately plunged from the height of happiness to the immeasurable depths of misery. The punishment of Tantalos was everlasting hunger and thirst, while at the same time he saw the clear flood rising to his lips, but receding as soon as he attempted to taste it, and the branch loaded with fruit hanging over his head, but was never able to grasp it.

IXION AND SISYPHOS.

Ixion, who reigned in Thessaly, was subjected to a fate similar to that of Tantalos. He was expelled from Olympos, and when he had the temerity to boast on earth of what he had attempted in heaven, Zeus precipitated him into Tartaros, where Hermes fastened him with brazen bands to an ever-revolving fiery wheel.

Sisyphos, like the Danaïdes, was condemned to perform an endless task. Hades required him to roll a huge rock up a mountain, a never-ending, still beginning toil; for as soon as he has nearly reached the top, and rejoices in the hope of being permitted to rest from his hard labor, the rock, in spite of all his endeavors, rolls back again to the plain.

MIDAS.

Pan, favorite of Midas, king of the Phrygians in Macedonia, wished also to compete with Apollo in the art of which the latter was master. Pan commenced the contest, and Midas repeated his songs with enthusiasm, regardless of his celestial rival, when, to his surprise, the latter felt a pair of ears, long and shaggy, pressing through his hair. Alarmed at this phenomenon, Pan fled. The prince, desolate at the loss of his favorite, made his wife the confidante of his misfortune, begging her not to betray his trust. She longed to tell the secret, but dared not, for fear of punishment: and, by way of relief, sought a retired and lonely spot, where she threw herself upon the ground, and whispered, "King Midas has the ears of an ass. King Midas has the ears of an ass."

Not long after her visit, some reeds arose in this place, and as the wind passed through them, they repeated, "King Midas has the ears of an ass." Enraged, no less than terrified at this occurrence, Midas sacrificed to Bacchos, who, to console him, desired him to ask whatever he wished. According to his desire, every thing he touched turned to gold, even his food and drink. He then prayed to Bacchos to deliver him from the plague. Bacchos directed him to wash in the river Pactolus, and hence that river has golden sands.

MERCURY AND HERSE.

As Mercury met the maidens that were carrying the sacred baskets to the temple of Minerva, he beheld Herse, the beautiful daughter of Cecrops. Admiring her charms, he resolved to have her for a wife, and for that purpose entered the royal abode, where dwelt the three sisters, Aglauros, Paudrosos, and Herse. Mercury was first met by Aglauros, who felt great displeasure at his preference for her sister. He entreated her good offices, which she promised on condition that he would reward her with a large quantity of gold, and immediately drove him from the palace till he should obtain it.

Minerva, incensed at the cupidity of Aglauros, and provoked with her also for other causes, sent Envy to fill her bosom with that baleful passion. Unable then to endure the happiness of her sister, she sat down at the door, determined not to permit the god to enter. He besought her to admit him, but his eloquence was vain. At length, provoked by her obstinacy, he turned her into a black stone.

NARCISSOS.

The beautiful youth Narcissos was son of the river-god Cephissos, and the sea-nymph Liriope.

According to Pausanias, Narcissos had a sister of remarkable beauty, to whom he was tenderly attached. She resembled him in features, was similarly attired, and accompanied him in the hunt. She died young, and Narcissos, deeply lamenting her death, frequented a neighboring fountain to gaze upon his own image in its stream. The strong resemblance that he bore to his sister made his own reflection appear to him, as it were, the form of her whom he had lost. The gods looked with pity upon his grief, and changed him to the flower that bears his name.

ACTÆON.

Actæon was the son of Aristæos and Autonoë, daughter of Cadmos. He was reared by Cheiron, and becoming passionately fond of the chase, passed his days chiefly in pursuit of wild beasts that haunted Mount Cithæron. One sultry day as he was rambling alone, he chanced to surprise Artemis and her nymphs while bathing. The goddess, incensed at his intrusion, threw some water upon him, and changed him into a stag. She also inspired with madness the fifty dogs that attended him, who devoured their master.

INDEX.

THE LATIN NAMES ARE IN ITALICS.

	PAGE
Absyrtûs,	273
Acheloös,	44, 235
Acheron,	31, 100
Acherusia,	103
Achilles,	146, 293
Achilleus,	154, 293
Acis,	36
Acrisios,	46, 214, 218
Actæôn,	123, 30
Actor,	288
Admêtos,	123, 267
Adonis,	169
Adrastos,	259
Æacos,	249, 284
Æœa,	274
Æêtês,	250, 271
Ægeus,	251, 255
Ægialeus,	283
Ægis,	157
Ægisthos,	290, 291
Ægle,	31, 206, 295
Ægyptos,	213
Aëllo,	37
Æneias,	37, 87
Æolos,	59, 265
Æsculapius,	205
Æsôn,	264, 276
Æstas,	197
Æthra,	253, 260
Agamemnôn,	291
Aganê,	280
Agênôr,	46, 213
Aglaïa,	193
Ajax,	267
Aïdes	93
Alcathoë	244
Alcæcs,	46, 219, 223
Alcêstis,	235
Alcimêdê,	265
Alcmêna,	46, 211, 249
Alcyoneus,	41
Alôeô,	31

	PAGE
Aloeids,	177
Alpheios,	44
Althea,	277
Amaltheia,	61
Amazons,	222, 231
Ambrosia,	68
Amicitia,	209
Amphiaraös,	285
Amphictyôn,	59
Amphiôn,	281
Amphitrite,	36
Amphitryôn,	127, 211, [219, 223
Amycos,	262, 270
Anaxo,	223
Ancæos,	271
Anchisês,	169
Androgeôs,	250, 251
Andromeda,	217
Anteia,	221
Antæos,	235
Anterôs,	193
Antigonê,	284, 287
Antiopê,	261, 281
Aphareus,	263
Aphroditê,	123, 145, [165
Apollô,	121, 173, 180
Arachne,	30
Areiopagos,	30, 140
Areopê,	290
Arês,	140, 272, 279
Arethusa,	31, 45
Argês,	41
Argô,	267
Argonauts,	136, 262, [267
Argos,	46, 82
Argus,	48
Ariadne,	250, 252
Arion,	95, 287
Aristæos,	240, 280

	PAGE
Aristippe,	244
Artemis,	134, 145
Ascalaphos,	142
Asclêpios,	206
Asteria,	50
Asterion,	250
Astræa,	195
Astræos,	52
Atalanta,	277, 30
Atê,	225
Athamas,	243, 264
Athena,	145
Atlantides,	52
Atlas,	52, 53, 214
Atreus,	289
Atropos,	25
Augeas,	230
Aurora,	49
Autonoë,	280
Autumnus,	197
Avernus,	101
Bacchos,	242
Bacchantes,	247
Baucis,	296
Bellerophon,	220
Bellerophontês,	220
Bellona,	140, 144
Belos,	46, 213
Bia,	52
Bœotia,	279
Boreas,	49, 267
Briareôs,	41
Brontês,	41
Busîris,	235
Cabeiri,	163, 196
Cacus,	235
Cadmos,	242, 279
Caduceus,	175
Calaïs,	267
Calliopê,	200, 201

INDEX. 300

	PAGE		PAGE		PAGE
Callirhoë,	39	Dædalos,	251	Euênos,	236
Calydonian Chase,	259,	Damastês,	255	Eueres,	223
	[277	Danaö,	46, 214	Eumæos,	123
Calypsô,	52	Dannides,	102, 177	Eumenides,	31
Camênæ,	199	Danäos,	46, 213	Eumolpos,	110, 113
Canephores,	131	Daphne,	30	Eunomia,	165, 136
Capaneus,	285	Daphnephoria,	126	Euphrosyne,	193
Carpo,	197	Dardanos,	203	Europa,	46, 211, 243
Cassiopeia,	217	Deianeira,	235	Euryale,	33, 216
Castôr,	262	Deino,	33	Eurybia,	52
Cecrops,	58, 149	Delphi,	129	Eurydicê,	297
Celæcô,	37	Dêmêtêr,	105	Eurynomê,	193
Centaurs,	259, 30	Demogorgon,	22	Eurystheus,	219, 225,
Cephalos,	224	Deucalion,	53, 250		[290
Cêpheus,	217	Diana, 45, 134, 180, 229		Eurytiôn,	232
Cerberos,	39, 101, 233	Dikê,	196	Eurytos,	236
Cercyon,	255	Diomêdês,	156, 231	Euterpê,	201
Ceres,	62, 68, 105, 180	Diônê,	123, 165		
Ceto,	221	Dionysos, 40, 177, 242		Fates,	25
Chaos	19	Dionysia,	246	Fauns,	193
Charon,	34, 101	Dioscuri,	263	Felicitas,	209
Charites,	193	Dircê,	281	Feronia,	209
Charybdis,	274	Doris,	35	Fidelitas,	209
Chimæra,	39, 40, 221	Dryades,	42	Flora,	209
Cheirôn,	205	Dryas,	243	Fortitudo,	209
Chrysaôr,	39, 217			Fortuna,	209
Chrysippos,	290	Echidna,	39	Fountains,	44
Cilix,	269, 279	Echion,	290	Furies,	23, 292
Cithæron,	31	Egyptos,	46		
Circe,	274	Electra,	37, 291	Galatæa,	36
Clio,	201	Electryôn,	219	Ganymêdê,	161, 203
Clôthô,	25	Eleus,	224	Ganymêdês,	161, 203
Clymênê,	52, 294	Eleusis,	116, 119	Ge,	43
Clytemnestra,	262, 291	Elysian Fields,	103	Gelanôr,	213
Cocalos,	252	Encelados,	41	Genii,	183
Cocytus,	100	Endymion,	139	Geryon,	39, 232
Cœlus,	43	Enyô,	33, 140	Giants,	41
Coios,	41, 50	Eôs,	49	Glaucos,	250
Comus,	203	Eosphoros,	49	Golden Apples,	54, 232
Connidas,	253	Epaphos,	46, 213	Golden Fleece,	266
Consualia,	95	Ephesus,	140	Gorgons,	33, 215, 220
Consus,	95	Ephialtes,	30	Graces,	193
Corybantes,	163, 186	Epigones,	283	Græa,	33, 216
Cottos,	41, 68	Epimetheus,	52, 54	Gyes,	41, 63
Creôn, 41, 224, 276, 287		Epôpeus,	281		
Cretheus,	264	Eratô,	201	Hadês	93
Crios,	41, 49	Erebos,	99	Hæmôn,	41, 287
Cromedon,	41	Erichthonios,	164	Halcyonê,	000
Cromyonian Swine,		Erigonê,	244	Hamadryades,	42
	[251	Erisichthon,	112	Harmonia,	142, 279
Cupido,	197, 298	Erôs,	19, 197	Harpies,	37, 109
Curetes,	61, 186	Erymanthian Boar, 229		Hêlê,	262
Cybelê,	92	Erinnyes,	29, 101	Hecabê,	000
Cycnos,	241, 295	Eriphylê,	285	Hecatê,	56, 106
Cyclopes,	41	Erythein,	31	Heimarmeno,	25
Cytheræa,	163	Eteoclês,	284	Helena,	266, 29
Cyzicus,	269	Euades,	247	Heliades,	295

	PAGE
Helicon,	31, 94
Hêlios,	49, 106, 295
Hellanodicæ,	77
Hellê,	266
Hellen	59
Hephæstos,	154, 158
Hêra,	70, 79
Hêraclês,	219, 222
Hera,	82
Hercules,	59, 214, 222
Hermes,	172
Hersê,	30
Hêsionê,	235
Hesperides,	31, 54, 232
Hestia,	84
Hippocrênê,	94
Hippodamia,	259, 288
Hippodromus,	95
Hippolytos,	240, 261
Hippomedon,	285
Honos,	209
Hôræ,	196
Hyacinthos,	30
Hyades,	52
Hydra,	39, 40, 229
Hyems,	197
Hygeia,	206
Hylas,	269
Hyllos,	238
Hymen,	208
Hyperiôn,	41, 49
Hypermnêstra,	213
Hypsipylê,	286
Janus,	62, 207
Japetos,	41, 52
Iasion,	59
Iaso,	206
Iusos,	47
Jason,	264
Icarios,	244
Icaros,	240
Idas,	263
Idomeneus,	253
Ilaira,	263
Inachos,	44, 45, 58
Indigetes,	212
Inô,	243, 280
Iô,	46, 47
Iobatês,	221
Iocasta,	282
Iolaos,	264, 275
Iolé,	236
Iphiclês,	225
Iphigeneia,	291
Iphitos,	236

	PAGE
Irene,	196
Iris,	37, 109
Isis,	46, 136
Ismênê,	284
Isthmian Games,	79, 96
Juno,	62, 63, 79
Jupiter,	62, 67, 180
Jupiter Ægiochus,	157
Jupiter Ammon,	73
Jupiter Capitolinus,	73
Jupiter Fulminans,	73
Jupiter Fulgetra,	73
Jupiter Tonans,	73
Jurentas,	204
Ixion,	177
Kratos,	52
Kronos,	41, 60
Lachesis,	25
Laios,	281
Lampetia,	295
Laodamas,	288
Lapiths,	259
Lares,	184, 186
Lasthenes,	286
Latona,	50, 134
Leimonaides,	42
Lêthe,	100
Lêtô,	134, 294
Leucippe,	244
Leucippos,	263
Leucothea,	250
Libertas,	205
Libya,	213
Lichas,	237
Limniades,	42
Linus,	226
Luna,	49
Lupercus,	24
Lupercalia,	24
Luperci,	24
Lybia,	46
Lycomedes,	261
Lycos,	271, 281
Lycurgos,	243, 286
Lynceus,	214, 268
Machaôn,	205
Mænades,	247, 298
Maia,	172
Mars,	140, 180
Marsyas,	148, 192
Medeia,	272
Medúsa,	38, 215
Megæra,	30

	PAGE
Megara,	235
Melanippos,	286
Meliades,	42
Meleager,	59, 277
Meleagros,	267, 277
Melicertês,	97, 280
Melpomenê,	200
Menelâos,	166, 290
Menœtios,	52, 54, 267
Mercurius,	91, 172, 180
Mestor,	223
Metis,	63
Midas,	30
Minerva,	69, 145, 180
Minos,	243
Minotaur,	251, 256
Minyas,	244
Mnêmosyne,	41, 199
Moiræ,	25, 185
Momus,	34
Morpheus,	33
Mors,	32
Musagetes,	129
Muses,	199
Myrtilos,	289
Naiades,	42
Napææ,	42
Narcissos,	30
Nectar,	68
Nêleus,	264, 267
Nemæan Lion,	39, 228
Nemesis,	28
Nemesia,	29
Nephelê,	266
Neptunus,	62, 93, 180
Nereides,	35
Nêreus,	35, 217
Nessos,	236
Nestor,	239
Nikê,	52
Nisos,	251
Nox,	20
Nycteis,	281
Nycteus,	281
Nymphs,	42, 191
Nysa,	177, 243
Oceanides,	43
Oceanos,	35, 43
Ocypetê,	37
Œdipûs,	41, 282
Œneus,	235, 277
Œnomaos,	288
Ogyges,	58
Olympic Games,	75

INDEX

	PAGE		PAGE		PAGE
Olympus,	45	Phoroneus,	46	Semones,	212
Omphale,	177, 236	Phrixos,	266	Silênos,	192
Opheltes,	286	Pirithoös,	259	Sinis,	254
Opus,	235	Pittheus,	253	Sirens,	274
Oreiades,	41	Pleiades,	52	Sisyphos,	102, 220, 264
Orestês,	291	Pluto,	62, 98	Sol,	49
Orpheus,	267, 297	Plutus,	208	Somnus,	32
Orthrus,	39	Podaleirios,	206	Sphinx,	39, 40, 283
Ortygia,	45	Pœas,	233	Steropês,	41
		Pollux,	262	Sthenelos,	219, 224
Palæmôn,	97, 250	Polybos,	282	Stheïno,	33, 216
Pales,	203	Polydectês,	214	Strophades,	270
Palladium,	157	Polydeukês,	262	Strophios,	291
Pallas,	52, 255	Polydôros,	230	Stymphalides,	230
Pallas-Athênê,	146	Polyhymnia,	202	Styx,	34, 48, 52, 101
Pan,	22	Polyneicês,	284, 286	Sylvanus,	195
Panacea,	206	Polyphêmos,	36, 93	Symplegades,	270
Panathenæ,	150	Polyphontes,	282, 286		
Pandora,	56	Pomona,	209	Tantalos,	102, 288, 300
Parcæ,	25, 100	Pontos,	35	Taphians,	223
Paris,	166	Porphyriôn,	41	Taphios,	223
Parthenon,	158	Poseidon,	36, 46, 93	Tartarôs,	99
Parthenopæos,	285	Priamos,	177	Telamon,	267
Pasiphaë,	240, 250	Priapos,	193	Teleboans,	223
Patroclos,	27, 267	Procrustês,	255	Telephassa,	278
Pax,	209	Prœtos,	214, 218	Telesphoros,	206
Pegasos,	91	Prometheus,	52, 54	Terminus,	203
Peithô,	253	Proserpina,	100	Terpsichore,	200
	279	Proteus,	204	Terra,	19
	36	Psychê,	298	Tethys,	41, 43
	264, 276	Pterolaos,	223	Thalia,	193, 201
	259	Pylades,	292	Thaliô,	197
	283	Pyrrha,	53	Thamos,	278
	288	Pythia,	134	Thaumas,	37
	86, 186	Pythian Games,	9, 132	Theban War,	5
	44	Pytho,	121	Thea,	41
	214, 280	Pydna,	125	Themis,	5
	38			Thersandro,	
	253	Rea,	20	Tria,	293
	250	Rhadamanthys,	2	Thus,	262
	50, 52	Rhea,	11, 60, 21	Thetis,	36, 60, 203
	50, 90, 171	Rhene,	42	Thoas,	26
	33, 53, 213	Rhea,	41	Thyestes,	289
	250, 261	Rivers,	44	Thyone,	215
	294			Tiphys,	27
	293	Salmoneus,	261	Tisiphonê,	
	52	Salmydessus,	270	Titans,	
	296	Sarpêdôn,	27, 249	Titanides,	
	238	Saturn,	41, 60	Triptolemos,	10
	37, 270	Saturnalia,	63	Triton,	
	100	Satyrs,	193	Tros,	
	41, 50	Scamandros,	41	Tydeus,	7
	121	Seirôn,	254	Tyndareos,	2
	243, 279	Scylla,	251, 271	Typhon,	

	PAGE		PAGE		PAGE
Ulysses,	- - 28, 104	Vertumnus,	- - 203	Vulcánus,	- - 158, 180
Urania,	- - 172, 202	Vesta,	62, 68, 84, 150		
Uranos,	- - - 43	Vestalia,	- - - 91	Zelos,	- - - - 52
		Vestals,	- - - 87	Zephyros,	49, 209, 299
Venus,	142, 165, 180	Vestibulum.	- - 86	Zêtês,	- - - 267
Ver,	- - - 197	Victory,	- - 52, 209	Zethos,	- - - 281
Veritas,	- - - 209	Virtus	- - - 209	Zeus,	- - - - 67

www.ingramcontent.com/pod-product-compliance
Lightning Source LLC
Chambersburg PA
CBHW031905220426
43663CB00006B/778